SENSE AND CONTENT

Sense and Content

Experience, Thought, and their Relations

CHRISTOPHER PEACOCKE

CLARENDON PRESS · OXFORD

1983

Oxford University Press, Walton Street, Oxford OX2 6DP

London Glasgow New York Toronto
Delhi Bombay Calcutta Madras Karachi
Kuala Lumpur Singapore Hong Kong Tokyo
Nairobi Dar es Salaam Cape Town
Melbourne Auckland
and associated companies in
Beirut Berlin Ibadan Mexico City Nicosia

Oxford is a trade mark of Oxford University Press

Published in the United States
by Oxford University Press, New York

British Library Cataloguing in Publication Data

Peacocke, Christopher
Sense and content.
1. Concepts
I. Title
153.2'3   BF311
ISBN 0-19-824703-6
ISBN 0-19-824702-8 pbk

Typeset by Cotswold Typesetting Ltd., Cheltenham.
Printed in Great Britain
at the University Press, Oxford
by Eric Buckley
Printer to the University

For Teresa

Preface

The topics of this book lie in the intersection of three areas: the philosophy of mind, the theory of meaning and content, and the philosophy of psychology. I have tried not to presuppose advanced knowledge in any one of these areas: my aim has been to make the book intelligible to final-year undergraduates specializing in philosophy. I hope the work will also prove to be of interest to philosophically-minded psychologists concerned with methodological issues, in particular those arising out of developmental psychology.

This book grew out of a desire to treat the nature of the content of psychological states in much greater detail than was attempted in *Holistic Explanation*.[1] The present work is based on material presented in classes in Oxford University in the years 1979 to 1982. Some of the material in Chapter Two on colour experience is to appear in an issue of *Synthese*, edited by Crispin Wright, devoted to the later philosophy of Wittgenstein. The rest of the material in the book is published here for the first time.

There are many past writers whose views could be fruitfully considered in relation to those defended here. This is obviously the case for what I have to say on perceptual experience: from my own limited knowledge. What I have to say bears on the views of the classical British empiricists, the sense-datum theorists and such phenomenologists of perception as Merleau-Ponty. It has also been suggested that there are affinities between what I say and the views of Kant on sense experience. I am no historian of philosophy, and have no special competence to discuss these connections. The one exception I have made to this policy is that of Russell, whose views have always been discussed in the philosophical tradition in which most British readers of this book are likely to have grown up.

In order to maintain accessibility of the text I have attempted to minimize formal machinery. So I have allowed myself such loose forms of language as 'Mary believes that *m* is tall', where '*m*' denotes a mode of presentation, even though in the intuitive sense Mary's belief is about the object *m* presents, and not about a mode

[1]Oxford: OUP, 1979.

vii

of presentation. Equally I will write 'Mary thinks "I am hungry" ',
where 'I am hungry' is used to pick out a thought in the sense
explained in the text.

I have always been helped by the reactions to drafts of this
material from audiences and discussion groups in Oxford, and
from audiences during my visits to the University of California at
Los Angeles and to the Australian National University. I also wish
to acknowledge the generous provision of excellent research
facilities by that last institution. I am also grateful for detailed
comments and advice from Rogers Albritton, Michael Dummett,
Philippa Foot, Graeme Forbes, John McDowell, Colin McGinn,
Derek Parfit, Teresa Rosen and Stephen Schiffer. Adam
Hodgkin's encouragement and substantive advice have once again
been important. Finally, those who know his work well will
recognize that my conception of how philosophy in this area
should be done—as opposed to the particular views to be
held—has been greatly influenced by vigorous discussions until a
few months before his death with Gareth Evans: these much
missed conversations were a crucial source of stimulation for what
follows.

New College, Oxford   C.P.
July 1982

Contents

Introduction

This book is about the nature of the content of psychological states. Examples of psychological states with content are: believing today is a national holiday, judging that the pencil is beneath the book, intending to phone London, having a visual experience as of a desk in front of oneself. A distinctive feature of such states is that their most direct descriptions embed expressions such as 'desk', 'London', 'to phone', which refer to, or are true of, objects in the world.

The very familiarity of such states can cause one to overlook the general philosophical challenge they throw down. What is the connection between these states and the ground floor vocabulary for describing the world which their descriptions embed? Is there any systematic connection between the distinctions drawn in the world by such ground floor vocabulary and the nature of these states?

There is a broad division between psychological attitudes – judgement, belief, intention, desire, hope, and so forth – and their contents, mentioned in 'that'-clauses. This book concentrates on the latter, and says nothing directly about the nature of the former states. But as a matter of principle, this distinction must be artificial. No one would suppose that a good account could be given of what it is for a thought-content to be disjunctive without specifying the conditions under which a thinker is willing to judge that content by reference to the conditions under which he is willing to judge the constituent contents from which that content is composed. Equally, there are many concepts which occur as constituents of thought-contents and whose nature cannot be explained without adverting to conscious experience. It is for these reasons that the first chapter of this book is about some conceptual issues raised by conscious experience. In the second chapter, a distinction defended in Chapter 1 is applied, and later in the book we will often draw upon the considerations of that first chapter.

The outer boundaries of the scheme by which we attempt to explain rational actions by appeal to psychological states with content is, in effect, the topic of Chapter 3. It seems that any being to whom we are prepared to attribute psychological states with content must be capable of attitudes with spatial contents. Chapter 3 attempts to answer the question 'What, minimally, is required for the possession of states with spatial contents?'. The answer I propose suggests one way of meeting the philosophical challenge of two paragraphs back: the minimal requirements for the possession of spatial concepts refer to spatial abilities and to spatial properties and relations themselves.

Chapters 4 through 6 are also concerned with an ability which it seems must be present in anyone capable of psychological states with content: the exercise of observational concepts, and of demonstrative and indexical thought about objects. This latter area is currently under intense discussion in the literature. Chapters 6 and 7 outline an epistemological approach to demonstrative thought. This approach appeals to a wider range of considerations, and aims to explain a different range of phenomena — including some Cartesian phenomena — than those currently appealed to and explained in formal semantical treatments. This approach is complementary to, rather than in competition with, those formal treatments.

Chapter 7 offers a neo-Russellian account of the conditions under which an object itself can be said to be a constituent of some content to which the subject has a psychological attitude. It is heavily dependent upon the earlier chapters. In this it differs from the final chapter. This is self-contained, and attempts to chart a middle course between the extreme positions of the views about propositional attitude psychology held on the one hand by the instrumentalist and on the other by the theorists of a language of thought.

In working on this material I have often felt myself to be in the position of a blindfolded man who is driven around a large city. Occasionally, the blindfold is lifted, and for a few minutes he sees rows of buildings, junctions and parks. This man is asked to draw up a map of the city. In fortunate cases, he has encountered the same junction from different directions; in unfortunate cases, he has had isolated glimpses, while travelling in he-knows-not-what direction, within an area of which he knows nothing. The map of the city drawn up by this man will have many blank areas, and streets he has often seen may be wildly placed relative to one another. Nevertheless, one who knows the city well may be able to say 'This section of the map accurately represents this corner of the city; and these features are correctly placed *vis-à-vis* one another, even though much between them is missing'. I hope and claim no more for my map.

1

Sensation and the Content of Experience:
A Distinction

Nothing is more fundamental to understanding the content of psychological states than sense experience. Time and again in this book we will need to appeal to it: in the accounts of observational concepts and of primitive demonstrative thought, and in the discussion of the Principle of Acquaintance. Elsewhere, in the account of the minimal conditions for the ascription of psychological states with content, we will need to make use of distinctions drawn from a particular theory of experience. If what I argue in this book is correct, we cannot fully understand these several areas if we remain unclear about experience.

But experience is not merely of instrumental interest. Having an experience is a psychological state in its own right, and one that raises many puzzles. How can senses as intrinsically different as sight and touch both serve as sources of knowledge about the spatial layout of our environment? Is the ancient tradition correct which holds that some concepts, those of secondary qualities, are more intimately related to experience than those of primary qualities? If so, must we acquiesce in the circular view that being red is to be explained in terms of looking red?[1]

These questions are the subjects of the next chapter. The present chapter develops some claims and distinctions needed both for the discussion of those questions and for some later topics. As such, it has the character of a prelude. Nevertheless, it too has a venerable subject, one that would have been discussed by a classical British empiricist under the heading 'Sensation and Perception'. My claim in this chapter will be that concepts of sensation are indispensable to the description of the nature of any experience. This claim stands in opposition to the view that, while sensations may occur when a subject is asked to concentrate in a

[1]For a clear statement of this last problem, see B. Williams, *Descartes: The Project of Pure Enquiry* (London: Penguin, 1978), at pp. 243–4.

4

particular way on his own experience, or may occur as by-products of perception, they are not to be found in the mainstream of normal human experience, and certainly not in visual experience. But first we need to clarify the issues.

Historically, the distinction between putative perceptual experiences and sensations has been the distinction between those experiences which do in themselves represent the environment of the experiencer as being a certain way, and those experiences which have no such representational content. A visual perceptual experience enjoyed by someone sitting at a desk may represent various writing implements and items of furniture as having particular spatial relations to one another and to the experiencer, and as themselves having various qualities; a sensation of small, by contrast, may have no representational content of any sort, though of course the sensation will be of a distinctive kind. The representational content of a perceptual experience has to be given by a proposition, or set of propositions, which specifies the way the experience represents the world to be. To avoid any ambiguity, I will use the phrase 'content of experience' only for the representational content of an experience, and never for a type of sensation: many past writers followed the opposite practice and used 'object' or 'meaning' for representational content. Corresponding to the historical distinction between sensation and perception, we can draw a distinction between sensational and representational properties of experience. Representational properties will be properties an experience has in virtue of features of its representational content; while sensational properties will be properties an experience has in virtue of some aspect — other than its representational content — of what it is like to have that experience.[2]

The content of an experience is to be distinguished from the

---

[2] Brian O'Shaughnessy in *The Will: A Dual Aspect Theory* (Cambridge: CUP, 1980) says that experiences with content are the causal consequences of sensations (vol. 1, pp. 172–3; vol. 2, pp. 68–74 and 139–42). I have set up the issues in such a way that sensational properties, if they exist, are properties of the very same thing, the experience, which has representational properties. That some properties of the experience are causally responsible for others would be an empirical psychological hypothesis, and one which involves simultaneous causation. O'Shaughnessy also writes, as I do not, of seeing sensations. Despite these differences and others noted later, much of what O'Shaughnessy says about sensation is congenial and complementary to the main theses of this chapter, in particular his emphasis on the inseparability of sensation from experience and on the nonconceptual character of sensation.

content of a judgement caused by the experience. A man may be familiar with a perfect *trompe l'œil* violin painted on a door, and be sure from his past experience that it is a *trompe l'œil*: nevertheless his experience may continue to represent a violin as hanging on the door in front of him. The possibility of such independence is one of the marks of the content of experience as opposed to the content of judgement. One of the earliest writers to state a distinction between sensation and perceptual experience, Thomas Reid, introduced it in terms which require that perceptual experience implies belief in the content of the experience.[3] In fact, we need a threefold distinction between sensation, perception, and judgement, to formulate the issues precisely.

This independence of the contents of judgement and experience does not mean that judgements cannot causally influence the content of experiences. In some cases they do. You may walk into your sitting-room and seem to hear rain falling outside. Then you notice that someone has left the stereo system on, and realize that the sound you hear is that of applause at the end of a concert. It happens to many people that after realizing this, the sound comes to be heard as applause: the content of experience is influenced by that of judgement. All the independence claim means is that this need not happen.

Among the many current uses of the term 'information', there is one in particular from which the present notion of representational content should be distinguished. There is a sense in which a footprint contains the information that a person with a foot of such-and-such shape and size was at the location of the footprint earlier; and in which a fossil may contain the information that there was an organism of a certain kind at its location in the past. This is a clear and important use of 'informational content', and it seems that it is, very roughly, to be explained along these lines (the details will not matter for us): x's being F at t has the informational content that there was something standing in R to x at some earlier time t' and which was then G, iff in normal circumstances an object's being F at some

---

[3]Essay II (ch. XVI) of *Essays on the Intellectual Powers of Man* (Edinburgh: Thin, 1895), p. 312: 'sensation, taken by itself, implies neither the conception nor the belief of any external object . . . Perception implies an immediate conviction and belief of something external— something different both from the mind that perceives, and from the act of perception.'

particular time is causally, and perhaps differentially, explained by there existing at some earlier time an object standing in R to it and which was then G.[4] An experience, or more strictly the occurrence to someone of an experience of a certain type at a certain time, will certainly have informational content in this sense. But informational content differs from representational content in at least four respects. First, the informational content of a visual experience will include the proposition that a bundle of light rays with such-and-such physical properties struck the retina; nothing like this will be in the representational content of the experience. Second, there are cases in which the representational content and the informational content of an experience are incompatible. This will be so for experiences of geometrical illusions. Such experiences are normally differentially explained by the presence of objects with properties incompatible with those they are represented by the experience as having. Third, though both informational content and representational content are specified by 'that'-clauses, the contents are of different kinds. A specification of informational content is completely referentially ⟵ transparent in genuine singular term position: this property it inherits from the corresponding transparency of 'causally explains'. In the representational content of an experience, on the other hand, objects are presented under perceptual modes of presentation. (This contrast applies not only to singular term position, but also to predicate position. We shall later wish to distinguish properties from modes of presentation of properties, and when that distinction is drawn, it will appear that only the properties themselves, and not properties under modes of presentation, enter causal explanations.) Finally, it is in the nature of representational content that it cannot be built up from concepts unless the subject of the experience himself has those concepts: the representational content is the way the experience presents the world as being, and it can hardly present the world as being that way if the subject is incapable of appreciating what that way is. Only those with the concept of a sphere can have an experience as of a sphere in front of them, and only those with spatial concepts can have experiences which represent things as distributed in depth in space.

[4]For differential explanation, see Ch. 2 of my *Holistic Explanation* (Oxford: OUP, 1979).

By emphasizing these differences, I do not mean to exclude the possibility that possession of representational content can be analysed in terms of informational content (whether this is so is a complex and difficult matter). The present point is just that any such analysis would not consist in an identity. So when I argue that all experiences have nonrepresentational properties, this is *not* a claim to the effect that the intrinsic properties of experience are not determined by their informational content. It is rather a claim about the range of intrinsic properties themselves.

Those who say that sensation has almost no role to play in normal, mature human experience, or at least in normal human visual experience, commonly cite as their ground the fact that all visual experiences have some representational content. If this is indeed a fact, it shows that no human visual experience is a pure sensation. But it does not follow that such experiences do not have sensational properties. It is one thing to say that all mature visual experiences have representational content, another thing to say that no such experience has intrinsic properties (properties which help to specify what it is like to have the experience) explicable without reference to representational content. To assert that all experiences have sensational properties is not necessarily to return to the views of Wundt and his followers.[5] My aim is just to argue that every experience has some sensational properties, and I will concentrate on visual experience as the most challenging case. We can label those who dispute this view, and hold that all intrinsic properties of mature human visual experiences are possessed in virtue of their representational content, 'extreme perceptual theorists'.

Again, we need to sharpen the dispute. One way to do so is to introduce for consideration what I will call the *Adequacy Thesis* (AT). The AT states that a complete intrinsic characterization of an experience can be given by embedding within an operator like 'it visually appears to the subject that . . .' some complex condition concerning physical objects. One component of the condition might be that there is a black telephone in front of oneself and a bookshelf a certain distance and direction to one's left, above and behind which is a window. Such contents can equally be the

---

[5]W. Wundt, *Outlines of Psychology* (Leipzig: Engelmann, 1907).

contents of perceptual or hallucinatory experiences.[6] The content need not be restricted to the qualitative properties of objects, their spatial relations to one another and to the location of the experiencer. It can also concern the relations of the objects and the experiencer to some environmental dimension: the experience of being in a tilted room is different from that of being in the same room when it is upright and the experiencer's body is tilted. Or again, a visual experience as of everything around one swinging to one's left can be distinguished from the visual experience as of oneself revolving rightwards on one's vertical axis. The specification of content may also need in some way to make reference to individuals whom the subject of the experience can recognize: a visual experience can represent Nixon as giving a speech in front of one. The representational content of a visual experience seems always to contain the indexical notions 'now' and 'I', and almost always 'here' and 'there'. (The relation of indexicals to experience will be given some discussion in Chapters 5 and 6.) It should be emphasized that the propositional contents available to the defender of the AT are not all restricted to those features of experience which do not result from unconscious cognitive processing. If there are indeed unconscious mechanisms analogous, say, to inference in the production of experience, then certainly many features of the representational content of an experience will result from the operation of these mechanisms. The important point about representational content, as the notion is used here, is not its freedom from processing but its simultaneous possession of two features. The first is that the representational content concerns the world external to the experiencer, and as such is assessable as true or false. The second feature is that this content is something intrinsic to the experience itself – any experience which does not represent to the subject the world as being the way that this content specifies is phenomenologically different, an experience of a different type. It is quite consistent with these two features that

[6]If we are to be strict, the attribution of a common existential content to perceptual and hallucinatory experience is too crude. There is a sense in which, as one incompetently says, a hallucination presents a *particular* nonexistent object, and so has more than a general existential content. (This can be important in explaining such sentences as 'He hallucinated a cup; he believed it to be medieval, and tried to pick it up; later he came to think it a fake.') To capture this the common content of perception and hallucination could be given by specifying perceptual *types* of modes of presentation of objects, types which do not in every context determine an object.

the presence of experiences with a given representational content
has been caused by past experience and learning. What one must
not do is to suppose that such explanations show that representational content is a matter of judgement caused by some purer
experience: even when an experience has a rich representational
content, the judgement of the subject may still endorse or reject
this content.

The extreme perceptual theorist is committed to the AT. For if
the AT is false, there are intrinsic features of visual experience
which are not captured by representational content. My initial
strategy in opposition to the extreme perceptual theorist will be to
argue against the AT by counterexamples. There is no obvious
defender of the AT whose views one can take as a stalking horse,
no doubt partly because the sensational/representational distinction seems not to have been sufficiently sharply formulated. There
are, though, strong hints of the thesis in Hintikka. He writes 'The
appropriate way of speaking of our spontaneous perceptions is to
use the same vocabulary and the same syntax as we apply to the
objects of perception . . . *all* there is (in principle) to perception (at
this level of analysis) is a specification of the information in
question' (Hintikka's emphasis). He is not here using 'information' in the sense of informational content, for he writes of the
information that our perceptual systems give *us*.[7]

There are at least three types of example which are *prima facie*
evidence against the AT. I will give all three before discussing
ways in which the extreme perceptual theorist might try to
account for each type; for any satisfactory account must accommodate all three types. The point in giving these examples is not
to cite newly discovered phenomena – on the contrary, all the
phenomena are familiar. The point is rather to consider their
bearing on the correct conception of the representational and
sensational properties of experience. Any novelty lies in claims
about this bearing.

Since I shall be arguing by counterexample, the extreme perceptualist's reasons for his view will not initially affect the argument.
But his views do not come from nowhere, and if the counterexamples are sound, the extreme perceptualist's reasons for his

---

[7] 'Information, Causality and the Logic of Perception', in *The Intentions of Intentionality
and Other New Models for Modality* (Dordrecht: Reidel, 1975), pp. 60–2.

views must be insufficient: in so far as there are true beliefs amongst his reasons, those beliefs cannot carry him all the way to his extreme perceptualism. The extreme perceptualist's main motivation is likely to be the thought that if the AT is false, then there are intrinsic features of an experience which are unknowable by anyone not actually having that experience. This thought may be backed by the following superficially plausible argument. We can tell what kind of experience someone has if we know his desires and intentions, and find that he is disposed to act in such-and-such ways when he takes his experience at face value. If, for instance, he wants to travel to a certain place, and takes the shortest available route even though this is not on a straight line, we can come to have reason to believe that he perceives an obstacle on the most direct route: this hypothesis could be inductively confirmed. But it seems that techniques of this sort could only ever reveal representational properties of the subject's experience: for the technique consists in checking that he acts in ways appropriate to the world being as his experience represents it. If this is the only way in which we could come to know the intrinsic properties or another's experiences, the nonrepresentational properties of another's experiences would be unknowable. If the counterexamples below are correct, there must be a gap in this argument. Though the massive general topic of our understanding of consciousness in others is beyond the scope of this book, I will try to indicate at suitable points how we might know of the sensational properties of others' experiences.

There is one last preliminary. Our perceptual experience is always of a more determinate character than our observational concepts which we might use in characterizing it. A normal person does not, and possibly could not, have observational concepts of every possible shade of colour, where shades are individuated by Goodman's identity condition for qualia.[8] Even concepts like 'yellow ochre' and 'burnt sienna' will not distinguish every such shade; and in any case not everyone has such concepts. Thus if the extreme perceptualist is not to be mistaken for trivial reasons, the most that he can maintain is this: the intrinsic properties of a visual experience are exhausted by a specification of its representational content together with some more specific determination of the properties mentioned in that content. I will not trade on this qualification.

[8] *The Structure of Appearance* (Indianapolis: Bobbs-Merrill, 1966), p. 290.

Here then are the examples:

(1) Suppose you are standing on a road which stretches from you in a straight line to the horizon. There are two trees at the roadside, one a hundred yards from you, the other two hundred. Your experience represents these objects as being of the same physical height and other dimensions; that is, taking your experience at face value you would judge that the trees are roughly the same physical size, just as in the *trompe l'œil* example, without countervailing beliefs you would judge that there is a violin on the door; and in this case we can suppose that the experience is a perception of the scene around you. Yet there is also some sense in which the nearer tree occupies more of your visual field than the more distant tree. This is as much a feature of your experience itself as is its representing the trees as being the same height. The experience can possess this feature without your having any concept of the feature or of the visual field: you simply enjoy an experience which has the feature. It is a feature which makes Rock say that the greater size of the retinal image of the nearer tree is not without some reflection in consciousness, and may be what earlier writers such as Ward meant when they wrote of differences in extensity.[9] It presents an initial challenge to the Adequacy Thesis, since no veridical experience can represent one tree as larger than another and also as the same size as the other. The challenge to the extreme perceptual theorist is to account for these facts about size in the visual field without abandoning the AT. We can label this problem 'the problem of the additional characterization'.

The problem of the additional characterization does not arise only for size in the visual field, or for properties such as speed of movement in the visual field which are defined in terms of it. It can arise for colours and sounds. Imagine you are in a room looking at a corner formed by two of its walls. The walls are covered with paper of a uniform hue, brightness and saturation. But one wall is more brightly illuminated than the other. In these circumstances, your experience can represent both walls as being the same colour: it does not look to you as if one of the walls is

---

[9] I. Rock, 'In Defense of Unconscious Inference', in *Stability and Constancy in Visual Perception* (New York: Wiley, 1977), ed. W. Epstein; J. Ward *Psychological Principles* (Cambridge: CUP, 1920).

painted with brighter paint than the other. Yet it is equally an aspect of your visual experience itself that the region of the visual field in which one wall is presented is brighter than that in which the other is presented. An example of the same type of phenomenon involving hearing might be this. You see two cars at different distances from yourself, both with their engines running. Your experience can represent the engines as running equally loudly (if you are searching for a quiet car, your experience gives you no reason to prefer one over the other); but again it seems undeniable that in some sense the nearer car sounds louder.

(2) All these illustrations of the problem of the additional characterization were in some way related to the duality of representational properties and properties of the two-dimensional visual field, but they were not cases in which the additional characterization apparently omitted by representational properties was something which could vary even though representational content is held constant. Yet there are also examples of this, examples in which a pair of experiences in the same sense-modality have the same representational content, but differ in some other intrinsic respect. Suppose you look at an array of pieces of furniture with one eye closed. Some of the pieces of furniture may be represented by your experience as being in front of others. Imagine now that you look at the same scene with both eyes. The experience is different. It may be tempting to try to express this difference by saying that some chairs now appear to be in front of others, but this cannot suffice: for the monocular experience also represented certain objects as being in front of others. Taking your monocular experience at face value, you would judge that some pieces of furniture are in front of others: objects do not suddenly seem to be at no distance from you when you close one eye. The experiential difference between monocular and binocular vision is independent of the double images of unfocussed objects produced by binocular vision. The extra way depth is indicated in binocular vision is present when you look into a child's stereoscope, and there need not be any double images when you do.[10] (There are not many examples of this

[10] In *The Perception of the Visual World* (Boston: Houghton Mifflin, 1950); J. J. Gibson says of the impression of distance in depth in binocular vision that 'You can reduce the distance somewhat by closing one eye' (p. 42). Even if this is in fact true in all cases, it cannot be definitional of the distinctive impression produced by depth in binocular vision: one can imagine that closing one eye eliminates this impression even though as a result nothing looks closer than it did before.

phenomenon with the other senses, but one such might be this. A stereophonic recording of a wave breaking sounds quite different from a monaural recording, even if one cannot locate aurally the various directions of the components of the whole sound.) The situation in the visual example is more complex than it may at first seem. The complexity can be brought out by reflecting that there are pairs of experiences which differ in the way in which the experiences of monocular and binocular vision of an ordinary scene differ, and in which only the binocular experience contains any dimension of depth. Consider two arrays of dots, one a random array and the other random except in some region in which the dots are arranged as they are in the corresponding region of the first array, but slightly displaced to take account of binocular disparity. These are the Julesz random-dot patterns.[11] When viewed with two eyes, some dots are seen as being in front of others: when the arrays are seen with only one eye, there is no impression of depth. There are two different attitudes one could take to this example. One, incompatible with what we have so far said, would be that the example shows that though there is indeed an additional way in which depth is represented in binocular as opposed to monocular vision, the extra feature is purely representational; and it is this additional purely representational feature which is present in binocular vision of the random-dot patterns. The second attitude is that even in the random-dot case, the difference between monocular and binocular vision is both sensational and representational. This is the attitude for which I shall argue.

On the second attitude, there is a sensational property which in normal human experience is indeed associated with the representation of depth. If it is granted that visual field properties are sensational, we already have other examples of such association, since in normal humans perceiving an ordinary scene, the visual field properties are associated with a representational content. The difference between the two attitudes lies in the fact that according to the first, it ought to be impossible to conceive of cases in which the alleged sensational property is present, but in which a representation of certain objects as being behind others in the environment is absent. According to the second attitude, this ought to be conceivable.

[11] B. Julesz, 'Texture and visual perception', *Scientific American,* February 1965.

But it does seem to be conceivable. It could be that there is a being for whom visual experience is in certain respects like the experience enjoyed by a congenitally blind user of a tactile–vision substitution system (TVSS).[12] A TVSS consists of a television camera, the output of which is connected to a two-dimensional array of vibrating rods on the user's back. After using the TVSS for a short time, the congenitally blind subject has intrinsically spatial sensations resulting from the vibrations, sensations which are not those of pressure or vibration on his back, and which are reported to be quite unlike those of touch. These sensations are arranged in a two-dimensional space, and they do not seem to the experiencer to be of objects in the space around him. That is, the space of the sensations is not experienced as bearing any spatial relations to the physical space in which the experiencer is located.[13] The subjects report that the sensations are not as of anything 'out there'. Now it seems that we can also conceive, at least as a logical possibility, of such sensations (perhaps resulting from the output of two cameras) existing in a three-dimensional space, which is nevertheless still not experienced as the space around the perceiver. Finally, it seems that we can conceive of someone's visual experience being like that of the subject in his hypothetical three-dimensional case: someone with tactile experience of the world around him and suddenly given stereoscopic vision of unfamiliar objects (such as small blobs randomly distributed in three-dimensional space) could conceivably be so. Here then a sensational third dimension would be present; but there would be no representation of depth in the sense that the experience itself represents some things as being further away than others in the forward direction in the physical space in which the experiencer is located. There is, then, a dangerous ambiguity in the term 'depth'. It is indeed true that whenever the extra feature which distinguishes binocular from monocular vision is present, there will be an impression of depth; but since on the sense in which this must be so, depth is a sensational property, the

---

[12]P. Bach-y-Rita *et. al.*, 'Vision Substitution by Tactile Image Projection', *Nature* 221 (1969), 963–4; G. Guarniero, 'Experience of tactile vision', *Perception* 3 (1974), 101–4.

[13]Cp. Guarniero, p. 104: 'By this time objects had come to have a top and a bottom; a right side and a left; but no depth– they existed in an ordered two-dimensional space, the precise location of which has not yet been determined.'

point cannot be used to argue that the difference between monocular and binocular vision is purely representational.[14]

(3) The third type of problem is illustrated by the switching of aspects under which some object or array of objects is seen. Consider an example in which a wire framework in the shape of a cube is viewed with one eye and is seen first with one of its faces in front, the face parallel to this face being seen as behind it, and is then suddenly seen, without any change in the cube or alteration of its position, with that former face now behind the other. The successive experiences have different representational contents. The first experience represents a face ABCD as nearer oneself than the face EFGH, the later experience represents the presence of a state of affairs incompatible with its being nearer. Yet there seems to be some additional level of classification at which the successive experiences fall under the same type; indeed that something like this is so seems to be a feature of the experience of a switch in aspect – as Wittgenstein writes, 'I *see* that it has not changed'.[15] We have here another example of apparently nonrepresentational similarities between experiences.

The challenge to the extreme perceptual theorist is to explain how there can be nonrepresentational similarities between experiences without giving up the AT. He might propose simply to introduce a new classification of visual experience by means of a content which still conforms to the spirit of the AT, but which relates

---

[14]My position here is incompatible with that of O'Shaughnessy, *The Will*, vol. 1, pp. 171–3, where he argues that (in my terminology) depth is never a sensational property. He offers three reasons, the first two of which aim to show that 'concepts play a causal role in the genesis of visual depth experience'. The first reason is that '*any* visual depth experience depends upon one's seeing one's visual depth sensations *as* contributing the colour of physical items situated at some distance from one'. This begs the question by presuming that the third dimension in the space of the sensations must represent to the experiencer depth in the physical space around him. The text above gives an imagined counterexample to this claim of necessary coincidence. The second reason given is that 'two visual fields of sensations could be internally indistinguishable and yet thanks to the diverse concepts and beliefs of their owners cause different *veridical* visual depth impressions'. But when there are stereoscopic depth impressions resulting from binocular vision, the three-dimensional visual field properties are not compatible with different depth impressions, at least in respect of the distribution in three dimensions of the surface actually seen. O'Shaughnessy's third reason is that his view is corroborated by the optical facts: but he considers only the bundle of light rays reaching a single eye. In the nature of the case, monocular vision is insufficient for stereopsis; and the optical facts when we consider binocular vision not only make depth as a sensational property intelligible, but also explain why the property should peter out at greater distances.

[15]*Philosophical Investigations* (Oxford: Blackwell, 1958), p. 193; cp. also *Remarks on the Philosophy of Psychology* (Oxford: Blackwell, 1980), vol. 1, section 33.

to some time just before the occurrence of the experience: the content would presumably be that the scene around oneself has not altered. But this view ignores the fact that, in normal circumstances, with memory errors aside, the presence of the impression that the scene has or has not altered surely depends on the character of the successive experiences. If we just added this new type of experience to our characterizations, we would still have to say on what properties of successive experiences its presence or absence depends. This suggestion also fails to cope with an aspect switch accompanied by loss of memory of the earlier experience: for here there need be no impression that the scene has not altered. Finally, the suggestion does not capture the nonrepresentational similarity between the experiences of two different subjects looking at the cube, one seeing a certain face in front, the other seeing it as behind. It is not only between successive experiences of a single person that there are nonrepresentational similarities. We do then have a third type of problem for the extreme perceptual theorist.

Why have I chosen to use the example of monocular vision of a three-dimensional wire frame to make these points, rather than the traditional duck–rabbit figure? The reason lies in this: when a subject undergoes an aspect switch while looking at that figure, there is nothing which is seen first as a duck, and then as a rabbit – rather, something is seen first as a representation of a duck, and then is seen as a representation of a rabbit. But then what is so seen, an arrangement of lines on paper, remains constant in the representational content of the successive experiences. So the example does not serve the purpose of showing that there can be nonrepresentational similarities between experiences, since someone who denies that could simply say that in this example the component of representational content concerning the arrangement of the lines on paper remains constant, and accounts for the similarity. In the example of the wire cube, this reply is not available: for after the aspect switch, the wires do not all seem to be in the same relative positions as before.[16]

A natural reaction of the extreme perceptual theorist to examples of these three types is to claim that all the statements whose truth

---

[16] The possibility of the notion of representation itself entering the content of an experience would allow one to give this explanation of the difference between seeing one area as figure and another as ground: the whole is seen as a representation in which the former area is represented as being in front of the latter.

seems to conflict with the Adequacy Thesis can be translated into statements which do not attribute to experiences any features going beyond those countenanced by the AT.[17] Let us consider this translational response as applied to size in the visual field and the two trees on the road. It might be suggested that the statement 'The nearer tree takes up more of the visual field' could be approximately translated by the counterfactual 'For any plane perpendicular to the subject's line of sight and lying between him and the two trees, a larger area of that place would have to be made opaque precisely to obscure the nearer tree than would have to be made opaque precisely to obscure the more distant tree'. It is not clear how the translational response could be implemented in the second kind of example; but does it succeed even for the first kind?

Of what is this translational suggestion offered as an explanation? A first possibility is that it might be offered as an explanation of why we use the same spatial vocabulary as applies to extended objects in space in connection with the visual field. As an explanation of this it is satisfying, and can be extended to such relations as *above* and *next to* in the visual field. But the defender of the AT needs more than this. If this account of the content of experience is to be adequate, he needs this suggestion to supply an account of what it means to say that one object is larger than another in the subject's visual field. This is the second possibility. As a meaning-giving account, the suggestion seems quite inadequate. When we reflect on the possibility that light rays might bend locally, or that the experiencer might have astigmatism, it seems clear that the counterfactual which is alleged to translate the statement 'The nearer tree takes up more of the visual field than the further tree' is in general neither necessary nor sufficient for the truth of that statement. There is also an objection of principle to a counterfactual analysis of an intrinsic property of experience. Whether one object is larger than another in the subject's visual field is a property of his experience in the actual world, be counterfactual circumstances as they may. An account of size in the visual field should make it dependent only upon the actual properties of the experience itself.

[17] In effect, some philosophers reacted this way to Gibson's use in his earlier writings of the concept of the visual field; D. W. Hamlyn for instance wrote '. . . the properties which Gibson ascribes to the visual field are all logically derivative from those ascribable to the visual world'. See 'The Visual Field and Perception'. *Proceedings of the Aristotelian Society*, supplementary volume 31 (1957) at p. 121. (I should add that Hamlyn later changed his mind on this question.)

The distinction between the acceptable and the unacceptable components of the translational view can be explained in terms of a partial parallel with Kripke's distinction between fixing the referent of an expression and giving its meaning.[18] Kripke noted that though one may fix the reference of a proper name 'Bright' by stipulating that it is to refer to the man who invented the wheel, nevertheless the sentence 'It might have been that Bright never invented the wheel' is true. Now to understand this last sentence, we have to have some grasp of the possibility of a person who actually meets a condition failing to meet it. Similarly, experiences of such a type that the nearer tree is larger in the visual field than the further do actually meet the condition that more of the previously mentioned plane must be obscured precisely to block perception of the nearer tree. This condition fixes the type of the experience, but this type might have failed to meet that condition, just as it might have been that Bright was less inventive. What the translational defender of the extreme perceptual view fails to supply is any account of sameness of experience which allows for the possibility that the type of experience which in fact meets his translational condition fails to do so.

A different strategy in defence of the Adequacy Thesis would be to expand the range of representational contents. It would be conceded that the three types of example make trouble for the AT if we confine ourselves to representational contents of the sorts already considered; but there would be no difficulty, it may be said, if for instance we included in representational content the angle subtended by an object. Such is the view of Rock, who regards perceived visual angle and perceived objective size as simply different aspects of perception. He follows the practice of calling experiences of the former type 'proximal mode experiences' and writes 'Proximal mode experiences are best thought of as perceptions rather than sensations'.[19] Despite his important contributions on the issues of this section, Rock's views here are open to criticism. As we emphasized, it is a conceptual truth that no one can have an experience with a given representational content unless he possesses the concepts from which that content is built up: an experience cannot represent the world to the subject of experience

---

[18] *Naming and Necessity* (Oxford: Blackwell, 1980).

[19] 'In Defense of Unconscious Inference', p. 349, and also in his *Introduction to Perception* (New York: Macmillan, 1975), pp. 39, 47, 56.

as being a certain way if he is not capable of grasping what that way
is. This conceptual point entails that adding contents concerning
the visual angle to representational content to save the AT is illegitimate: for an unsophisticated perceiver who does not have the
concept of subtended angle it is nevertheless true that one object
takes up more of his visual field than another, just as it does for a
more sophisticated theorist.[20] This criticism would equally apply to
a view once endorsed by Boring, who, after asking what
'observation would demonstrate' that a subject is perceiving the
size of his own retinal image, continued: 'For a man to perceive the
size of his own retinal images his perception of size must remain
invariant under all transformations that leave the size of the retinal
images invariant'.[21] If this is a sufficient condition, it is one that can
be met by a man who has never heard of a retina. It would also
involve a fundamental overdeterminacy of the representational
content of experience, since transformations that leave the size of
the retinal image invariant will equally leave suitable cross-sections
of the light rays in a given plane within the eye unaltered in area,
and by Boring's lights this could equally be taken as the content of
the perception. These problems result from trying to construe a
sensational property, size in the visual field, as a representational
property.

It will help at this point if we introduce a simple piece of notation. If a particular experience e has the familiar sensational property which in normal circumstances is produced by a white
object (such as a tilted plate) which would be precisely obscured
by an opaque elliptical region (r, say) of the imagined interposed
plane, let us express this fact in the notation 'elliptical' (r, e) and
white' (r, e)'. These primed predicates 'elliptical'' and 'white''
should not be confused with their unprimed homonyms. In using
the notation, we are not thereby saying that experiences have

[20] Even if the perceiver does have the concept of the subtended angle and it enters the
representational content of his experience, it is not clear that the suggestion works. For it
would rule out *a priori* the following possibility. There is someone who suffers from
unsystematic distortion in a particular region of his visual field. He knows this, and after
a time objects presented in that region of his visual field are no longer presented as being
as determinate in size in the way those presented elsewhere are so represented. If this is
possible, then an object may be presented outside the distorting region, and be presented
as subtending a certain angle, and it may occupy the same size of region of the visual
field as an object in the distorting region which is not presented as subtending any
particular angle.

[21] 'Visual Perception and Invariance', *Psychological Review* 59 (1952), 141–8, at p. 145.

colour properties or spatial properties. With this apparatus we can express what would more traditionally have been expressed by saying 'There is a yellow elliptical region of the visual field next to a white square region'. Thus, using logical notation:

$$\exists\, r\, \exists\, s\, (\text{elliptical}'\, (r, e)\,\&\, \text{yellow}'(r, e)\,\&\, \text{square}'\, (s, e)\,\&\, \text{white}'\, (s, e)\,\&\, \text{next}'\, (r, s)).^{22}$$

We said earlier that the means by which these expressions containing primes have been introduced serves only to fix which properties they pick out. The point of invoking Kripke's distinction between fixing the referent and giving the meaning was to emphasize a modal point: that we can conceive of circumstances in which, for example, a tilted plate does not produce an elliptical region of the visual field. But the phrase 'it fixes the referent rather than gives the meaning' is potentially misleading: it may suggest that there is more to understanding 'red'' than knowing that it is the sensational property of the visual field in which a red thing is presented in normal circumstances. But there is not more than this. Anyone who knows what it is like to have an experience as of something red and has the concept of the visual field knows what it is like to have an experience which is red' (relative to some region). In this respect the means by which we have fixed which property 'red'' refers to does indeed play a special role in understanding that primed predicate. It would be equally true to say that the property of being red' is that property of the visual field normally produced by the presence of an object with such-and-such physical reflectance properties. This description would not convey understanding of 'red'', except in the presence of additional knowledge of which sensational property it is that meets the physically specified condition.

The sensational properties of an experience, like its representational properties, have reliable and publicly identifiable causes. We argued that the property of being presented in a large region of the visual field cannot be identified with the property of being represented as subtending a large visual angle: but nevertheless the fact

---

[22] The visual field sensational properties caused by an object can of course be influenced by the properties of the other objects perceived: geometrical illusions again illustrate the point. A more complex means of introducing the primed properties would take account of this relativity.

that an object does subtend a large visual angle does causally explain its presentation in a large region of the visual field. This explanatory fact is one which concerns the physical spatial relations of the perceiver to the physical objects in his environment. Nor is it true that the sensational properties of an experience cannot explain a subject's behaviour. We can conceive of someone who does indeed want to obscure precisely certain objects by attaching opaque surfaces to a glass plane which is perpendicular to his line of sight. At first, he may have to learn from experience with several particular objects what shape of surface to place on the plane. But it seems clear that we can also imagine that his learning successfully transfers to shapes quite different from those cases in which he learned which shape to choose, and that he comes to need no more than his ordinary visual experience in order to make a selection of the shape. At this stage, the sensational properties of his experience would have to be cited in the explanation of why he chooses one shape rather than another to obscure precisely some particular kind of object seen for the first time behind the glass. It is not clear that the sensational properties of experience are in principle any more problematic epistemologically than are the representational properties (which are, certainly, problematic enough).

These points about sensational properties have been tailored to the first type of example offered against the Adequacy Thesis. But they apply equally to the second: they apply *pari passu* if we introduce a primed relation 'behind'' and fix its reference in terms of the physical conditions which normally produce the sensational property it stands for – the conditions for binocular vision of objects at different depths. I suggest that in the third kind of case, nonrepresentational similarity of experiences consists in sameness or similarity of sensational properties. In all the standard cases of switches of áspect, the successive experiences have the same primed sensational properties, those fixed in terms of the imagined interposed plane. Such identity of sensational properties is also not confined to successive experiences of one individual. This explanation of the third type of case also generalizes to an example with which it is hard to reconcile the AT. A person can have the experience of waking up in an unfamiliar position or place, and his experience initially has a minimal representational content. The content may be just that there are surfaces at various angles to him, without even a rough specification of distances. Suddenly, everything falls into place, and he has an experience with a rich representational content: he sees that nothing has altered in the scene in the sense in which one sees this when experiencing an aspect switch with the wire cube. Again, the primed sensational properties of the successive experiences are identical.

If this treatment of the examples is correct, then neither one of representational content and sensational properties determines the other. The cases of change of aspect show that sensational properties do not determine representational content, while the case of binocular vision of depth shows that representational content in a given sense-modality does not determine sensational properties. Concepts of both types are needed for a full description.[23]

Sensational properties are ubiquitous features of visual experiences: indeed it seems impossible to conceive of an experience devoid of all sensational properties. This is one reason why the visual properties which have been argued here to be sensational should be distinguished from the early Gibsonian conception of the visual field. Concepts of the Gibsonian visual field apply not to ordinary visual experience, but only to a special kind of experience we can have when we adopt the attitude a painter adopts to his experience. 'By adopting the appropriate attitude, one can have either kind of visual experience . . . The visual field is a product of the chronic habit of civilized men of seeing the world as a picture . . . The visual field is a picture-like phenomenal experience at a presumptive phenomenal distance from the eyes, consisting of perspective size-impressions.'[24] Gibsonian visual field experiences can occur only to those who

---

[23] A listener hearing an earlier version of this chapter drew my attention to David Lewis's unduly neglected 'Percepts and Color Mosaics in Visual Experience', *Philosophical Review* 75 (1966), 357–68. Lewis's notion of experiences which are modification-equivalent and his claims concerning it are clearly close to what I would call the relation of having the same sensational properties and the claim that sensational properties are distinct from representational properties. But readers wishing to compare his views with those of this chapter should note that Lewis's percept and my representational content are not to be identified. He writes of percepts which are pure percepts of colour mosaic and nothing else (p. 363): such experiences do not in my sense have representational content. Like the early experiences of the TVSS user, they do not represent the world in the environment of the subject as being a particular way. Correspondingly they are not directly assessable as veridical or otherwise. (Less direct relations of correspondence could though be defined).

[24] J. J. Gibson, 'The Visual Field and the Visual World', *Psychological Review* 59 (1952), 149–51.

have the concept of a planar representation of the environment. It would perhaps be open to a Gibsonian to hold that the pictorial attitude and the special experiences it produces merely emphasize features already present in ordinary visual experience. This is indeed the position I have been defending, but on such a defence the account of the nature of these features cannot make essential reference to pictorial representation.

Where do the phenomena to which the Gestalt psychologists referred with the label 'grouping' fall within this classification? One such phenomenon is given by the fact that we see the array

                    .   .   .
                    .   .   .
                    .   .   .

as three columns of dots rather than as four rows. Two points make it plausible to classify grouping phenomena as generally sensational properties of experience. One is that it is manifested simply in the exercise of experientially-based discriminative capacities. Someone who perceives the array grouped into three columns will find this array subjectively more similar to

                    | | |
                    | | |

than to

                    _____
                    _____
                    _____
                    _____

Instances of a three-place relation of comparative subjective similarity can be manifested in experientially-based discriminative reactions. Quine emphasized this point in *The Roots of Reference*,[25] and in this he was in agreement with the experimental techniques of the Gestalt psychologists themselves.[26] A second reason for saying that grouping properties are sensational rather than representational is that they are found in experiences which have

[25] La Salle, Illinois: Open Court, 1974.
[26] W. Köhler, *Gestalt Psychology* (New York: Liveright, 1947), Ch. 5.

no representational properties. In listening to the rhythms produced by a solo drum player, each sound is grouped with some but not with other sounds.[27] It is true that in our initial example, the very description of the case 'seen as three columns rather than four rows' seems to suggest that we are concerned with a representational, not a sensational, property: the concept of a column enters the content. But this is because experiences with a particular sensational property also have, in normal mature humans, a certain representational property. Many ,of the examples given by Gestalt psychologists are ones in which there are distinctive grouping properties, groupings in particular curves and shapes, and in which the subject of the experience has no concept in advance with which to pick out the curve or shape in question.[28]

Grouping phenomena do however raise two closely related problems for what I have so far said about the category of sensational properties. In some cases we can perceive one and the same array as differently grouped in successive experiences. This array

```
o       o       o       o

•       •       •       •

o       o       o       o

•       •       •       •

o       o       o       o

•       •       •       •
```

[after Rock, *Introduction to Perception*]

---

[27] Compare also hearing a chord as an augmented fourth rather than as a diminished fifth. Someone can have this experience without having the concept of an augmented fourth. His hearing it that way is necessarily linked to the resolutions of that chord which sound right to him. If it is true that different groupings are sensational properties, any proposal to include both grouping phenomena and switches in the aspect under which an object is perceived under the common label of 'organization in experience', needs some positive justification. Note also that the fact that there seems to be a conceptual distinction between grouping and seeing something as an instance of a particular concept may underlie Wittgenstein's otherwise somewhat obscure remark in his discussion of seeing-as — that one has to distinguish 'purely optical' aspects from those '*mainly* determined by thoughts and associations': see *Remarks on the Philosophy of Psychology* vol. 1, sections 970, 1017.

[28] For sample illustrations, see Köhler, op. cit. and Rock, *Introduction to Perception*.

can be seen as either rows or columns. The first problem now is this: we earlier said that in switches of aspect the sensational properties of the successive experiences remained constant. But now, in the case of switches of grouping, we are distinguishing switches *within* the class of sensational properties of experience according to the account so far given. No doubt aspect – and grouping – switches are to be distinguished, but the impression after a switch of either type that nothing has altered seems to have a similar basis; yet the account seems to leave no room for saying that it does. That is the first problem. The second problem, now that grouping is included as a sensational property, is how the particular sensational properties an experience may possess are to be explained. For the primed properties of the successive experiences, for someone who views our most recent array and undergoes a switch of grouping, may be identical; and yet their sensational properties are different.

A full treatment of these problems would give a detailed theory of the types of sensational properties and the relations between them. Here I will just note a distinction which can be applied to the problem. The facts about grouping show that many different types of experience may be produced in normal circumstances by a given pattern of light on the imagined frontal glass plane. We can capture the nonrepresentational differences between these types by using again the fact that if an experience has a particular grouping, it will be subjectively more similar to a second experience with different primed properties than it is to a third. There are at least two levels of classification of visual experience in sensational terms: a basic level, at which terms for the properties have their references fixed by means of the imagined frontal glass plane; and a second level, determined by different possible patterns of comparative subjective similarity between experiences falling under these basic types. The difference between the case in which a given array is seen to be grouped in columns and the case in which it is seen to be grouped in rows is captured at this second level. The difference remains a difference within the class of sensational properties.

2

The Distinction Applied

I turn now to some applications of the sensational/representational distinction and to some problems it poses. The three applications are to the perception of spatial properties and relations, to the perception of secondary qualities, and to some asymmetries between the experience of primary and secondary qualities. These applications are not intrinsically unconnected. In the first two applications, the distinction is applied in an attempt to help resolve problems which are caused by failure to draw it. Clearly there are two ways of ignoring the distinction: one way is to assimilate all intrinsic properties of experience to the sensational, and the other is to assimilate them all to the representational. The former assimilation is the source of problems in the topic of the first application; while the treatment of all intrinsic properties on a model suitable only for certain representational properties is a source of problems in the second application. The third application employs principles which emerge from the second application.

We start then with the perception of spatial properties. The existence of sensational properties, distinct from representational properties, relieves one of the main sources of pressure towards the view that one sense-modality must be conceptually prior to the others in the perception of space. One of the reasons which moved Berkeley in *An Essay Towards a New Theory of Vision* to hold such a view was that

> the extension, figures and motions perceived by sight are specifically distinct from the ideas of touch, called by the same names, not is there any such thing as one idea, or kind of idea, common to both senses.[1]

What is true is that the sensational properties of visual and factual experience are *toto caelo* distinct; in this sense no ideas are common

---

[1] Section 127.

to touch and sight. It does not follow that the representational contents of visual and tactual experiences, including their spatial content, do not overlap. If the distinctness of visual and tactual experience is captured at the sensational level, there is no pressure to take one sense as conceptually prior to the other in the perception of space. A failure to distinguish sensational properties from representational content is of course not merely incidental to Berkeley's thought. Drawing the dinstinction is tantamount to accepting that there is a sense in which what is perceived can be something that exists independently of states of mind.

The second application of the distinction requires a more extensive discussion. I shall claim that the notion of a sensational property can be used to resolve a problem about the relation between looking red and being red. 'Red' here is just an example; the problem is one which arises for any secondary quality, and it is this.

There seems to be a straightforward dilemma about the relation between being red and looking red. There are arguments for saying that each must be more fundamental than the other. Someone does not know what it is for something to be red and does not fully understand the predicate 'is red' unless he knows what it is like to have a visual experience as of a red object; and the occurrence of such an experience suitably caused is registered by saying that an object looks red to someone at some particular time. The connection here is specifically with visual experience. Consider these two biconditionals:

A perceptible object is red iff it looks red in standard circumstances

and

A perceptible object is square iff it looks square in standard circumstances.

Both seem to be true, but they are not of the same status. For

A perceptible object is square iff it feels square in standard circumstances

is as acceptable as the visual version in the case of squareness; whereas 'feels red' makes no sense. Again, the congenitally blind can understand 'is square' (though they may think of the property in a different way from the sighted). For these familiar reasons, visual experience seems to occupy a special position in an explanation of what it is for something to be red which no particular sense-modality occupies in an explanation of what it is for something to be square. The point is not just that squareness is accessible to more than one sense: rather, what it is for something to have the property of being square cannot be explained in sensory terms at all. (Other differences are consequential on this.) These points are precisely what we should expect if looking red is conceptually more fundamental than being red. Yet on the other hand the expression 'looks red' is not semantically unstructured. Its sense is determined by that of its constituents. If one does not understand those constituents, one does not fully understand the compound; and conversely, with a general understanding of the 'looks' construction and of some predicate for which 'looks' makes sense, one can understand the compound without the need for additional information. So from this angle it appears that looking red could not be more fundamental than being red. How is this dilemma to be resolved?[2]

If colour is a coherent notion at all, it seems there are three possible types of response to this problem. Each response takes a different relation to hold between the concept of being red on the one hand and concepts of experience on the other. The three types of response are as follows.

(i)   The concept of being red is philosophically prior to that of looking red and to other experiential concepts. This is true not just in the uncontroversial sense that the phrase 'looks red' contains 'red' as a semantic constituent.[3] On this first type of view, it is true

---

[2]There is a passage in *The Concept of Mind* (London: Penguin, 1963) in which Ryle brings out the dilemma, but curiously leaves it untreated: '. . . when I describe a common object as green or bitter . . . I am saying that it would look or taste so-and-so to anyone who was in a condition and position to see or taste properly . . . It must be noticed that the formula "it would look so-and-so to anyone" cannot be paraphrased by "it would look *green* to anyone", for to say that something looks green is to say that it looks as it would if it were green and conditions were normal.' Having denied that this paraphrase is correct, Ryle is left explaining 'green' by a definition which takes the phrase 'looks so-and-so' as an unexplained primitive. This is the unacceptable price he pays to avoid the threatened circularity.

[3]For emphasis on the importance of this relatively uncontroversial point, see Anscombe, 'The Intensionality of Sensation' in *Analytical Philosophy (Second Series)*, ed. R. Butler (Oxford: Blackwell, 1968), p. 172, and W. Sellars 'Empiricism and the

also in the more substantial sense that an account of what makes an experience an experience as of something red must ultimately make use of the concept, applicable to physical objects, of being red. This we will label 'the anti-experientialist option'.

(ii) Neither being red nor any relevant family of concepts whose instantiation entails the occurrence of experiences ('experiential concepts') is prior to the other. Both have to be characterized simultaneously by means of their relations to one another and to other notions. This is the no-priority view.

(iii) The concept of being red has to be explained in terms of experiential concepts. This can be done in a way not undermined by the fact that 'looks red' semantically contains 'red', and without any circular use of the concept of being red. This might be called 'the pure experientialist view' — 'pure' because the no-priority view is a partially experiential view. But for brevity we will call a view of this third type simply 'the experientialist view'.

These three exhaust the possibilities. In labelling the views, we have not used the terminology of objective and subjective. It may sit well with some intuition to say that the anti-experientialist is the objectivist about colour: but it is obvious that even the experientialist can admit some sense in which a physical thing is objectively red if, in certain conditions, it produces experiences of the kind he chooses to designate.

These three positions exhaust the possibilities only for given notion of priority. I have written, very loosely, of the relations 'more fundamental than', 'conceptually prior to' and 'philosophically prior to'. To be more precise, my topic here is a priority of definability. We can say that concept A is definitionally prior to concept B iff B can be defined illuminatingly in a given respect in terms of A. The fixed relation of priority with which we are concerned is definitional priority, and the respect in which we want to be illuminated is what it is to have the concept of being red. There are other notions of priority in the offing: I will return to one of them later.

Philosophy of Mind' in his *Science, Perception and Reality* (London: Routledge, 1963), pp. 141ff. Sellars' later explanation (p. 147) of why, as he puts it, it is a necessary truth that something is red iff it looks red to standard observers in standard circumstances is this: that standard conditions are just conditions in which things look as they are. That may be true, but it applies to any predicate F for which 'looks F' has some application: it does not explain why the concept of being red has a closer connection with visual experience than does the concept of being square.

I take first the anti-experientialist view. One form such a view might take has been developed by Shoemaker: he holds, by implication, that the fact that an experience is as of something red consists in the fact that it would, in the absence of countervailing beliefs, give rise to the belief that the presented object *is* red.[4] Alternatively, such an anti-experientialist might try to characterize such experiences as those playing a certain role in an experientially-based ability to discriminate red from non-red things. In either case, the property of being red is employed in the account of what it is for an experience to be as of something red.

What, then, can the anti-experientialist say about the property of being red? His view collapses into the third option, that taken by the experientialist, if he attempts to explain redness in turn by appeal to the properties of experiences. One cannot assess the anti-experientialist's view, and nor can he establish the special connection with visual experience, until he gives some positive account of colour properties of objects.

One response which is not immediately circular is to say that the predicate 'red' in fact picks out either a dispositional property of objects to reflect light of a certain sort, or picks out the categorical ground of this disposition. This is Armstrong's view, later adopted by Smart.[5] Such a view may have a relatively sophisticated structure. It may be said that after being introduced to certain sample objects as being within the extension of 'red' one goes on to act in accordance with the definition: 'red' picks out that state S of these objects which causes human observers to be in some experiential state, and this experiential state tends to give rise to the belief that some object has S, or tends to give rise to an ability to discriminate things with the property S. Such methods of introducing 'red' are not formally illegitimate and avoid circularity; provided that the states quantified over can be characterized in terms other than 'states which produce experiences of such-and-such kind'. For instance, in verifying that some physical state T conforms to this more sophisticated definition, one has to check that T is possessed by the initial sample objects and that it produces in humans the belief that some object has T, or produces an ability to discriminate

[4] 'Functionalism and Qualia', *Philosophical Studies* 27 (1975) 291–315.

[5] D. M. Armstrong, *A Materialist Theory of the Mind* (London: Routledge, 1968); J. J. C. Smart, 'On Some Criticisms of a Physicalist Theory of Colour', in *Philosophical Aspects of the Mind–Body Problem,* ed. Chung-yin-Chen (Honolulu: University of Hawaii, 1975).

objects with the property T. The objections at this point are not those of circularity.

Told only that a word refers to a certain object, we are not in a position to know what way of thinking of the object that word is used to express. Similarly we can draw a distinction between physical properties themselves and ways of thinking of them; and the move we are envisaging the anti-experientialist as making gives an account of which physical property the word 'red' picks out, but gives no account of a way of thinking of that property the word expresses. We just said cautiously on behalf of the anti-experientialist that 'red' picks out that state S of some initial sample of objects which causes human beings to be in some experiential state and this experiental state tends to give rise to the belief that some object has S, or tends to give rise to the ability to discriminate things with the property S. But someone would equally be 'acting in accordance with' such a specification if he employed some instrument which is sensitive to the reflectance properties of surfaces, and whose output is given in auditory form through a small loudspeaker. He may acquire beliefs about the properties of surfaces, beliefs which are caused by the auditory experience produced by the instrument, and which are not based on inference. Yet this person does not fully understand 'red' if he knows only that the word picks out the property which explains the noise from the loudspeaker when he uses the instrument. This way of developing the anti-experientialist view lacks any component which would explain why understanding of the word 'red' is so closely tied to visual experience.

Since the anti-experientialist has an account only of the property that 'red' picks out, but does not have any account of the way an understander is required to think of that property, the only propositional-attitude and more generally psychological contexts containing 'red' which he can explain are those in which it occurs transparently: contexts which say that someone believes of the property that such-and-such object has it, or of the property that it falls under so-and-so higher-order condition. This leads to a difficulty in carrying out the anti-experientialist's programme of explaining the property of looking red in terms of being red, even when we confine our attention to visual experience.

Suppose that, initially, surfaces with a given physical reflectance property R look red, and those with a given physical reflectance property G look green. Then at a certain time, perhaps because of some effect on people's brains, things with R look green, and things with G look red. This is a case of universal intrasubjective change; it is detectable, and, we suppose, actually detected. The most difficult problem for our anti-experientialist is not whether in these circumstances things with R are no longer red — a question on which intuitions vary — but what account of 'looks red' he can give which squares with the possibility of the case; for as the case is described, it is not in dispute that objects which have R no longer *look* red after the change (whether or not they really are red). How can the anti-experientialist secure this consequence?

The anti-experientialist may reply that immediately after the change, experiences of a kind which before the change were produced by objects with R still tend to produce after the change the belief about the property R that the presented object has it. Such a belief, after the change, is false; but the anti-experientialist can argue that the case is analogous to those considered in discussions of proper names. If someone just like Quine kidnaps Quine early on in Quine's life and starts to act Quine's role, we will falsely believe this man to be Quine; in acquiring beliefs about him we also acquire beliefs that Quine is thus-and-so. The problem is that if the impostor continues long enough, the beliefs expressed in utterances of 'Quine is thus-and-so' come to concern the impostor. So similarly in the anti-experientialist's account of the colour example: after a time it is correct to say that experiences in which something looks red tend to produce the belief that the presented object has physical property G, the one which before the change produced experiences as of green objects. In whatever sense Armstrong, for instance, would say that before the change experiences as of something red tend to produce beliefs (in a transparent sense) about physical property R, a long time after that change, in that same sense, such experiences will tend to produce beliefs about the different physical property G. For exactly the same relations hold between experiences in which things look red and the physical property G at a much later time, as held before the change between such experiences and physical property R. This remains true if the change in the effects of R and G had been unnoticed. (The same general point can also be made if the account of looking red in terms of red speaks of abilities to discriminate objects with property R.) But then the anti-experientialist account delivers the wrong answer on the question of the qualitative similarity of two experiences, one

(*e*) before the change and another (*e'*) a sufficiently long time after-
wards. The experiences *e* and *e'* may both be as of something red,
but *e* tends to produce the belief of the presented object that it has
physical property R (by Armstrongian standards), while (*e'*) tends
to produce the belief that it has physical property G. It does not help
to try to appeal to what would be the case if experience of the kinds
of *e* and *e'* occurred simultaneously to someone; for the *kinds* here
will have to include determinate specifications of the experienced
colour, and that is what we were asking the anti-experientialist to
explain, and not just take for granted.

At this point the anti-experientialist may be tempted to argue
that he can admit the possibility of intrasubjective inversion of the
colour experiences produced by a given type of physical surface in
fixed lighting conditions. He may argue that this possibility is
allowed for in the fact that different brain states may be produced by
looking at such a physical surface at different times. But of course
brain states may alter while experience remains the same: a change
of brain state produced by the surface is not sufficient for a change in
colour experience. To make this account work, our anti-
experientialist needs to distinguish just those changes in brain state
which produce, or are correlated with, change in the colour the
object looks; and he cannot legitimately do so in explaining 'looks
red'. The problem here is one of meaning or significance. We have
a conception of colour experience on which such a change of brain
state is not constitutively sufficient for a change in colour experience
(which is not to say that it may not in some circumstances be good
evidence for it). A general principle is applicable here. Suppose one
can conceive of evidence which counts in favour of a hypothesis;
that does not suffice to show the hypothesis to be significant if it is
also true that our conception of what it is for that hypothesis to be
true allows that either that evidence could obtain and the hypothesis
be false, or vice versa. The rationale for this principle is obvious: if
either the hypothesis or the evidence can obtain independently of
the other obtaining, then to cite possible evidence does not exhaust
the content of the hypothesis. We could call this general principle
the Principle of Significance. It is not itself intrinsically a
verificationist principle: rather, if functions as a constraint, a
condition of adequacy, on any substantive general theories of
meaning held simultaneous with views about the content of

particular sentences.[6] The Principle gets a grip here because the anti-experientialist was citing, as possible evidence for intrasubjective inversion, altered brain states, which are not, as we ordinarily conceive them, sufficient for such inversion.[7]

The anti-experientialist may complain that too much is being asked of him. 'Why', he may ask, 'cannot the concept of being red have the priority I claim for it and yet that concept not be further explicable? To someone who does not possess it, one can convey it only by suitable training (or brain surgery).' The problem with such a position is that it still does not account for the special features of the ability such training or brain surgery induces. No one has the concept of redness unless his exercise of that concept stands in quite special relations to his visual experience. It is hard to see how the anti-experientialist can explain why this is so without moving, by bringing in experience, from the first position to the second or third of the possibilities we described. The difficulty seems endemic to the anti-experientialist view.

The second option was a no-priority view. A no-priority view must offer more than the observations that 'Red things in standard circumstances look red' and 'Being red cannot be eliminated from an account of what it is for an experience to be as of something red' are both constitutively true. For corresponding claims are true of being square, and yet being square does not have the special relationship with visual experience that being red does. It is a virtue of the pure experientialist view, the third option, that it is not left as a mysterious, inexplicable necessary truth that one cannot experience objects as red in modalities other than the visual. The impossibility is rather a simple consequence of an account of what it is for an object to be red which mentions specifically a feature of

[6] The principle should also be accepted by criterial theorists of meaning, in the sense in which 'criterion' is understood by, for instance, P. M. S. Hacker in *Insight and Illusion* (Oxford: OUP, 1972). Such a theorist would (or should) not admit the possibility that someone be in pain yet none of the criteria, however far one investigates possible defeating conditions, indicate that he is.

[7] These remarks apply to Shoemaker, 'Phenomenal Similarity', *Critica* 20 (1975), at p. 267. They could also be applied *mutatis mutandis* to his remark in 'Functionalism and Qualia' that if two persons could fuse into a single subject of consciousness, 'the behaviour of the resulting person could presumably settle [the question of whether their colour spectra were inverted relative to each other]' (p. 264 in the reprinting in *Readings in the Philosophy of Psychology*, vol. 1 (Cambridge, Mass.: Harvard UP, 1980), ed. N. Block).

visual experience. A no-priority theorist must explain the special relationship with visual experience.

A different no-priority theorist, one aware of this requirement, might try to explain both 'red' and 'looks red' in terms of the type of experience which is present when a certain experientially-based ability is exercised: something looks red to someone when this ability would be exercised with a particular result, and it is really red when it would be exercised with that result in standard circumstances. Now what would the ability be? Such a theorist cannot say: the ability on the basis of visual experience to discriminate red from non-red things. The occurrence of 'red' in his description of the ability would prevent the resulting claim from being described as a no-priority view – we would be back at an anti-experientialist view. But we ought to consider a bold modification of this idea, one on which we try to characterize the ability extensionally. We say that someone has a *reactive recognitional ability* (RRA) for a class *A* of objects in a given period (with respect to given physical circumstances) if and only if, when trained to act in a particular way when he has a visual experience caused by objects in some sample subset of *A*, he goes on to act in the same way, on the basis of the visual experience caused in him in the given physical circumstances by the remaining members of *A*, all in that period. An RRA is something one has in relation to a class, and so long as there is a class of red objects, one can speak of the existence of an RRA for a given class, and in terms of it explain 'looks red' and 'red' without initially using 'red' and 'looks red'. Presumably the idea would be that there is a class with respect to which we have an RRA, a class such that, when an object causes us (after training) to give on the basis of the visual experience it causes in us a positive response to it, we say it looks red; and it is red if it meets a similar condition in some standard specified circumstances. So the idea of this particular no-priority theory would be that both 'red' and 'looks red' are explained by reference to an RRA, and in such a way that certain connections – such as that a red object looks red in standard conditions, etc. – are preserved between them.

This is a tempting theory, but the problems seem insuperable. If the properties of being purple and being shiny were coextensive, the corresponding RRAs would be identical, since they are identified by classes. The account needs to be thickened to distinguish between looking purple and looking shiny. This could not be done by appealing to counterfactual circumstances in which the responses for 'purple' and 'shiny' would come apart. This is not because they would not come apart – they would – but because the antecedents of the counterfactuals specifying the circumstances in which they come apart would either contain colour predicates or mention of the physical grounds of looking a particular colour. If they contained colour predicates, the account would be circular, while the physical grounds of looking purple may alter.[8]

There is also a second problem. The definition of an RRA requires the ability to learn to produce a new response to red objects when conditioned anew. But the ability to learn new responses seems distinct from the enjoyment of colour experience, and may be absent in a creature though it does enjoy such experiencs. It would be too weak to require only that in some circumstances the creature gives the same experientially based response to precisely the things in a certain class; for in some circumstances the response may not be to the colour of the object.

This does not exhaust the plausible no-priority theories. In particular, there is a form of no-priority view which tries to take on board the considerations in favour of the third option, that of the experientialist, and then goes on to claim that these considerations can all be accommodated within the no-priority view. We will be able to formulate this properly only after developing that third option.

The experientialist can say that when a normal human sees a red object in daylight, there is a certain property possessed by the region of his visual field in which that object is presented to him. This is the property we labelled 'red'': the canonical form was that token experience e is red' relative to region r, and the crucial point is that red' is a *sensational* property of experience. It is true that we picked out the property by using the ordinary notion of redness; but it does not follow that someone could not manifest a sensitivity to the red'ness of his experiences without already possessing the concept of redness. The experientialist may now say this: in mastering the predicate 'red' of objects, one comes to be disposed to apply it to an object when the region of one's visual field in which it is presented is red' and circumstances are apparently normal (or when one has evidence that it would meet this condition were it so

[8]Extensionality also produces other problems: it is difficult to give a satisfactory account of how an object that is in fact red might not have been.

presented). The experientialist will say that this explains the inclination we feel initially to explain 'red' in terms of 'looks red'. He will say that what is correct is to explain red in terms of red'; and since normally when something looks red, the region of the visual field in which it is presented is red', he will say that this inclination comes as no surprise. Since for him the property red' of experiences, and a sensitivity of one's judgements to its presence, are the fundamental notions, rather than that of looking red, this experientialist does not need to deny the obvious fact that 'red' is a semantically significant constituent of 'looks red'.

The experientialist is not committed to the consequence that anyone who can exercise the concept of redness also has to have the sophisticated concept of experience. All this experientialist requires for the possession of the concept of redness is a certain pattern of sensitivity in the subject's judgements to the occurrence of red' experiences. This sensitivity can exist in a subject who does not himself possess the concept of experience. This experientialist can then agree with the letter of Wittgenstein's claims in these passages:

315. Why doesn't one teach a child the language-game 'It looks red to me' from the first? Because it is not yet able to understand the rather fine distinction between seeming and being?

316. The red visual impression is a new *concept*.

317. The language-game that we teach him then is 'It looks to me . . . , it looks to you . . .' In the first language-game a person does not occur as perceiving subject.

318. You give the language-game a new joint. Which does not mean, however, that now it is always used.[9]

It is important to note that the experientialist is operating with three, and not two, notions: that of being red', that of looking red, and that of being red. The second of these is not in any simple way definable in terms of the first. However plausible it may seem at first blush, it is not true that anything which looks φ must be presented in a region of the visual field which is φ'. If one looks through a sheet of red glass at an array which includes a sheet of

[9] *Remarks on the Philosophy of Psychology*, vol. 2.

white paper, the sheet will be represented in the experience itself as being really white: anyone who has such an experience will, taking his experience at face value, be disposed to judge that the sheet really is white, and 'white' here refers to the property of physical objects. It should be emphasized that this is not a matter of conscious inference: the surface of the paper is *seen* as white.[10] In such a case, it would be wrong to insist that the region of the visual field in which the paper is presented is white′ and wrong to insist that it is red′. We have here a new kind of experience, and any extension of these primed properties from the cases where the conditions of viewing are more normal seems partly stipulative. Certainly to insist that in this case the region of the visual field is obviously white′ seems to rely tacitly on the representational content of the experience in determining the application of the primed predicates; and since this representational content contains the concept of being white, the experientialist cannot on pain of circularity use such applications of primed properties in explaining colour predicates. The experientialist should, rather, agree that something can look φ without being presented in a φ' region of the visual field, and explain how this can be so as follows. In so far as he is prepared to offer a definition of 'x is red', it would be along these lines: 'x is disposed in normal circumstances to cause the region of the visual field in which it is presented to be red′ in normal humans'. Now this concept of being red may enter the representational content of a subject's experiences. That it may so enter is an instance of a general phenomenon of concepts entering the representational content of experience. In possessing for instance the concept of complacency, one has the concept of a person who is unconcerned about something when there are available to him good reasons for concern: this is a trait that manifests itself in the man's thoughts. But one can also *see* a face or a gesture as complacent, and one can

[10] The red of a pane of red glass is a transparent film colour (*Flächenfarbe*) rather than a surface colour in the sense of psychologists of colour perception. The *locus classicus* is D. Katz, *The World of Colour* (London: Kegan Paul, 1935), p. 17 ff. In seeing a snowman through a pane of red glass, one sees the pane as having a transparent film colour red and the snowman as having the *surface* colour white behind it. A red snowman by contrast would have the surface colour red. If the pane of glass is thick, the colour red may appear as a volume colour— one that is presented as occupying a volume of space. (See Katz, or again J. Beck, *Surface Color Perception* (Ithaca, NY: Cornell UP, 1972), p. 20.) Anyone who doubts these points should look at a white surface through a coloured transparent bottle, or consult Plate 1 of Beck's book.

hear an utterance as complacent. The experientialist should say that the property red′ stands to being red as the components of an account of being complacent stand to being complacent; while the property of an experience of representing something as red stands to being red, in certain respects, as the property of representing a gesture as complacent stands to being complacent. One must, then, beware of pinning on the experientialist an overly simple account of the property of representing something as red. In normal circumstances (and — unlike complacency — constitutively so) a thing presented in a red′ region of the visual field is indeed seen as being red, but it is not always so, and the experientialist can acknowledge the fact.

We noted earlier that not all views of the no-priority type had yet been discussed. What we considered earlier were no-priority views which claimed that being red and looking red have to be simultaneously explained, views which we found left these two concepts pointing at each other. It now appears that a much stronger type of no-priority view would be one on which the concepts which have to be introduced simultaneously are not those of being red and looking red, but rather those of being red and of being red′. Red objects are ones which in normal viewing conditions are presented in red′ regions of the visual field; and red′ is that property of regions of the visual field instantiated in regions in which red objects are presented in normal circumstances. Such a no-priority view can take over much of what we have already attributed to the experientialist, including the threefold distinction between red, looking red and red′.

But can these relations between red and red′ really sustain the claim that we have here a no-priority view? We said that the sense in which the definition of being red in terms of red′ was relevant to possession of the concept of redness is not that anyone who possesses it must be able to supply that definition, but rather that it captures a sensitivity to red′ experiences which must be present in judgements that a presented object is red. Is it equally true that if someone possesses the concept red′, there must be some appropriate sensitivity of his judgements involving *it* to the presence of redness, as opposed to other properties? One way to see that this is implausible is to consider a community, the members of which not only often see things in normal daylight, but also often see them under ultraviolet light (perhaps at night). They might use 'red$_{UV}$' as a predicate true of objects which are presented in a red$'$ region of the visual field when seen under ultraviolet light. Now we can ask: is it true that anyone who possesses the concept red$'$ must have a special sensitivity of his judgements involving it to the presence of redness as opposed to red$_{UV}$ness? This seems to have no plausibility. If someone learns that red$'$ is that property of the visual field instantiated by regions in which red$_{UV}$ objects are presented in ultraviolet light, he can fully understand 'red$''$'. Indeed anything which tells him what that experiential property is, whether or not it mentions redness, will suffice to give him understanding. This seems to undermine the status of the view under consideration as a no-priority view: though one can indeed give definitions of each of 'red' and 'red$'$' in terms of the other, a sensitivity to red$'$ness is essential in grasping the concept of redness, whereas a sensitivity to redness is not essential to grasping the concept of red$'$ness in the same way. The result seems to be a priority of red$'$ness, an experientialist rather than a no-priority conclusion.[11]

An objector might agree that it is false that red rather than red$_{UV}$ has to be used to explain red$'$; but he may nevertheless say that what is definitionally prior to both red and red$_{UV}$ is a certain *character*, in a suitable generalization of Kaplan's notion.[12] Different utterances of 'I' may refer to different persons, but there is a single uniform rule for determining which person is referred to at any given context of utterance. The objector's point may be that we should adapt Kaplan's notion by replacing 'context of utterance' with 'condition of perception taken as standard'. We could then say this: words differing as 'red' and 'red$_{UV}$' differ may refer to different properties, but there is a single uniform rule for determining which property such a word refers to if any given condition of perception is taken as standard. Thus in a certain sense the characters of our 'red' and their 'red$_{UV}$' are one and the same, and it is this character which is prior to red$'$.

This view would indeed circumvent the objection. But the difficulty for it lies in stating what the common character of 'red'

[11] This point does not depend upon taking 'red' and 'red$'$' as natural kind terms. The view for which I am arguing is that for an object to be red is for it to be presented in a red$'$ region of the visual field in certain conditions (external and internal to a perceiver). In the case of red and red$_{UV}$ these conditions are different, and so the properties of being red and of being red$_{UV}$ are different in at least one sense. There is no commitment in saying that an object is red$_{UV}$ to how it would look in normal daylight.

[12] 'On the Logic of Demonstratives', *Journal of Philosophical Logic* 8 (1978), 81–98.

and 'red$_{UV}$' is. What is the common rule which, applied to different conditions of perception taken as standard, gives the different properties of being red and of being red$_{UV}$? The objector can hardly say that for given conditions of perception the rule picks out the property of looking *red* under those conditions; for that brings back all the old problems of circularity. But if the objector were to say that the rule should advert to the property of being presented in a red′ region of the visual field, he has not shown red to be definitionally prior to red′.

There are other types of priority than the definitional. We can say that a concept A is *cognitively prior* to B iff no one could possess the concept B without possessing the concept A. In the simplest case, this will be because a property thought of by way of the concept B has to be thought of as the property bearing certain relations to concept A. One should not assume that definitional priority and congnitive priority must coincide. It may be that in some cases one concept is definitionally prior to a second, while that second concept is cognitively prior to the first. This may be the case where the first concept is red′ and the second is that of being red.

If concept A is definitionally prior to concept B because a thinker has to use its definition in thought when he employs the concept B, and if one concept can be cognitively prior to another only because the latter has to be defined in terms of the former, then it might be that definitional and cognitive priority have to coincide. But in the case of red′ and red, the first antecedent of this conditional is false. A definition of an object's being red as its disposition to present itself in a red′ region of the visual field under certain conditions is good, not because it captures the way everyone must think concerning an object's being red; rather, as we said, the judgements of one who has the concept of being red are responsive to experience and evidence in exactly the same ways as would be the judgements of one who explicitly used this definition. If one wishes to maintain that red′ is definitionally prior to red, but cognitively posterior to it, then the fact that one can have an experience in which a region of one's visual field is red′ without one having the concept red′ is crucial in avoiding circularity.

The reasons which might be given for saying that red is cognitively prior to red′ are subjects for other work.[13] It might, for

---

[13] I have discussed some of them in a forthcoming paper at present entitled 'Other Minds'.

example, be held that a necessary condition of possessing a conception of other minds according to which others can have red' experiences in exactly the same sense as one can have them oneself is that red' experiences, one's own and others, are alike thought of as experiences which bear certain relations to the property of objects, perceivable by oneself and others, of *being* red. (Such a reason would, if correct, have an *a priori* status, as required by the characterization of cognitive priority.) What matters for the present is just the possibility of such a position. For if it is possible, one must be careful before drawing any anti-experientialist conclusions from considerations of priority, and correspondingly careful in ascribing the anti-experientialist view to others. For someone's insistence that red is prior to red' may be an expression of cognitive priority. Such a theorist may not be rejecting definitional priority in the reverse direction. If he is not, then it would be wrong to ascribe to him anti-experientialist views. Indeed it may well be that Wittgenstein should be regarded as holding just such a combination of views. In a passage already displayed, he insists that 'red' has to be learned before certain concepts of experience: while elsewhere he seems to hold at least that seeming to be a certain colour cannot be left out of an account of what it is to have that colour:

97. Don't we just *call* brown the table which under certain circumstances appears brown to the normal-sighted? We could certainly conceive of someone to whom things seemed sometimes this colour and sometimes that, independently of the colour they are.

98. That it seems so to men is their criterion for its *being* so.

99. Being and seeming may, of course, be independent of one another in exceptional cases, but that doesn't make them logically independent; the language-game does not reside in the exception.[14]

If Wittgenstein did believe, or would have believed, in the cognitive priority of red over red', but was nevertheless not an anti-experientialist, then according to the arguments I have been endorsing, his position was consistent.

The experientialist view also has consequences for the explanation of experience. In the case of primary qualities, it is

[14] *Remarks on Colour* (Oxford: Blackwell, 1977), tr. L. McAlister and M. Schättle, p. 29e.

legitimate, and arguably mandatory in normal cases, to explain someone's experience of an object as square by the fact that it really is square (or by something entailed by its being square). But on the experientialist view one could not explain in a central case an object's looking red to someone by citing the fact that it really is red – at least, not if this explanation were intended to leave open the question of whether there is any primary quality ground of redness. Genuine explanations cannot have a *virtus dormitiva* character. On the particular experientialist theory I suggested, for something to be red is for it to produce experiences of a certain kind, red′ experiences, in standard circumstances. In central cases – those by reference to which possession of the concept of redness was analysed – for a thing to look red to someone is for it to produce red′ experiences. So on the experientialist option, the conditional 'If circumstances are standard, in a central case if an object is red, then it look red' is *a priori*: it reduces to a logical truth of the form $\forall x ((Sx \,\&\, (Sx \supset Rx)) \supset Rx)$. An expression might of course be introduced as an abbreviating ('descriptive') name for whatever physical state (if any) is the ground of objects' producing red experiences. It is not clear, and perhaps not determinate, whether 'red' is used in this way in English, but if it were, what would make it legitimate to say 'It's red' in explanation of something's producing red experiences in standard conditions would be the existence of some other, physical, characterization of the object that produces red′ experiences.[15]

This concludes my discussion of the second application of the sensational/representational distinction. We will use some of the views developed in this second application in the next, which also concerns a Berkeleyan point.

[15] In *Form and Content* (Blackwell: Oxford, 1973), Bernard Harrison argues that colours are not 'natural nameables'. These last are objects which are 'defined as distinct objects of reference . . . independently of linguistic convention'. The experientialist does treat colours as natural nameables under this definition; the fact that something is a natural nameable in Harrison's sense does not exclude the possibility that an account of the nature of the object may have to make reference to human experience.

Harrison's own model of colour-naming is as follows: we fix a set of shades as name-bases, and apply the colour word associated with that name-base to any shade which more closely resembles that name-base than any other. He takes this to justify his view that colours are not natural nameables; yet it seems clear that the experientially-caused actions of a non-linguistic creature could manifest sensitivity to exactly the colour distinctions which are determined by Harrison's model of colour-naming as applied to, say, English.

Berkeley wrote:

> For my part, I see evidently that it is not in my power to frame an idea of a body extended and moving, but I must withal give it some colour or other sensible quality . . .[16]

Berkeley's view was that we can neither conceive of nor perceive primary qualities as instantiated in objects without those objects also instantiating secondary qualities. It would no doubt be largely agreed today that Berkeley was wrong about what we can conceive; but that is not my present topic. The third application of the sensational/representational distinction is to Berkeley's much more plausible claim that we cannot perceive primary qualities without perceiving secondary qualities. We can explain the truth on which Berkeley insists as a consequence of the following principles:

(1) For an object to have a certain secondary quality is for it to have the power to produce, in specified circumstances, experiences with certain sensational properties; and for every sensational property which may be possessed by an experience having representational content, there is a corresponding secondary quality (named or unnamed).
(2) Every experience has sensational properties.

From (1) and (2) it follows that every experience which has a representational content is also an experience with some sensational property. If we grant that every experience of primary qualities is an experience with representational content, then Berkeley is literally correct in holding that there can be no experience of primary qualities without experience of secondary qualities. Since it is plausible that (1) and (2) are necessary truths, and we are concerned with an entailment, we can also draw the stronger conclusion that it is necessary that every experience which has a representational content also has sensational properties. Berkeley was right in making the stronger modal claim that, at least as far as experience is concerned, primary qualities are 'inseparably united' with the secondary.

---

[16] *The Principles of Human Knowledge,* section 10.

We can now turn from applications of the sensational/representa-
tional distinction to some of the questions it raises. One of these
questions is concerned with the distinction which exists between
those senses which are intrinsically spatial and those which are
not. The experiences of sight and touch seem to be intrinsically
spatial in a way that ordinary monaural experiences are not. Sometimes those who say that only some senses can be regarded as
intrinsically spatial say that the special features of sight and touch
are not restricted to those senses. The philosophical psychologist
Ward, for instance, while seeing that it is absurd to apply spatial
predicates underivatively to sensations, nevertheless held that the
property of 'extensity' possessed by sensations of touch and sight
could be shared by taste too. He gave as examples of variation in
extensity not only the difference between the ache of a large bruise
and the ache of a small bruise, and again the difference between
total and partial immersion in a warm bath, but also the spreading
of the taste of a drop of sugared water placed on the tongue.[17] But to
auditory experiences he did not attribute such extensity. In fact,
whatever the appropriate use of the term 'extensity', we ought to
distinguish sharply between monaural and binaural hearing in
respect of intrinsic spatiality. Sounds experienced binaurally have a
radial location, and it is legitimate to speak of an aural field as we
also speak of a visual field; though of course the aural field has a less
rich structure than the visual.[18] For mature humans, a sound with a
particular radial location will be heard as coming from a particular
direction in physical space. But radial location of a binaurally heard
sound is a more primitive feature than possession of a representational content concerning a place in physical space, in the
environment of the subject. A symptom of this is the fact that we can
make sense of the possibility that an infant with no spatial concepts,
perhaps with only certain sensations and motor skills, experiences a
sound which in fact comes from one angle differently from a sound

---

[17] *Psychological Principles*, pp. 78ff.

[18] Here I oversimplify the facts. Even in monaural hearing, the pinna allows restricted
localization of the sound (see R. Butler, 'The Influence of the External and Middle Ear
on Auditory Discriminations' in *Handbook of Sensory Physiology*, vol. V/2 eds. W. Keidel
and W. Neff (Berlin: Springer, 1975)). What matters is that we can conceive of monaural
auditory experience which is not intrinsically spatial at all, while we cannot do so for
visual experience.

coming from a different angle. This difference can be reflected in his behaviour: we will return to this point.

The existence of intrinsically spatial senses poses a problem for the sensational/representational distinction because it seems at first blush impossible to accommodate their intrinsic spatiality on either side of the distinction. Suppose we do try to capture the distinction, whichever side taste falls, between those senses which are intrinsically spatial and those which are not, in terms of the categories I have so far employed. We cannot capture it by saying that only in the representational content of intrinsically spatial senses do spatial concepts feature; for the obvious reason that there are monaural experiences with the representational content that there is a man walking towards oneself. It may be correct in the case of monaural experiences to say that the occurrence of such experiences is parasitic on the capacity to have experiences with a spatial representational content in some intrinsically spatial sense-modality: but it would be circular to try to use this point in explaining what it is for a sense to be intrinsically spatial.

There are equally difficulties in expressing the distinction at the level of the concepts used in fixing the reference of words for sensational properties. It is not true that any sensational property which can be fixed as the reference of a word, by making use of spatial concepts in ways analogous to those by which we introduced the primed properties, must itself be a property of experiences in an intrinsically spatial sense. That this is indeed untrue should be initially plausible, since the claim concerns only reference-fixing and not meaning-giving conditions. We can give one example to illustrate the point. Let us first compare monocular vision with the eye at a given point with monaural hearing with the ear also at a given constant position. If a French horn is played to the right of the ear of the person thus listening monaurally, and simultaneously an oboe is played to its left, the experience produced will be of exactly the same type as if the oboe were on the right and the horn on the left. By contrast, such insensitivity of the experience to the location of its causes is not exhibited by the visual experience produced by the horn and the oboe; even the sensational properties of the visual experience will be sensitive to the locations of the instruments in the plane parallel to the observer's face. In fact one could in normal circumstances recover the locations of the seen instruments from the sensational properties of the visual experience and sufficient knowledge of the human visual system. The same is not true of the auditory experiences. Now it seems evident that these facts about monaural experience are contingent. We can imagine a possible world in which our nervous systems are so constructed that all these conditions are met: the closer an object, the louder it sounds; the further to the right in the plane parallel to one's face, the richer its timbre; and the higher it is in that plane, the higher its pitch. In such a world, any of the sensational properties of high pitch, rich timbre, or great volume could be fixed as the reference of a word by employing, *inter alia*, the correlated spatial concepts. But this would not make the monaural experiences intrinsically spatial; indeed, since the experiences in this imagined world could be intrinsically the same as they are in the actual world, any of their properties which vary between these worlds cannot be an intrinsic property of the experiences themselves.[19] So the task of elucidating the intrinsic spatiality of some senses remains.

The intuitive reason for counting a sense-modality as intrinsically spatial is that the experiences of that sense have features we want to describe in terms of a system of locations which bear relations to one another isomorphic to the spatial relations between places in some conceivable space. Thus qualitatively identical red triangles can be located at different places in the visual field, just as distinct but qualitatively identical objects can exist at different locations in a two-dimensional space. But there is a serious danger of begging the question if we try to convert this intuitive idea into a criterion: the danger is that of giving no meaning to 'qualitative' other than 'not intrinsically spatial'. If we do not beg the question this way, how are we to exclude any sensations which are ordered in some 'quality space' from the status of sensations in an intrinsically spatial sense-modality? We want to say that monaural experiences are not intrinsically spatial, and we want to say that it is no argument against that fact that we can define quality spaces with axes of pitch and volume such that qualitatively similar sounds (of similar timbre, etc.) can occur at different places in this quality space. But we do not yet have a criterion that justifies us in

---

[19] These points do not cast doubt on the philosophical thesis that any objective world is spatial, nor on the thesis that any world thought of as objective must be thought of as spatial. They do not undermine these theses even if it is allowed that such monaural experience is sufficient to allow possession of the concept of an objective world. But if this *is* allowed, then the imagined world must undermine the thesis that anyone with a conception of an objective world must be capable of having (or know what it is like to have) intrinsically spatial experiences.

wanting to say this. Could we perhaps say this: what defines the axes of a quality space varies in degree, while there is no variation of degree in any direction in the space of an intrinsically spatial sense? No: it is quite intelligible to speak of a sensation of light as being to the far left, as opposed to the middle left, of one's visual field.

A different approach would be to exploit the notion of informational content we set aside earlier. Does the informational content of experiences in an intrinsically spatial sense-modality always involve spatial properties and relations? The problem with this is that we can imagine the actual external causes of auditory experiences, viz., pressure waves in the air, causing in other beings intrinsically spatial visual experiences. In such an imagined world, the location of a sound source need not be correlated with the spatial visual field properties which it causes.

Another possible line of attack on the problem concerns an asymmetry with respect to the notion of intensity. In an auditory sensation, the note middle C may be experienced intensely (i.e. loudly). But a region distinguished at the centre of one's visual field cannot provide a case in which its location is experienced intensely: rather some property such as brightness is experienced as intense. The sensation of red (say) is intense; neither the location nor the association of the sensation with it can be more or less intense. By contrast with this visual example, we could not in a parallel fashion say in the case of monaural experience that though the sound is located at middle C in the quality space, the sound but not its pitch is experienced intensely. The phenomenal sound is nothing over and above its pitch and timbre – there is nothing further that could be intense, mild or faint, it may be said. But in fact this idea does not work either. There is no relevant sense in which timbre varies in intensity. One sound which is more intense than another is just louder, with or without the same timbre. The test the idea presently under consideration suggests would then count timbre as an intrinsically spatial dimension. Actually, even if there were asymmetries with respect to the notion of intensity it is hard to see any very specific connection with intrinsic spatiality. It is also unclear that there *is* a uniform concept of intensity across modalties: Which is the visual analogue for colours of loudness of sound – lightness or saturation? What determines the right answer?

A stronger suggestion is that to give an account of the intrinsic

spatiality of some experiences we have to mention the dispositions
—> of the experiencer to perform actions in space. Intrinsically spatial
sensations are intermediate in character between experiences with
representational content (seeings-as, hearings-as, etc.) on the one
hand, and pure sensations in some non-spatial sense on the other.
They resemble seeings-as in the respect that just as it would be
much too weak an account of seeings-as to say that they are
sensations which tend to cause judgements, so it would be too
weak an account of intrinsically spatial sensations to say that they
tend to cause dispositions to spatial behaviour. In both cases,
what is said to be caused in these too-weak accounts is in some
way incorporated into the experience itself. But intrinsically
spatial sensations are like pure sensations in that they do not
require for their enjoyment the possession of any particular
concepts on the part of the experiencer.

What then are the dispositions to behaviour which it is claimed
we need to mention? They are such dispositions as these: if a
sound with a radial location is heard, to turn one's body or head
towards it if it is pleasant, away from it if it is unpleasant; to move
one's limbs further up rather than down if an attractive or
interesting object is in one's upper visual field, in comparison with
the way in which one would move one's limbs to reach an object
the same distance from oneself but lower in the visual field.
Complex though a fuller description of some of these dispositions
—> must be, the dispositions are less complex than those required for
possession of concepts of an objective spatial world, and it is for
this reason that an infant can have intrinsically spatial binaural
experiences without possessing spatial concepts.[20] So perhaps we
can say that a sensory dimension is intrinsically spatial if an only if
variation along that dimension is *a priori* correlated with variations
in dispositions to bodily actions, where the actions vary in some

[20] The possibility of such an intermediate position is overlooked by G. Pitcher in his
book *A Theory of Perception* (Princeton: Princeton UP, 1971), pp. 186–95. More generally,
if the main claim of the previous chapter is correct, there is another objection, beyond
those already current in the literature, to Pitcher's (and Armstrong's) theory that
perception consists in dispositions to acquire beliefs. The objection of course is that the
propositional content of the belief will not capture the sensational properties an experience
will have. This problem might be avoided if the beliefs were made to include perceptual
modes of presentation of objects, but use of such a notion would mean that experience
would not after all have been eliminated in favour of dispositions to believe, perceptual
modes of presentation having to be explained in terms of types of experience.

genuinely spatial respect? This is an analytical suggestion, not an empirical hypothesis. It does not have the same status as, for instance, hypotheses about the role of efferent nerve instructions to the eye in the production of visual experience. The dispositions need to be construed sufficiently broadly so that a paralysed person can have intrinsically spatial experiences: other things equal, these experiences would dispose him to act as a normal person if he had such a person's capacities. A contrary view would be that the intrinsically spatial character or otherwise of the paralysed man's experience is quite independent of how he would be disposed to move if he could move. It is important here to note that the arguments for adverting to dispositions to movement need not be verificationist arguments alone. There are also arguments from the intrinsic character of the experience itself. There seems to be an unimaginability, from the *inside*, of having an experience of a sound with a particular radial location in the aural field, and yet having no dispositions in suitable circumstances to move one's head one way rather than another.

This action-based account may well be right in its view that dispositions to movement can be incorporated into the intrinsic properties of experiences in the way that concepts can. But it is very hard to believe that it gives an adequate theory of all intrinsically spatial senses. It seems both conceivable and imaginable from the inside that there should be someone who has visual experiences with sensational visual field properties and who is not so much as capable of movement. And even as we actually are, the intrinsically spatial properties of our visual experiences are much more fine-grained than any correlated abilities to act. The visual sensational properties produced by the foliage on a bush may be clearer, finer, and more detailed than anything we could trace out with an outstretched pointing finger. (The finger may tremble across the boundaries and tiny shapes.)

The conclusion to which all these objections to the various suggestions about intrinsic spatiality point is that we should not be afraid of acknowledging that there are sensational spaces, and their spatiality cannot be explained away as derivative or artificial. The sensational spaces are not, of course, populated by the sensations themselves. Rather, for each intrinsically spatial sense-modality, there is a space such that all experiences in that modality have intrinsic sensational properties characterized by reference to that sensational space. The sensational spaces of different modalities do not bear spatial relations to each other: it makes no sense to ask of a location in visual *sensational* space what spatial relation it bears to a location in tactual sensational space (e.g. the tactual location when a certain place on the neck is touched). In this, the sensational spaces stand in sharp contrast with the space — everyday public, physical space — which the representational content of experiences in different modalities concerns. It is the very same relation 'closer to', concerning the very same space, which enters the representational content of a visual experience as of someone walking closer to one and an auditory experience as of someone walking closer to one. This sharp contrast between the one space which representational content concerns and the many sensational spaces further highlights Berkeley's mistake in moving from the premise that in one respect no ideas are common to touch and sight, to the conclusion that one modality must be prior in the philosophical explanation of the space about which we learn from both touch and sight.

The primed properties of the previous chapter — elliptical' and the rest — are then in one way genuinely spatial properties. They concern shape and size in visual sensational space. We may even say that being elliptical' is being elliptical in visual sensational space. There is no ambiguity here since different spaces are in question: we exercise a concept of something being elliptical which is applicable in arbitrary spaces which sufficiently resemble familiar spaces 'for the notion to make sense. Were different spaces not in question, there would indeed be many complications. The unsuccessful strategies of the last chapter, those appealing to translation or to additional representational content, were in effect attempts to explain the property of being elliptical' solely by means of public, physical space.

These points suggest two observations on other positions which have been taken in the literature relating to these topics. The first observation is one sympathetic to sense-datum theorists of perception. Despite the immensely tangled skein into which some such theorists wove themselves, one of their central views, if my discussion has been correct, is a genuine insight. These theorists characteristically applied spatial vocabulary to sense-data, which they would describe as square, or elongated, and so on. The insight consists in the recognition that there is a need, if one is fully to specify the intrinsic properties of experience, for spatial notions which cannot be captured at the level of representational content. Indeed the more plausible of the claims the sense-datum theorists made can be translated into the vocabulary I have used to talk about sensational properties.[21]

The second comment concerns the area of developmental psychology. Many questions arise in that area about the stage at which the infant perceives spatial relations and has some conception of objects as located in a space around him. This comment is that it is not sufficient to establish that an infant has these concepts that, for example, that he responds differently to binocular and monocular vision of the Julesz random-dot patterns. If he responds differently, he is indeed likely to be responding to the difference between an experience with a dimension of depth and one without; but this difference, compatibly with this evidence, may be purely at the level of a difference in sensational space. A difference in response would not be evidence that the infant saw objects as distributed in space around him.[22]

There remain many unsolved problems about the relation between sensational and representational properties. The relations between action and representational content plainly need elucidation. A good account of this matter should also provide a philosophical understanding of the experiments with inverting spectacles. But there are also problems outside that area. Here are two. Can one give some analysis of what it is for an experience with given sensational properties also to possess a given representational property? From what will be said later in this book, some suggestions for necessary conditions will emerge, but not sufficient conditions. The second question is a subquestion of the first. There exists a distinction between those representational properties which are grounded in a sensational property in a particular experience, and those which are not. The impression

---

[21] The tangles begin if one does not explicitly recognize that the space which these additional notions concern is sensational space. If one does not immediately acknowledge that this is distinct from public, physical space, one will not realize that questions such as 'Are sense-data surfaces of material objects?' and 'Do we *perceive* sense-data?' are spurious.

[22] These remarks apply to the tests suggested in A. Yonas and H. Pick, Jr., in 'An Approach to the Study of Infant Space Perception', in *Infant Perception: From Sensation to Perception*, vol. II, ed. L. Cohen and S. Salapatek (New York: Academic Press, 1975).

of a hut as having a certain physical size is grounded in part in the size of the region of the visual field in which it is presented; whereas when a whole scene is experienced as tilted, and when there is no dominant vertical or other familiar feature, this impression is not grounded in any sensational property (its causal origins lie of course in the workings of the inner ear). Again, what is the nature of this distinction? We will not fully understand perceptual experience until either we have answers to these questions or we understand why it is a mistake to think that there are answers.

I close this chapter with some more general remarks. I suggested earlier that the present account of sensational and representational properties distinguishes them without requiring a return to the views of the Wundtian tradition. Since the distinction has been explained in terms of the contrast between representational and nonrepresentational intrinsic properties, acceptance of the distinction does not entail that visual sensational properties are some form of aggregate of atomistic, puctual experiences of light and colour; nor does it imply that the sensational properties of one part of the visual field are causally independent of the physical antecedents of sensational properties of its other parts; nor that sensational properties are not influenced by the causes of representational content; nor that representational content is the result of conscious interpretation of sensations. To reject these theories of the sensational/representational distinction is not to reject the distinction itself, without which experience cannot be adequately described.

3

Spatial Contents and Constraints

A territory may have boundaries of two kinds: external boundaries which delineate it and internal boundaries which subdivide it. This chapter is concerned with two questions about the boundaries of the domain of beings enjoying psychological states with content. The first question is an external boundary question: what, if any, are the principles which distinguish a being enjoying states with content from one who does not? What more is required for the possession of such states than a collection of stimulus–response (S–R) links? Writers can be found who maintain that it is correct to attribute attitudes to a thermostat: it has one constant desire, to keep the room at 70°F, and may believe that the room is too hot, too cold, or just right.[1] What exactly has gone wrong here? These are external boundary questions, and answers to them will have consequences we will consider for what is involved in confirming that an infant, or organism, has attitudes with a content concerning its environment.

The second question is about internal boundaries, for it concerns distinctions to be drawn within the domain of the legitimate attribution of psychological states with content. The question is: what makes it correct to attribute to a given organism a set of states with particular contents rather than a different set with different contents? What, for example, is it for an infant to have attitudes about places identified by their relation to the walls of a room in which he is located, rather than attitudes about places identified by some other reference frame, or rather than no attitudes about places at all? Again, it is probably not controversial that informational states of some kind can be attributed to dogs, even though it may be a mistake to ascribe to them the full human panoply of judgement, belief, conjecture and the rest. But as Lloyd Morgan wrote, it is wrong to say of a dog trying to pick up

[1] J. McCarthy in *Philosophical Perspectives on Artificial Intelligence*, ed. M. Ringle (Brighton: Harvester, 1979).

a stick in its jaw that it is trying to discover the stick's centre of gravity.[2] The problem in discussing the internal boundary question is to formulate sharp, general and motivated constraints upon the ascription of one set of contents as against another.

The internal boundary issue takes us to the level of subsentential distinctions. In stating that some propositions can, while others cannot, be regarded as the contents of a given organism's attitudes, one is incurring commitments about which concepts, as constituents of those propositions, the organism possesses. One incurs commitments about which subsentential expressions can be used in giving the contents of the organism's attitudes. Earlier writing on how attitudes can explain actions has concentrated on the level of the whole sentence, rather than subsentential components. Thus Davidson wrote 'R is a primary reason why an agent performed the action A under the description d only if R consists of a pro attitude of the agent toward actions with a certain property, and a belief of the agent that A, under the description d, has that property.'[3] Everything in what follows is not in conflict with, but is rather additional to, such views of explanation by attitudes. In considering the internal boundary issue, we are in effect considering what constraints there are upon the particular concepts which feature in the description d of Davidson's definition of a primary reason.

In discussing these boundary questions, I will move in two stages. The first stage will consist of an attempt to give conditions necessary for an organism to have psychological states with contents relating at least to objects and places in his immediate environment. The case in which an organism has such attitudes I will label 'The Basic Case'. The second stage will consist of an attempt to define a binary relation of comparative tightness between sets of attitudes – those sets of attitudes which are candidates for the sets to be ascribed to a given organism at a given time. 'Sets of attitudes' here and in what follows should be taken to include not only specifications of particular beliefs, hopes, fears, and so forth, but also specifications of which events are actions, and the descriptions under which they are intentional; and also specifications of both of these first two kinds in various

---

[2] C. Lloyd Morgan, *Introduction to Comparative Psychology* (London: Scott, 1894), p. 241.

[3] D. Davidson, 'Actions, Reasons, and Causes', reprinted in his *Essays on Actions and Events* (Oxford: OUP, 1980), p. 5.

counterfactual circumstances. My claim will be that a set of attitudes is not to be attributed to a given organism if there is a tighter set which can be attributed to it. The relation of comparative tightness thus appears in a principle which constrains the ascription of attitudes beyond the primitive ones ascribed in the Basic Case. It should be emphasized that the constraints to be offered at each of the two stages are very far from providing sufficient conditions for the ascription of any particular psychological state with content. Any given psychological state with content will be ascribed using several particular concepts – of kinds of objects, tenses, various logical notions – and there will be further constraints on ascription relating to each such concept. All that is claimed here is that the constraints at the two stages are indispensable components of any further set of sufficient conditions for the ascription of a particular psychological state possessing content.

The Basic Case

Let us first consider the Basic Case – the question of what it is for a subject to have attitudes about places and perceptible objects in his immediate environment. It is plausible that the Basic Case is fundamental in a way that can be acknowledged quite independently of the two-part strategy we have adopted. It seems that an agent must be capable of having some attitudes of the kind dealt with in the Basic Case if he is to have any attitudes about any matters at all.

We can plunge into the issues by discussing 'a methodological problem raised by the developmental psychologist T. G. R. Bower. The problem is this: when does someone's behaviour manifest grasp of a spatial distinction? I shall question Bower's formulation and his solution, but the problem is genuine.

Suppose an infant could form a conditioned discrimination between a sound on his right and a sound on his left. What would this tell us? It would tell us that the infant could differentiate between a sound on the left and a sound on the right, on some basis; it does not tell us what the basis is. The baby could differentiate on the basis of spatial position, which is what we are interested in, or it could differentiate equally well on the basis of the succession of sounds at its two ears, with no localization at all. Discrimination experiments cannot tell us the *basis* of a discrimination. . . . If we are interested in the distal perception, in this case the localization of a sound source, we must use a distally oriented response — in this case a localizing response.[4]

If an infant reaches out for an object intentionally, no matter how inaccurately, there can be no doubt that the infant sees the object in the third dimension.[5]

The genuine problem Bower is raising corresponds to an ambiguity in the phrase 'can discriminate *F*s from *G*s'. In one sense, anyone who can tell men from women can discriminate persons with XX chromosomes from persons with XY chromosomes, but this does not imply that the discriminator has the concept of a chromosome. In a similar sense an infant may be able to discriminate sounds on his left from sounds on his right without possessing spatial concepts. Concerned as we are with the attribution of concepts in the Basic Case, any appeal to discriminative abilities must be an appeal to the stronger sense, and we must explain what this involves in the case of spatial concepts.

This point is not happily formulated, as Bower attempts to formulate it, in terms of the 'basis' used by the agent for his discriminations. If 'basis' means 'inferential basis' then the agent need not have any: the knowledge that the sound is on the left can be noninferential. (It certainly need not be inferred from beliefs about differences between the times at which each ear is stimulated, about which the agent may know nothing.) So this construal of 'basis' will not favour the spatial description of what is discriminated. On the other hand if 'basis' is construed causally, a different point arises: it is undeniable both that the presence of a sound on the left causally explains the agent's response, and that the time difference in aural stimulation causally explains the response. (Since these *explanantia* relate to different times, there is no over-determination.) So causal considerations will not uniquely favour a spatial characterization of what is discriminated either. The genuine problem concerns not inference or causation but the ascription of content.

In other contexts, it would be important to distinguish two ways in which a spatial content could be ascribed to the subject's

---

[4] *Development in Infancy* (San Francisco: Freeman, 1974), p. 29.
[5] Ibid., p. 80.

psychological states. The auditory experience itself could have a representational content to the effect that there is a sound coming from the left; or, what is weaker, the experience caused by the sound coming from the left could, in combination with the subject's other attitudes, give him the information that there is a sound coming from his left. But to fall under either case the subject of the experience has to possess spatial concepts and the question we shall be concerned with in discussing Bower's problem is the general one of what it is to possess spatial concepts. ⟵

In asking after the nature of the distinction between psychological states with content and the states of a creature satisfactorily describable by an S–R psychology, we are not asking about the location of the line between those systems which are information-processing and those which are not. On the contrary, a being with only an S–R psychology may have complex information-processing systems which are employed in the identification of stimuli and the selection of responses. Nor is the distinction we are concerned with the same as that between organisms which are conscious and those which are not. An S–R psychology may specify responses not to physical stimuli, but to sensations, and being with sensations has some primitive form of consciousness. Our problem is with the attribution of propositional content, and not all experiences ⟵ have representational content. A type of experience may be enjoyed by a being with a purely S–R psychology provided instances of that type have only sensational and not representational properties, in the sense of Chapter 1 above.

Is Bower's own solution, that an appropriate spatial response confirms the attribution of a spatial content, correct? The difficulty is that when someone makes a discriminatory response, just as there are many stages of the incoming causal chain, there are also many stages of the outgoing causal chain. Just as what is responded to might be the degree of binocular parallax, or aural time differences, so the responses might be a certain neural instruction, or the performance of an action with such-and-such 'response image'[6] or even (what may be the result of a bodily movement) an alteration of one's pattern of retinal stimulation in a certain way. One needs some reason for giving the spatial description of the response a special status. It will be noted too

[6]Cp. A. Goldman, 'The Volitional Theory Revisited', in *Action Theory*, ed. M. Brand and D. Walton (Dordrecht: Reidel, 1976).

that some of these stages, besides the external objects and places, have the property of involving objects which play a role in both the incoming and outgoing chain — for instance the retinas of the eyes.

The suggestion is not that an agent for whom the attitudes in the Basic Case are in question might nevertheless have attitudes whose content relates to motor instructions, response images, or retinal stimulations. The point is rather that we have to give some account of the possession of propositional attitudes about the places and objects immediately around one which does not make stimulus–response connections between certain sensory stimulations, and motor instructions which in fact result in spatial, distal responses, sufficient for the attribution of spatial concepts. (If this were sufficient for the attribution of spatial concepts, they could be attributed to an infant simply by virtue of his possession of the 'doll eye' reflex, the reflex by which, when the head is tilted back, the eye moves in its socket to maintain the line of gaze.) Bower's remark that 'If an infant reaches out for an object intentionally . . . there can be no doubt that the infant sees the object in the third dimension' is not in dispute: the question is what constitutes the subject's having an intention with the content 'reaching out for an object'. A spatial response caused by spatial properties of an object is not sufficient for that intention. It is also not sufficient for attribution of a spatial intention that the subject is distressed when he reaches out for an attractive object and feels nothing there. Such distress would equally be predicted by the supposition that the subject has a stimulus–response link functionally relating degrees of binocular parallax with the direction of reaching and grasping. Whether such a link is wired in at birth or is acquired, one does not need to attribute spatial concepts to account for the distress; if such a link has been rein-forced with rewards either in the subject or members of previous generations from whom it has been inherited, we should not be surprised at the presence of the distress.[7]

Thus if, as seems plausible, Bower was right in thinking that there is a problem about the stages of the incoming chain, there is a corresponding problem about the stages of the outgoing chain,

[7] This point provides a criticism of the experiments of T. G. R. Bower, J. M. Broughton and M. K. Moore, 'Demonstration of Intention in the Reaching Behaviour of Neonate Humans', *Nature* 228 (1970), 679–81.

and neither problem can be solved solely by reference to the other. A different form of approach is required.

These arguments against Bower illustrate a general tactic which is helpful when thinking about content ascription. Presented with any theory which purports to give sufficient conditions for the ascription of attitudes with content, one should always ask: 'Could these conditions be fulfilled by a being with a purely S–R psychology?'. If they could, the conditions cannot be sufficient.[8] Another example of such insufficiency is provided by the way Jonathan Bennett introduces the notion '*a* registers that *p*' in his stimulating discussion of teleology in *Linguistic Behaviour*. He explains '*a* registers that *p* in terms of *p* by saying

if *a* is in an environment which is *relevantly similar* to some environment where *p* is *conspicuously* the case, then *a* registers that *p*[9]

where *p* is conspicuously the case in environments in which it is true and *a* can respond behaviourally to features in virtue of which it is the case; relevantly similar environments are ones which do not differ in any respects to which *a* is sensitive from some environment in which *p* does hold.[10] If this is all that constrains the notion of registration, then organisms which produce a conditioned response to sensory stimulations by a certain type of physical object will count as registering the presence of an object of that type. There is also room for the notions of educability and inquisitiveness, Bennett's suggestions for what needs to be added to registration to reach belief,[11] in an S–R psychology. A highly educable organism will respond quickly to changes in the association of types of stimuli with types of reward; an inquisitive one will try many different responses in different environmental conditions.

A different approach to these problems makes use of the idea of a structured ability. This approach I shall criticize, but the criticism will lead us to the formulation of a condition of adequacy which must be fulfilled by any better account.

---

[8] In answering this conceptual question, one must consider the full range of conceivable S–R theories. Stimulus–response psychology has historically been associated with responses to absolute and not relative values of magnitudes: but it need not have been.

[9] (Cambridge: CUP, 1976), p. 53.

[10] Ibid., pp. 53–4.

[11] Ibid., pp. 84–9.

The general idea of a structured ability arises out of the thought that when we attribute an ability to someone, and this ability is manifested in the exercise of many different particular abilities, we can draw a distinction. We can distinguish the case in which the general ability is merely the sum of these component abilities from the case in which these component abilities are themselves the result of interactions between members of a smaller set of more powerful abilities possessed by the agent. A clear example of the distinction is provided by the case of understanding a language which has only finitely many sentences, an example which, thanks to the work of Evans and Davies, is now relatively well understood.[12]

Suppose we are concerned with a language whose sentences can be regarded as built from finitely many predicates and finitely many proper names. It contains no other kinds of expression, no iterative or recursive devices such as connectives, operators, or functors. We have learned that we can distinguish the case in which someone's ability to understand the sentences of this language is structured from the case in which it is unstructured. (Note that here in a certain sense we speak of the structure of the ability itself, not the structure of expressions we use to pick out the ability.) The evidence that someone's understanding is structured, that he understands not just complete sentences as unstructured wholes, but understands individual proper names and predicates, would be given in normal circumstances by such facts as the following. If he were taught a new sentence, consisting of new proper names concatenated with a familiar predicate used in the construction of sentences in the fragment with which he is already familiar, then he would go on to use and understand yet other new sentences containing the new name in cancatenation with other familiar old predicates. Or again, if he were to revise his opinion about the meaning of a particular sentence in the language, there would be corresponding revisions in the way he would understand other sentences built up from some of the same vocabulary. One would not expect such conditions to be fulfilled by someone who had learned to understand the finitely many individual sentences one by one, as unstructured wholes. These

[12]G. Evans, 'Reply to Wright', in *Wittgenstein: To Follow a Rule* (London: Routledge, 1981), ed. S. Holtzman and C. Leich; M. K. Davies, *Meaning, Quantification, Necessity* (London: Routledge, 1981), chapter on understanding.

facts are of course all just evidence for structure in the ability, and are not constututive of it. What would be constitutive of it would be the presence of some state in the understander such that for any sentence containing a certain semantically significant component expression, that state enters the explanation of his understanding the sentence in the way he does. 'Explanation' here does not mean, or does not need to mean, explanation by inference on the part of the understander; the state may just be a neurophysiological state that enters the causal explanation of the subject's coming to have a noninferential belief to the effect that a certain sentence of the language says that such-and-such. The distinction between structured and unstructured understanding has been more sharply formulated in the cited writings of Evans and Davies and I shall take it that these reminders are enough here. What matters from the standpoint of our present enterprise is that the linguistic case gives a clear example of a more widely found phenomenon, that of the importance of drawing a distinction between two cases that may arise when an agent has a given ability: the case in which the ability has some further structure, and that in which it does not.[13] Now how might this apply to the Basic Case?

The suggestion would be that there is a complex ability, the ability to move and manipulate objects in one's immediate environment. This ability will generally be manifested in actions on attractive or unattractive objects, or objects the motion of which is a means to the manipulation of such objects. The ability is a complex one, since there are many places relative to one's body between which objects may be moved and many different movements and limbs that one may employ in manipulating the objects. The question then arises whether this ability is a structured one or not. The suggestion I want now to consider is that when a certain kind of structure is present in these sensori-motor abilities, it is correct to attribute to the subject attitudes about the objects and places in his environment. It is correct to go beyond the

[13] It does not matter for the present point if it is correct to say that when the ability is unstructured it is not literally the same language which is understood as in the structured case. There is indeed some point in saying that the language is not the same. We can still make corresponding points to those in the text about persons who understand either one of these two different but, at a level which is not the most refined, equally expressive languages.

attribution merely of sensori-motor skills and to attribute beliefs and desires about the external objects, just as the structure of the ability in the linguistic case made it correct to attribute under-standing of the individual expressions composing the sentences.

What then might be the evidence for the presence of structure in the Basic Case? One obvious source of evidence which might be cited by the structural theorist of the Basic Case would be the fact that if someone for instance extends his arm to grasp an object he believes to be at a certain place, and contrary to his expectations finds nothing there, then he will not then reach out with some other limb and try again at the same place. Similarly he will not try again with the same limb, tracing a different path in space that ends at the same place (relative to his body). The structural theorist will say that this is precisely what one would expect if the bodily movements of the subject are manifestations of his beliefs and desires about the objects and places around him. Yet again, it may be said, when by reinforcement we induce in the subject new stimulus–response connections, it may be that in the normal case, what is reinforced by a training programme is not a particular motor response, a particular kind of movement of a certain limb, but rather any movement which has certain results either for particular physical objects in the agent's environment or for his own location. Different movements of limbs are ordinarily treated as equivalent by the subject if they have the same end results for the objects and places around him.

There are also more sophisticated suggestions about such structural evidence. Suppose someone wants to reach out to a particular place and does so. Suppose too that after doing so he then rotates through some angle, and wants to reach out to that same place again, or has been trained to reach out to that particular place for a certain kind of reward. Then in reaching out the second time after some rotation, he will move some limb out at an angle different, in relation to the front of his body, from the angle of his previous movement. I will call theories which cite structural evidence of the kinds mentioned, and which regard structure in the ability to manipulate objects and to act on places as constitutive of the presence of propositional attitudes, 'purely structured ability theories' (PSATs). It is important, since we are here concerned with the Basic Case, that the kinds of structure cited as essential by a PSAT theorist must not be ones that need not be present whenever a subject has attitudes about his environment. It is not obvious that structure relating, for example, to the use of implements by the subject fulfils this condition.

There is a fundamental criticism of the form of the conditions offered by the PSATs. It is unintelligible that someone should have beliefs about just one particular place in his environment (identified as a place bearing a certain relation to his body), while not having any beliefs at all about other places — not even the belief that there are other places spatially related to the one about which he does have beliefs. Yet nothing in the conditions offered by the PSAT theorist excludes this as a possibility. There is no reason why the absence of a different movement, or a movement by another limb, to a place after one has failed once, should not be a feature of one place and not others. The same holds for the rotation suggestion. Of course, this possibility might be excluded as one in which propositional attitudes are manifested simply by stipulation on the part of the PSAT theorist. But this would be unsatisfactory in that the unintelligibility does not seem to be satis-factorily explained just by the inclusion of a stipulation. If indeed it is not possible for someone to be capable of beliefs about just one place, then we ought to be able to say why this is impossible on the basis of our account of belief and places. Someone who has mastered the 'believes' construction and also understands discourse about places will be in a position to understand state-ments about people's beliefs concerning places; there is no plausibility in the view that in understanding such statements he has to grasp some additional stipulation about what it is to have beliefs about places, something not determined by his general knowledge of what it is to be a place and his understanding of 'believes'. If this is correct then it is theoretically desirable that the impossibility of having beliefs about just one place be displayed as a derived consequence of a theory about belief and places, rather than as a stipulation. The impossibility is presumably connected in some way with the thought that a place is essentially spatially related to other places. I will, then, take it as a condition of adequacy on any account of what it is to have attitudes about places in the Basic Case that it excludes the possibility that one could have attitudes about one place only, and that it achieves this not in a purely stipulative way.[14]

---

[14] There may also be other difficulties if we accept the stipulative view. Can this view explain the significance of the distinction between attributing attitudes to someone and simply ascribing stimulus–response mechanisms to him?

There are other difficulties with some of the PSATs I have formulated. It seems quite wrong, for example, to say that we cannot ever attribute beliefs about places and objects in his environment to a creature with just one limb and only one way of moving that limb to any given place in his environment. This is especially clear when we remember that the creature could still have a complex perceptual mechanism, and these simple movements could be explained by the creature's possession of a complex theory of the world around him. Yet a PSAT theory either rules this out as a possibility if it makes essential to the ascription of attitudes in the Basic Case the points about different movements of the same limb or movements of different limbs (or else it wrongly attributes attitudes to *any* such simply equipped creature). Finally no PSAT theory accounts for our intuition that it is right to attribute attitudes to creatures only if they are capable, or were once capable, either of having perceptions of the world, or of being in states which carry information about the world in a way systematically similar to that in which perceptual experiences carry such information.

I have considered only one kind of PSAT. It may be that there are other PSAT accounts of the Basic Case which are not vulnerable to these criticisms, and which avoid them by citing different structural features. But I turn now to state my own positive account of the Basic Case and the fulfilment of the adequacy condition. This account is based on a notion I will call 'perspectival sensitivity'. Here is an illustration. Suppose the agent is located at place A in the diagram, and is demonstratively presented in perception with an object B (see Figure 1).

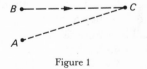

Figure 1

Suppose too that the agent regularly obtains food or occasionally fulfils some other desire at place C. The requirement of perspectival sensitivity demands that if he moves from A to the demonstratively presented object B, by a path he recognizes as taking him from A to B, then in going off from B to get food or fulfil his desire, he goes in the direction of the broken line from B to C and not along a line parallel to AC. Such perspectival sensitivity is required, at least in central cases, if any action by the thinker on the demonstratively presented object at B is to be more than, different in kind from, a stimulus–response mechanism.

This is just an illustration of perspectival sensitivity: it is not a general account. A general account ought to make explicit the dependence of bodily movements on changes in experience. One would like to say that if one first has an experience in which a particular array of objects is represented as bearing certain spatial relations to oneself, and one's experience gradually alters to become an experience in which that array is presented as bearing different spatial relations to oneself, then there is a corresponding alteration in one's dispositions to perform bodily movements: that is what it is for one's movements to display perspectival sensitivity. But here we meet an obstacle. Experiences may, and in general do, already have a representational content: they represent objects of such-and-such kinds as being spatially related thus-and-so to oneself. In attributing such experiences to someone one is already attributing states with content, a content containing concepts; and an analysis of the ascription of these contents in the Basic Case is our present aim. Someone could not have such experiences without already possessing concepts of spatial relations and objects in his immediate environment. Use of an undifferentiated notion of experience threatens to prevent our obtaining the illumination of the Basic Case which we sought.

This obstacle is removed if we appeal not to representational but to sensational properties of experiences. Let there be a subject presented in perception with three objects – a house, a lake, and a mountain. These objects are presented in experiences of types Π_h, Π_l, and Π_m respectively. These types are intended fully to capture the intrinsic properties of the experiences in which the objects are presented, and thus specify both sensational and representational properties. If our subject is located at A in Figure 2 overleaf, then the arrows show the distances and directions in which he would move if, for each one of the three objects, he had an intention to move to that object as presented in perception. Figure 2 displays part of the subject's *intentional web* at a given time. His intentional web at that time consists of a set of labelled lines, each one of them originating in his location at that time. The labels consist of the

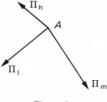

Figure 2

ways objects are presented to him in perception, a given line showing the direction and distance he would move if he acted on an intention to come into contact with the object presented in the label of that line.

Our subject now moves to a new location. The house, lake, and mountain produce new experiences in him at the new location. Let the new experiences be Π_h', Π_l' and Π_m' respectively. These new experiences will normally differ in their *sensational* properties from Π_h, Π_l and Π_m. The sensational properties of the new experiences will normally in the circumstances determine a unique place B, the place from which experiences of these types and of the house, lake, and mountain would be obtained. If our subject earlier had an intention to move to the lake, and the time for acting arrives after he has moved to his new location, then he moves in the direction and distance given by the line labelled Π_l' in Figure 3; and similarly for other such intentions. We can express this concisely thus: our subject's intentional web at the later time results from his web at the earlier time by *recentring* his earlier web on the place B. Figure 3 illustrates the recentring of part of the subject's earlier intentional

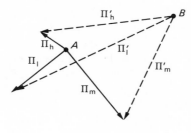

Figure 3

web on the place B. The web shown by broken lines is part of his intentional web at the later time. It does not follow from what has been said so far that B is identical with our subject's actual location at the later time; tricks of the light or perceptual errors may have produced in him experiences with sensational properties not normally produced by motion along the path he has followed. But discrepancies between actual location and the place of recentring of the intentional web will tend to be corrected.

So a simplified general statement of the requirement of perspectival sensitivity would be this: if the subject moves from one place to another, his intentional web must be recentred on the place determined in normal circumstances by the change in the sensational properties of his experiences. A creature with the concepts of the Basic Case might never move, but it must be true that such a being would display perspectival sensitivity were he to move and to be capable of action. Perspectival sensitivity is literally a matter, in actual and counterfactual circumstances, of the sensitivity of the subject's intentional actions to variations in his perspective on the world.

Many variations are possible on the theme played by this basic constraint. In fact the best metaphor for the relations between experience and the subject's information about his own location seems to be Quine's of someone scrambling up the inside of a chimney. In some cases experiences, impressions and accelerations, flow patterns and the rest will determine such positional information, while in others that information will determine the significance of the experiences. It would also be possible to investigate some complementary relationships implicit in perspectival sensitivity. If, for instance, a subject were very familiar with all the types of objects in his environment and how they would appear from different angles, it seems that he would need much less in the way of efferent-based information about changes in his own position to display perspectival sensitivity.

The oversimplifications in the present formulations are myriad. Our subject may forget how far he has moved, or may not move along the line labelled by Π_1' in Figure 3 because he knows there is a spatial obstacle to doing so; or he may be like a travelling salesman who wishes to visit many places by the shortest journey. The simple model applies only to beings with perfect memories and single goals operating in a desert with a few small objects strewn over the surface. But there can be independent evidence that there have been failures of memory, or that there are believed to be obstacles, or that there are multiple goals. Such qualifications of the principle, which seem analogous to qualifications one needs elsewhere in stating psychological principles, do not make the requirement of perspectival sensitivity vacuous.

Perspectival sensitivity as we have so far characterized it is necessary for the attribution of attitudes in the Basic Case; but it is a weaker necessary condition than we seek. For consider the hypothetical case of the fruit-eating creature. This creature is repeatedly exposed to a particular kind of plant which always has an attractive fruit at the same place inside it. The creature eats the fruit when it finds it; and after a certain amount of training, the creature acquires the ability to reach the fruit, which may be obscured from it visually by the shortest possible route, regardless of its angle of approach to the plant. When this ability has been acquired, then for all I have said so far, we can say that the behaviour of the fruit-eating creature displays perspectival sensitivity: its behaviour is spatially dependent on the particular experiences it has. But it seems undeniable from this description that the fruit-eating creature might have no more than an ability for which a stimulus–response characterization is quite appropriate. It is not vacuous to say that there is *some* requirement for the attribution of attitudes which concerns perspectival sensitivity; but this example shows that we have not yet made fully explicit what that requirement *is*.

There is no prospect of ruling out this kind of example by developing the reflection that the behaviour of someone with attitudes is dependent upon his beliefs about the spatial distribution of objects around him, and so his behaviour is sensitive to his past experience while that of the fruit-eating creature is not. The fruit-eating creature would not behave as it does in moving towards the food, had it not had various experiences during the conditioning of the response to the stimulus of its perception of the plant. Perhaps a narrower idea was intended by the suggestion: that the example can be excluded because the creature's behaviour is not causally sensitive to its recent spatial relations to objects not currently perceived. But again this condition would be met by the fruit-eating creature if on the way to the fruit it turned its head in another direction without stopping on its way. This can hardly make the crucial difference for the attributability of spatial concepts. What one would so like to say is that the behaviour of a person with attitudes about objects depends specifically upon the spatial distribution of objects around him. But this is the kind of thought we found, in the discussion of Bower, to lead nowhere. The behaviour of the fruit-eating creature certainly depends causally on the spatial orientation of the plant relative to the creature. Until we say more, this idea of specific dependence upon spatial facts seems to rest on the intuition to be explained, viz., that spatial concepts enter the content of the attitudes of someone whose actions require more than just a stimulus–response characterization.

Another idea that may seem tempting is the view that the spatial abilities and dispositions of someone with spatial attitudes can only be specified by making reference to the spatial relations of the subject to objects in his environment. But to yield to this temptation can result in a dogmatic position. Consider a creature for whom there is some exhaustive and no doubt higher-order specification of the sequences of experiences, characterized by their sensational properties, which would produce in it a given set of spatial beliefs. Suppose too we could exhaustively demonstrate the effects on bodily movements of any given intention in the presence of a given set of spatial beliefs. It could be that using such characterizations we could build up a complete account of the role of spatial attitudes in this creature's psychology, without at all mentioning its spatial relations to particular objects or places in its environment at any given time. The possibility of such a complex description of the spatial dispositions of the creature need not undercut its claim to be accorded psychological states with contents containing spatial notions.

We should ask the question: if it were correct to attribute attitudes to the fruit-eating creature, what else would we expect him to be capable of doing? What are the consequences of such an attribution? We would expect that if, for example, some new attraction were located permanently at a place which the creature passed through on some of his routes to the fruit, then he must be able to find his way to this new attraction from various starting points, even when the attraction is obscured by the plant that has the fruit. This condition would need to be fulfilled for each place about which we attribute thoughts to the creature. Perspectival sensitivity must be preserved when the objects of the agent's desires are located at places about which he is already capable of having attitudes. Yet this would still not be enough. Suppose that the fruit-eating creature were able to identify the plant containing the fruit only from a certain range of angles — say the shaded range in Figure 4.

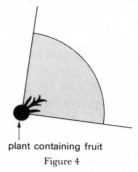

plant containing fruit
Figure 4

In these circumstances, it could well be the case that the requirement we last mentioned, that of the preservation of perspectival sensitivity when desirable objects are located at places about which the subject is capable of having thoughts, is fulfilled by all places within the shaded area. This is consistent with the requirement remaining unfulfilled for places in the unshaded area; and if it were so unfulfilled, then the attributability of spatial attitudes would be problematic if no further explanation were forthcoming.

It would be problematic, for how in such a case does the creature itself think of the space in which it is located? It is contradictory to suppose a given space is the whole of physical space, while supposing also that it has a boundary beyond which there are further points.[15] We could not attribute such an unintelligible view to the creature. Perhaps then the creature does not believe there are places beyond the region within which he displays perspectival sensitivity? But, as he moves, the changing sensational properties of his experience which are produced by the objects outside the region will be just the same as those produced by similar objects at the same distance withing the region. So unless the creature distrusts his senses outside the region (which we could independently confirm), such a limitation of perspectival sensitivity entails that the changing

[15]This is not to deny that physical space could be a bounded metric space in the sense of the topological sense, i.e. that the maximum distance between any two points in it is finite. It is not denied, because in that case the bounded space *is* the whole of physical space.

sensational properties are not always a sufficient cause of appropriately adjusted movement: the sensitivity is not general. There may of course be explanations of these limitations on the creature's behaviour, explanations which defeat the *prima facie* objection to ascribing spatial attitudes to it. Independently certifiable motor failures or failures of the senses outside the given region would be such defeating explanations. (A more recherché case would be that in which there are perceptual and motor distortions, near the edge of the given region, of such a kind that the creature *could* reasonably think the whole of its space to be bounded in the topological sense.) But unless some such defeating explanation exists, spatial attitudes should not be attributed to the creature. The fact that such defeating explanations are conceivable shows, incidentally, that we could not have excluded the modified version of the example of the fruit-eating creature simply by requiring that perspectival sensitivity be displayed in all regions the creature may occupy. When there are defeating explanations, such a condition would be too strong.

When one tests empirically whether the behaviour of a subject satisfies the conditions of this perspectival account, here as elsewhere in propositional attitude psychology one can derive empirical predictions only from a set of psychological hypotheses. If a subject on a particular occasion fails to engage in bodily movements which are perspectivally sensitive, one should not necessarily revise any hypothesis to the effect that he has spatial attitudes. It may be that his desires have changed, his memory has failed him, that his motor mechanisms are not functioning, and so forth. What one empirically tests is a conjunction of hypotheses concerning the subject's beliefs about objects and places around him, his desires, abilities, perceptual sensitivities, . . . According to the perspectival theory, one has reason for ascribing spatial attitudes in the Basic Case only if one has reason for believing a set of hypotheses of the kind just mentioned, which entail that in some circumstances the subject intentionally moves in a way manifesting perspectival sensitivity, and that he would in other circumstances too, were it not for the failure or limitations of various subsystems on which intentional actions depends.[16]

[16] The methodology both of W. Köhler in his celebrated *The Mentality of Apes* (New York: Liveright, 1976 repr.) and of more recent work such as that reported in E. Menzel, 'Chimpanzee spatial memory organisation', *Science* 182 (1973), 943–5, meshes well with the perspectival theory.

The requirement of perspectival sensitivity concerns the behaviour of the subject at more than one place. It immediately excludes the possibility that the subject is capable of attitudes about only one place, has the concept of only one place. Unlike the PSAT accounts we considered earlier, this consequence has not been secured by stipulation additional to some prior account. Failures and limitations of the subsystems and one recherché case aside, general perspectival sensitivity also excludes the possibility that there is a region within space such that a particular being is capable of spatial attitudes only about things in that region.

Though we have said that the spatial behaviour of a creature with attitudes in the Basic Case must vary in a certain way with variations in the sensational properties of his experiences, we have so far left open the question of whether those variations in experience must cause the changes in dispositions to spatial behaviour. It is conceivable there should be an individual we will label 'The Pure Realigner'. The Pure Realigner's actions are appropriately adjusted to his location in space, but change in the sensational properties of his experiences plays no part causally in this adjustment. The adjustment need not be a miracle: judgements about location might be caused as a side-effect of efferent nerve instructions to move, stop, change direction and so forth. Is it right to exclude the Pure Realigner from having psychological states with a content concerning his immediate environment? It depends upon what happens in the counterfactual circumstances in which the impressions caused by efferent instructions and the evidence from perception of the external world point in different directions. Suppose the Pure Realigner moves two hundred yards to a place p, but has the impression (caused by efferent mechanisms) that he has moved only one hundred yards, to p'. He is surprised by what he finds; as he moves more, the evidence becomes overwhelming that initially he moved to p, not p'. There are then two cases to consider, according as he does or does not adjust his actions appropriately to his new circumstances. If he does, it seems plausible to say that he meets the requirements of the Basic Case: although the behaviour is not in fact caused by changes in his experiences of the world but by something in the actual world systematically correlated with such changes, in counterfactual circumstances the tie with experience is dominant. If he does not adjust his actions, the ascription of attitudes about objects and places in the world is questionable. To possess some conception of oneself as located in the world, one must employ such concepts as those of spatial location, directions and relations. It is constitutive of those concepts that no non-spatial conditions which are experienced or which may cause judgements are conclusive for the application of these spatial notions; one can always make sense of the suggestion that any given indicator is misleading.[17] It is just this inconclusiveness that is shown in the first case; but if the Pure Realigner responds as in the second case, it is not manifested. In the second case the Pure Realigner is like a bird on a long-distance flight, responsive by a S–R mechanism to variations in (say) the earth's magnetic field. Such behaviour would be perspectivally sensitive to actual circumstances; but if it were not also perspectivally sensitive in circumstances in which magnetic field is clearly no guide to direction, that behaviour would not by itself suffice for the ascription of attitudes in the Basic Case.[18]

When a creature's behaviour displays perspectival sensitivity, adjustments in his behaviour will be correlated not only with changes in the sensational properties of his experiences, but with anything else with which sensational properties are correlated. Complex properties of the pattern of retinal stimulation would be one such example. One should not leap to the conclusion that on this perspectival theory, one could equally say that an organism meeting the requirements of the Basic Case has attitudes about his patterns of retinal stimulation. As was emphasized at the start of this chapter, the constraints offered here are necessary, not sufficient, conditions for the ascription of content; there will be further constraints relating to various particular contents. For example, before we can conclude that a perceptually-based judgement 'that dog is white' could equally be construed as a judgement concerning retinal stimulation patterns, we have to give an account of other contents containing the component 'that dog', including past-tense contents. Any conclusions about indeterminacy of the ascription of content are premature in advance of consideration of the full range of occurrences of a component in other contents. Whether there is indeterminacy when the full constraints on the

[17] See my *Holistic Explanation*, Chapter 1.

[18] We would have here a special case of what Jonathan Bennett calls 'frozen intelligence' (*Rationality* (London: Routledge, 1964), pp. 33–42). Note that to sustain this type of argument, one has to establish that the concept whose attribution is in question does not have conclusive conditions of application: 'looks red' does not meet this requirement. (All the examples in Bennett's text do meet it.)

ascription of content are considered is clearly a subject for further work.[19]

It is harmless to summarize the claim that an organism displays perspectival sensitivity or has spatial attitudes by saying that it has a mental map of its environment.[20] But two stronger statements are not legitimized by this harmless way of expressing perspectival sensitivity. First, nothing I have said seems to require that an organism which displays perspectival sensitivity has a global image of its environment which functions as a map, if to have an image is to be in a conscious state. Ulrich Neisser, for example, takes it as plain that 'Every organism that can anticipate its environment has cognitive maps'; in the sense of 'cognitive map' on which this is plausible, it is not also plausible that cognitive maps 'are a species of images'.[21]

Second, in the case in which someone has an external, physical map of his environment, his possession of the map cannot be a general explanation of the perspectival sensitivity of his actions. To use a map, one has to be able to keep track of one's own location on the map, and this requires the ability to recognize one's altered spatial relations to the objects one perceives. But if one can do this, one will already be capable of perspectival sensitivity in some range of cases; and if one cannot, one will be unable to use the map. It follows that possession of the map cannot explain all cases of perspectival sensitivity.

The perspectival theory can be described as having a two-tier holistic structure. There is the familiar holism always present in belief–desire psychology. But there is also implicit in the theory a kind of holism which remains even when we hold the desires of the agent constant. The familar belief–desire holism is shown by the

[19] It is plausible that in normal circumstances when a human being judges of a perceptually presented dog on the basis of his experience that it is white, there will be a correlated region of his retinas, with a certain kind of shape property D, and a certain colour property W. Does it follow that we could replace the content 'that dog is white' in circumstances of this type with 'some region of my retinas are D and W'? No: for 'In the past, that dog was white' will not in general be even materially equivalent to 'In the past, some regions of my retinas were D and W' – the subject may never have seen that dog before.

[20] A practice followed by E. C. Tolman ('Cognitive Maps in Rats and Men', *Psychological Review* 55 (1948), 189–208) and many later psychologists. For brief surveys, see U. Neisser, Chapter 6, 'Cognitive Maps', in his *Cognition and Reality* (San Francisco: Freeman, 1976), and Chapter 2, 'Spatial Behaviour', of *The Hippocampus as a Cognitive Map,* by J. O'Keefe and L. Nadel (Oxford OUP, 1978).

[21] Op. cit., pp. 131, 134.

fact that any action is intentional under a particular description only if the agent has certain appropriate attitudes, and the presence of these attitudes requires various other actions in other circumstances. Similarly, even when we hold the desires of the agent fixed, the statement that a certain movement is a manifestation of propositional attitudes about external objects, rather than a mere response to a stimulus, is answerable to facts about what the agent would do if differently situated with respect to the objects and places on which he is acting. This answerability has, according to the perspectival theory, a constitutive character which it also has in the belief–desire case.[22]

Perspectival sensitivity is necessary for the ascription of content, but it may reasonably be questioned whether it is sufficient for thought in the way that human beings are capable of thinking. The condition of perspectival sensitivity could be fulfilled by a being whose cognitive psychology is completely describable by the fact that he updates a map of his environment on the basis of his experiences, and this map interacts with his desires to produce action. There is indeed genuine content here, but not judgement: in particular, this being never witholds assent from the proposition which is the content of an experience, in order to weigh up the evidence or to explain away recalcitrant experiences. Recalcitrant experiences are first taken at face value, and later ignored if they cause errors, but they are not reflected upon. It would be dogmatic to claim that the word 'belief' in English exludes the states of such a being, but there is clearly a real distinction between the intermediate case of this being and our own thinking.[23] Hume's concep-

---

[22] I do not mean to imply in contrasting the perspectival theory with PSATs that the beliefs and desires manifested in the perspectivally sensitive bodily movements do not need to be realized by states of the brain; on the contrary. Indeed I would be prepared to write into the perspectival theory the requirement that there be physical states of the creature in question, related as are beliefs and desires in propositional attitude psychology, and which explain the movements of the creature which has this perspectival sensitivity.

[23] This real distinction may be what underlay Bernard Williams' formulation in terms of belief and assertion in his paper 'Deciding to Believe' (reprinted in his *Problems of the Self* (Cambridge: CUP, 1973)). Williams envisages a creature whose epistemic states are manifested in assertion-like performances, but with the difference from assertion that the creature cannot lie. He claims that the states manifested by these assertion-like performances cannot be beliefs. This argument has been justly criticized by Jonathan Bennett (*Linguistic Behaviour*, p. 9). But Williams was right to connect belief in humans with our ability to withhold *something*— but the withholding should be of judgement rather than assertion.

tion of belief as determined by brute custom is applicable to this being in a way it is inapplicable to us. But such a being does register facts about its environment, and has psychological states with content.

The Tightness Constraint

We turn now from the Basic Case to discuss the internal boundary question: the question of why, if a being has psychological states with content at all, it is correct to attribute to it a collection of attitudes with one set of contents rather than another set. My strategy will be to introduce a relation, *tighter than*, between sets of attitudes which are candidates to be a certain creature's attitudes. This relation will feature in a constraint to the effect that a set of attitudes should not be attributed to a creature if there is another, tighter, set which can be attributed to it. Since the relation *tighter than* is to feature in this constraint, it would lead to vacuity if we were to take for granted in the explanation of comparative tightness the concept of an action being intentional under a particular description. But we can legitimately use a relative notion: that of an action being intentional under a given description *according to* a given set of candidate attitudes. We can compare, for a given subject, the relations of different sets of candidate attitudes to his actual and possible behaviour.

I will introduce the relation *tighter than* by giving three examples and I will then go on to suggest a generalization from them. The three examples concern respectively places, numbers and material objects. There is a uniform principle underlying the different subject matters of the examples.

Example 1. Suppose someone to be in a room and a circular table to be in the same room. The table top can revolve about its centre. Suppose too that the person can act on, manipulate and rearrange objects which are on the table. The person has beliefs about the objects on the table. If attractive objects are regularly to be found under whatever thing bears such-and-such spatial relations to other items on the table, the person will reliably look under that thing and not under others, and will do so from whatever angle he views the table. So the conditions proposed by the perspectival theory for the Basic Case are fulfilled: his behaviour is sensitive to the spatial arrangement of the objects themselves, and he does not simply act on whatever object bears such-and-such spatial relation to his own body. We can say in brief that he is sensitive to *table-relative* properties of objects – that is, he is sensitive to the spatial relations between the objects on the table.

This is consistent with his not being sensitive to what we can label *room-relative* properties of objects. That is, although he can recognize a configuration of objects on the table as the same configuration, even when seen from different angles, he does not distinguish the case in which such a change in relative orientation is a result of *his* motion relative to the room from the case in which it is a result of the *table's* motion, or indeed of both. Thus, for instance, if an atractive object is placed always under the thing on the table nearest to the north side of the room, he does not reliably look under that thing, even though, as we can imagine, the sides of the room are qualitatively different and cause different kinds of experience in the subject. I suggest that it would be incorrect in these circumstances to attribute to the agent actions intentional under room-relative, as well as table-relative, descriptions. Such attribution would be unconstrained by the presence of actions sensitive to the distinctions drawn by the room-relative descriptions. The attribution would not fit the actual and counterfactually possible intentional actions of the agent as tightly as some alternative attribution.

It may well be that we are prepared to say of the agent in this example that when he is perceiving the room in normal circumstances, it is table-relative and not room-relative conditions which psychologically explain his actions. But it is plausible that our willingness to draw this distinction amongst explaining conditions is dependent upon our willingness to attribute only table-relative attitudes to the agent. Can we give a sharper and clearly nonvacuous formulation of why is it wrong in this first example to attribute room-relative attitudes?

Let us consider a set of table-relative attitudes Σ and a set of room-relative attitudes Σ' as candidates for the set of attitudes to be attributed to our subject in the first example. The set of concepts attributed in Σ' and the set of concepts attributed in Σ are distinct. The former set, call it $C(\Sigma')$, will contain notions, such as 'is roughly three feet from the radiator on the west wall', where are not in the second set (which we can label $C(\Sigma)$). We can say that the set of concepts $C(\Sigma')$ has greater expressive power than the set of concepts

$C(\Sigma)$ in a sense similar to that in which we might say this of two languages: there will be conditions frameable using only the concepts of $C(\Sigma')$ to which no conditions framed using only the concepts of $C(\Sigma)$ are equivalent, while the same (we shall take it) does not hold for $C(\Sigma)$ *vis-à-vis* $C(\Sigma')$. An example of a condition which can be formulated using the room-relative concepts and not the table-relative ones will be, say, 'The cup is two feet from the middle of the north window and two feet from the door'. No table-relative condition can possibly be equivalent to this since such a condition will only state the relative positions of objects on the table. Since the table can revolve, any table-relative condition can continue to hold while some room-relative condition varies in truth value. The reason which I offer for the superiority of the table-relative attitudes in this first example lies in the fact that the greater expressive power of the concepts $C(\Sigma')$ is nowhere manifested in the subject's actions. To attribute room-relative attitudes in these circumstances is to allow unempirical slack into our attribution of propositional attitudes; and there remains unempirical slack so long as there is no intentional action rationalized by the attitudes in the room-relative set which would not equally be rationalized by table-relative attitudes.

The attribution of room-relative attitudes in this example is unempirical only if the absence of actions rationalized by room-relative but not table-relative attitudes cannot be explained by operational limitations. Operational limitations will include limitations of memory, attention, and inferential ability (provided the missing inferences are not constitutive of the concepts in the more sophisticated set of attitudes). If on some particular occasion the subject does not perform an action one would expect from a subject who possesses the more sophisticated set of attitudes, then if the absence is explained by operational limitations, the absence need not cast doubt on the subject's possession of the more sophisticated set. This *caveat* does not render a tightness constraint vacuous, for the presence of operational limitations can be independently confirmed.

Anyone who accepts that in examples like this first one it is acceptable to attribute table-relative but not room-relative attitudes will be committed to the view that there must be something to be said about rational psychological explanation in addition to general principles about reasons of the sort we quoted from Davidson earlier, the sort which does not descend to the subsentential level. For it is undeniable that certain room-relative attitudes would be of a correct form to explain the agent's behaviour in this example. The problem is that they would employ concepts that combine in other circumstances to rationalize behaviour that would not be there. A similar point will apply to the examples to come.

An illustration of tightness can be given, analogous to its role in this first example, which is more closely tied to empirical research in psychology. Suppose that what Bryant calls the 'match–mismatch hypothesis' concerning infants' judgements of the relative orientation of successively presented oblique lines is correct.[24] This is the hypothesis that infants register whether lines are parallel or not, and can give a positive answer to the question whether a pair of successively presented oblique lines have the same orientation, only if in both cases the lines are parallel to some given line that remains unchanged in both presentations. If this hypothesis is true, then it would be a violation of the tightness constraint to hold also that the same infants can register whether an oblique line runs northwest–southeast (NW–SE) or northeast–southwest (NE–SW). For if the infants can register and remember such facts, then they should be able to report that successively presented lines running NW–SE and NE–SW differ in direction; but if neither is parallel with a constantly present line they will not do so, under the match–mismatch hypothesis. One set of attitudes not attributing the concepts NW–SE and NE–SW to the infants will be tighter than another set which does.

Example 2. This kind of example is familiar from the philosophy of arithmetic. There one sometimes has reason to consider a person all of whose numerical beliefs can be formulated using the four forms of expression: 'there is one F', 'there are two Fs', 'there are three Fs', and 'the Fs are equinumerous with the Gs', together with various non-numerical forms of compounding these basic expressions with others. What can we say of the actions of a person whose numerical beliefs do conform to this restriction? I suggest that in general his intentional actions, including his utterances, will be insensitive to conditions in the world which are expressible using, for instance, complex arabic numerals, but which do not have consequences

[24] See P. Bryant, *Perception and Understanding in Young Children* (London: Methuen, 1974).

expressible using the restricted set of four numerical concepts ('using the numerical operators', as we will abbreviate it).[25] Thus, for example, our person may believe that the gold pieces he owns are equinumerous with the pebbles in his hand. Suppose the number of both is in fact twenty. The kind of insensitivity our person's actions display would be shown in such facts as the following (in the simplest case). Suppose our person owned only nineteen gold pieces, and had paired them one-to-one with some pebbles, which he then collected together in his hand. Then all his intentional actions in given circumstances would remain as they actually are – that is, there would be no intentional action he would perform in these counterfactual circumstances which could not be suitably explained by attitudes the content of which is built up using the numerical operators. Of course, an antecedent of a counter-factual expressed using arabic numerals may in particular circumstances have empirical consequences for conditions expressed using the 'equinumerous' operator, and then the person's actions may well be different. It might be that the person has a box of twenty standard pebbles used for pairing, each pebble couched in a particular slot; and so if he owned only nineteen pieces of gold, and paired these with his pebbles, he would notice that one pebble remained unused in the box. In these circumstances his owning only nineteen gold pieces would have the consequence that he came to believe, for instance, that his gold pieces are not equinumerous with the slots in the box, and his latter belief could have consequences for action. But it would remain the case that there would be no difference in his intentional actions without a difference formulable using the four numerical operators. Intui-tively, for our person a particular set of attitudes specified using the numerical operators and not complex arabic numerals will be tighter than any set which does attribute concepts of particular numbers greater than three, just as table-relative attitudes were tighter than room-relative attitudes in the first example.

This second example also shows how one can have substantive and empirical reasons for attributing to someone a belief by using in the content-sentence an unstructured rather than a structured, albeit necessarily and *a priori* coextensive, expression. 'Equi-

[25] Obviously we must take it that the means for combining these concepts do not stretch far enough to permit the standard first-order definitions of the finite numerical quantifiers.

numerous' can be treated as an unstructured second-level operator on a pair of first-level predicates. But if instead of using an expression treated that way we attributed to our person the belief that there is some number n such that n is both the number of pebbles in his hand and the number of gold pieces, we would be open to the charge of representing him as having beliefs specified using distinctions to which he is not in fact sensitive — that is, to the charge of making non-empirical attributions of belief.

Example 3. This example concerns predication. Evans argued that we should not take a given linguistic construction as a predicate of a certain kind of object unless this condition is met: there are sentences in the language whose truth value turns on the distribution of various features within, or relational properties of, a boundary of the sort possessed by objects of that kind.[26] There is a correspondingly compelling and motivated generalization of this principle to the attribution of attitudes about objects of a given kind more generally. Very roughly, the idea is that just as the ascription of semantical properties is answerable to the existence of certain kinds of sentence, in a corresponding way the attribution of concepts is answerable to the existence of certain kinds of action. The generalization would run: we should not construe someone as having propositional attitudes , the content of which is specified by using the concept of objects of a given kind with certain boundaries, if there is a tighter set of attitudes we can ascribe which does not involve attributing a concept determining objects with the same boundaries. Evans' requirement is indeed a special case of this requirement, restricted to the semantical, since saying something or assenting to something is an intentional action. But nonlinguistic actions can also be sensitive to the boundaries of an object. The actions of someone who is out to capture an unstained white rabbit will be sensitive to the distribution of features within the boundary of an individual rabbit. This sensitivity may be present without the presence of any predicate of rabbits in the agent's language, if any. This cannot be said of the actions of someone who has the feature-placing concepts 'rabbiteth' or 'it's rabbity here' and yet not the concept of an individual rabbit. If such a person's perceptual and intellectual apparatus is in order, his actions will be sensitive only to distinctions formulable in feature-placing terms.

[26] 'Identity and Predication', *Journal of Philosophy* 72 (1975), 343–63.

As we might expect, the arguments against violating the propositional attitude constraint, which we have identified in this third example, correspondingly generalize the kind of arguments Evans employed against the acceptability of Quine's interpretation of predication of rabbits in terms of predications of undetached rabbit parts. Evans complained that Quine's suggestions have the consequence that whatever is true of one undetached rabbit part is true of any other undetached rabbit part of the same rabbit – so the boundary between one such part and another, however fuzzy, is not required to play any part in the semantics of the language; that is, in understanding it. Just as the price of denying this is to make the identification of predicates of objects of a given kind empirically unconstrained, so a similar point may be made about using predications of objects of a given kind in the 'that'-clauses of sentences ascribing propositional attitudes to an agent. If we accept for an agent a set of attitudes specified using predications of rabbits, even though under that set counterfactually his actions are not sensitive to the boundaries of rabbits, our attribution seems to be empirically unconstrained.

We can now give a general definition of comparative tightness Suppose Σ and Σ' are distinct sets of attitudes that might be attributed to a given agent. Each set will attribute a certain family of concepts to the agent: $C(\Sigma)$ and $C(\Sigma')$, let us say. We will say (relative to the given agent) that Σ is *tighter than* Σ' iff the following conditions are met:

(1) There are some conditions frameable using $C(\Sigma')$ which are not equivalent to any condition frameable using $C(\Sigma)$, and no actual or causally possible token action is explained under Σ' by attitudes which have one of these conditions as their content;

(2) the clause resulting from (1) by interchanging 'Σ' and 'Σ'' is false.

These conditions need some elucidation. (1) in effect says that even under Σ' when events are taken as intentional under descriptions using concepts in $C(\Sigma')$, these concepts are always combined in ways that make the conditions equivalent to ones formulable using the concepts in $C(\Sigma)$. Clause (2) says that the converse does not hold of Σ *vis-à-vis* Σ': that is, the tightness requirement applies only where $C(\Sigma)$ and $C(\Sigma')$ are not incomparable in respect of expressive power, and so are not such that neither family of concepts has strictly greater expressive power than the other.

The formulation of clause (1) is not fully satisfactory. Even if we want to say that Σ is superior to Σ', and someone actually has only the concepts of $C(\Sigma)$, and not $C(\Sigma')$, nevertheless we will not want to deny that in some counterfactual circumstances someone may come to *acquire* the new concepts $C(\Sigma')$ — and then there may well be actions intentional under descriptions formulable using $C(\Sigma')$ but not $C(\Sigma)$. I will not discuss this problem in detail because it is not special to propositional attitude psychology. It arises for any concept introduced directly or indirectly by means of conditionals, and which we suppose to have some categorical basis. An account of our understanding of what it means to say that something is opaque must include the condition that if it is placed in light, objects cannot be seen through it. What is correct in this thought is surely not completely undermined by the fact that some ways of putting it in light may change its internal structure so that it becomes transparent.

Our examples illustrated the argument for saying that one should not attribute a set Σ' of attitudes to an agent if there is a set Σ tighter than Σ' which fits. Let us call this 'the Tightness Constraint'. Without this requirement, the attribution of concepts is unconstrained by the presence of intentional actions responsive to the distinctions in the world drawn by these concepts. There are also some formal and structural points to be noted about the relation *tighter than*. It is a transitive relation, but it may not be connected. One way of stating a thesis of indeterminacy of propositional attitude ascriptions would be to claim that there are pairs of sets of attitudes such that neither is tighter than the other, and no satisfactory set is tighter than them both. A final point of some importance is that the relation *tighter than* determines a partial ordering by expressive power of *families* of concepts, and does not necessarily determine an ordering of individual concepts one by one. Any partial ordering of individual concepts extracted from this material must be defined in terms of a relation between sets of concepts.

There are other applications of the Tightness Constraint. It does, for example, exclude certain incorrect attributions of scientific concepts to people. Suppose it were suggested that instead of ascribing to scientifically unknowledgeable persons various beliefs about material cubes or spheres, we attribute to them beliefs about cubic or spherically shaped arrangements of neutrons, protons and electrons. Now in this suggestion, in the content-sentence speci-fying the newly ascribed beliefs, either the phrase 'arrangement of neutrons, electrons and protons' is treated as semantically unstruc-tured or it is not. If it is treated as semantically structured, then such attributions are not correct unless there are, or in various counter-factual circumstances would be, actions of these people sensitive, for instance, to the presence of evidence of protons in the vicinity, or actions satisfactorily explicable only on the assumption that they have a concept of protons. For scientifically unknowledgeable persons, this condition is not met, and for any such person there will always be a tighter set of attitudes which does not attribute these concepts. On the other hand, if the phrase 'arrangement of neutrons, electrons and protons' is not treated as semantically structured, it will simply have the same sense as 'lump of matter', and the proposal will not after all involve attributing new concepts to the agents: it will simply suggest a new way of writing old attributions.[27]

[27] The tightness constraint bears a systematic resemblance to structural constraints on translation and meaning theories proposed by J. Wallace, 'On the Frame of Reference', in *Semantics of Natural Language*, eds. D. Davidson and G. Harman (Dordrecht: Reidel, 1972), at p. 225, and refined by M. Davies *Meaning, Quantification, Necessity*. This is no accident; my own route into this area started from questions of radical interpretation of natural language. Whether there are other points at which specific constraints on semantical and psychological attribution are analogous is a question deserving further study.

The Tightness Constraint may also be regarded as an elaboration of C. Lloyd Morgan's 'Canon'. In his *Introduction to Comparative Psychology* the Canon is italicized, and reads 'In no case may we interpret an action as the outcome of the exercise of a higher psychical faculty, if it can be interpreted as the outcome of the exercise of one which stands lower in the psychological scale' (p. 53). It is not clear that in this book Lloyd Morgan has a uniform view of the status of the canon. Sometimes he seems to regard it as constitutive. In response to an imagined critic who complains that it is too ungenerous, he replies that this could only be shown if we had rival principles for attributing 'higher' psychical faculties; and many of the examples to which he applies the Canon— such as the dog case above— fit well with a constitutive interpretation. But this impression is spoiled by his concession that some criticisms of his canon 'might be valid if we were considering the question apart from evolution' (p. 55).

4

Observational Concepts

Can we make sense of the idea of an observational concept? This familiar question is linked in several ways with the topics of this book. Those who have thought that there is a significant distinction between those concepts which are observational and those which are not have often made use of experience, or some surrogate for it, in explaining the distinction; so it is natural to hope that what we have said about experience might be brought to bear on the issue. It also seems that if any concepts are observational, some of those possessed by a being meeting only the minimal conditions of the Basic Case will be observational. Finally, to look ahead, the account of demonstrative content in the later parts of this book will appeal to the role of demonstratives in certain judgements, of which the most fundamental are those in which they are combined with observational concepts.

Anyone who sets out to defend an interesting notion of observationality finds himself swimming not just against the tide, but against a torrent. There can be few distinctions which have been so roundly rejected in recent philosophy of science as that between observational and theoretical terms. Now it is certainly true that many of those who drew the distinction often had questionable motives: they drew the distinction as a prelude to arguing that theoretical terms are only partially interpreted, that we should take an instrumentalist view of theoretical sentences, or even that some extreme epistemological foundationalism is true. But we can distinguish the correctness of drawing the distinction from the soundness of these motives for drawing it. The possibility is open that the distinction is correct, and is important for quite different reasons.

These other reasons have to do with the characterization of some distinctive features of observational concepts which can be acknowledged without claiming that observational judgements are infallible, or again not subject to withdrawal. Both Quine and

Dummett have given accounts of observationality which are not motivated by a desire to formulate an instrumentalist view of theoretical sentences.[1] My aim in this chapter is to formulate an account of observational concepts which explains some of their epistemological features. One can make a start on building an account by developing a response to the detailed attacks to which the distinction has been subjected.

These attacks fall largely into two broad types. The first type consists of attacks on the (alleged) permissiveness of standard ways of drawing the distinction. The attacker notes that a device may be seen as an X-ray tube, or as a geiger-counter; a landscape may be seen as glaciated; a circular ridge may be seen as a crater. In some cases, these concepts of 'X-ray tube', 'geiger-counter' and the rest enter the representational content of the subject's experience: the experience itself represents there as being an X-ray tube in front of the subject.[2] Such an experience may cause the subject to judge that there is an X-ray tube in front of him, and there is no more conscious inference here than there is when the subject is caused to judge by his experience that there is a table in front of him. The concept of an X-ray tube would classically be counted as theoretical, yet the fact that such a concept enters the representational content of experience and may be judged (and known) to be instantiated without inference means that it meets the standards set by some for observationality. By these standards, too, observationality would be dependent upon the sophistication of the observer. It would not be a feature of the concept itself, regardless of who employed it in thought.

Besides these attacks on permissiveness, there were also attacks on the vacuity of classical accounts of observationality; this second type of complaint was that nothing met the requirements. It may seem that both types of complaint could not be made by the same person at once, since it would be a poor critic who complained both that a defined category would let in too much and that it let in

[1] W. V. Quine, *Word and Object* (Cambridge, Mass.: MIT, 1960), Ch. 2, and 'Empirical Content', in *Theories and Things* (Cambridge, Mass.: Harvard, 1981); M. Dummett, 'What is a Theory of Meaning? (II)' in G. Evans and J. McDowell, eds., *Truth and Meaning* (Oxford: OUP, 1976).

[2] N. R. Hanson, *Patterns of Discovery* (Cambridge: CUP, 1958), Ch. 1. I have taken it that the most challenging formulation of the theory-laden quality of observation concerns the case in which theoretical concepts specify the content of experience, as opposed to milder formulations which emphasize that theoretical assumptions may enter someone's reasons for uttering a sentence traditionally classified as observational.

nothing at all. But in fact the attacks were directed at different features of classical explanations of observationality, and the attack on vacuity was directed at the idea that in mastering observational concepts, a subject makes no essential use of theory. Even in so simple a case as a concept of being square, it seems highly doubtful that anyone could possess this concept without being prepared to make judgements containing it which are those which would be made by someone operating with a simple theory of himself, as located in a spatial world that acts upon him. As Feyerabend declared:

Experience arises *together* with theoretical assumptions, not before them, and an experience without theory is just as incomprehensible as is (allegedly) a theory without experience: eliminate part of the theoretical knowledge of a sensing subject and you have a person who is completely disoriented and incapable of carrying out the simplest action.[3]

The attack on permissiveness and the attack on vacuity will be considered in that order. It already seems clear that the critical questions will have to do with the relations between experience and theory. There is first, though, a terminological point about which it will help to be explicit. I use the word 'concept' for a mode of presentation of a property. This employs the word 'concept' for a Fregean purpose, but in a way in which Frege did not use it. One and the same property may be presented in different descriptive modes of presentation, and in this case the distinction is familiar. But not all modes of presentation of properties are descriptive: some are perceptual. One way we think of the physical property of having high temperature is by a mode of presentation we can employ because we are capable of having sensations of heat. As Paul Churchland notes, other beings, if the rod cells in their retinas were sensitive to infrared radiation, could have visual experiences the nature of which is dependent upon the temperature of the object seen: hot objects cause in them experiences of the kind which white objects cause in us, and cold objects would similarly correspond to black ones.[4] For these beings, the physical property of high

[3] P. Feyerabend, *Against Method* (London: New Left Books, 1975), p. 168.
[4] Paul Churchland, *Scientific Realism and the Plasticity of Mind* (Cambridge: CUP, 1979), pp. 8ff. Churchland argues that the word 'hot', applied by these beings on the basis of their visual experiences, should be given a homophonic translation into our language. I agree with this conclusion, but would offer a different reason for it. Homophonic

temperature would be presented in the way whiteness is for us. I shall be interested in characterizing observationality as a property of certain concepts (in this sense) and not others. Since concepts have to do with thought, there is no commitment, in adopting such a distinction, to the view that objects falling only under non-observational concepts are any less constituents of reality than those which fall under observational concepts. There is, though, a commitment to saying that the phenomena crucial to explaining the notion of observationality are those to which the individuation of Fregean thoughts and their constituents are answerable: phenomena of cognitive significance and epistemic possibility. There is no reason why these phenomena should be closely matched by the correct use of the word 'observe' in English, and the account is not meant to predict that use.

A natural first response to the attack on permissiveness is to say this: 'Though there are indeed experiences as of an X-ray tube viewed from the cathode, and experiences as of trails resulting from the creation of a particle-pair, the capacity to have such experiences is not essential for possession of the concepts of an X-ray or of the creation of a particle-pair. But in the case of the observational (visual) concept of a square, the corresponding capacity is essential; one cannot possess that concept unless in normal circumstances visual experiences as of something square cause, if the question arises, the judgement of a thought, containing that concept, to the effect that the presented object is square.'

The response is plausible. In the case of the X-ray tube, such experiences do indeed seem to be inessential. It is quite sufficient for the possession of the concept that a thinker have an understanding of the components of which an X-ray tube could be built drawn from the theory of electricity. This understanding could be

---

translation is correct here because when we cannot in translation preserve both mode of presentation and property presented, it is more important for communication and understanding to preserve the latter. (Ideal translation would preserve both.) On this position one can consistently hold that in Churchland's example, homophonic translation is correct, while also holding (a) that types of experience still help to determine the mode of presentation of a property, and (b) that any given physical property presented to us in one way may be presented to other beings in some other way. (Some actual creatures are not far from the beings Churchland imagines. Certain snakes have pit organs sensitive to infrared radiation, and information from these is built up into a map of the snake's infrared environment. For a popular account see E. Newman and P. Hartline, 'The Infrared "Vision" of Snakes', *Scientific American* 246 (March 1982) 98–107.)

present while the capacity to see things as X-ray tubes is absent. There is indeed something which might be called a visual concept of things which are in fact X-ray tubes; this is the concept the janitor of a laboratory might employ in thinking about the contraptions he sees on the benches. But this is not the same concept as that of an X-ray tube exercised by the scientist. The janitor's visual concept is of things which look a certain way — whereas the scientist can make sense of the supposition that an X-ray tube might look entirely different from those he has seen in the past, provided it meets the right theoretical specifications.

But in fact matters are more complex than this. Possession of a suitable sensitivity to experiences as of a φ is required for the possession of the concept φ if φ is observational. This, however, is a necessary but not sufficient condition for the observationality of φ. That it is not sufficient is shown if one reflects upon natural kind concepts. It is essential to our concept of a tomato that tomatoes are thought of as things which look a certain way. Someone may think of the property of being a tomato in some gastronomic, biological, or biochemical way. These will be different ways of thinking of the same property or kind, and statements of the identity of a kind thus picked out with the kind picked out by our (partially) visual way of thinking of tomatoes will be informative. But the concept of being a tomato, unlike that of being tomato-like (perceptually indistinguishable from a tomato) is not observational, since an object's status as a tomato can depend upon its genetic structure, and possibly upon its ancestry. (This is not to say that normally we cannot know whether something is a tomato just by looking at it: there are many theories of knowledge which will permit one to know perceptually that a presented object is φ without φ being observational.) Everyday natural kind concepts are not the only ones which show the insufficiency of the condition appealed to in this natural first response. Similar remarks apply also to a biologist who looks down a microscope and says 'Let's call cells which are the same in such-and-such respects as these (visually presented) cells "*A*-cells" '. For him it is *a priori* that some *A*-cells look a certain way. We were also too harsh on the janitor. He too can introduce the concept of devices which function in the same way, whatever way that is, as those visually presented on the bench. It is perhaps just worth adding, to avoid misunderstanding, that the point here is not that it is necessary that all tomatoes look tomato-like — they do not, and the natural kind of model makes clear why not: the point is rather that, as Kripke might put it, the reference-fixing conditions for some natural kind concepts essentially involve perceptual experience. This affects, in Kripke's terms, not the metaphysical but the epistemic possibilities in which such concepts feature. It is this which makes the first response supply only a necessary condition of observationality.[5]

What then is the relevant difference between the visual concepts of squareness and of a tomato? It seems to be this. The concept of a tomato is not observational because its experiential component could be shared by someone who does not possess the concept 'is of the same underlying kind as' and who does not possess the conception that there may be underlying structures from which superficial properties flow. That experiential component, it seems, would be shared by someone who used the concept 'tomato-like' of physical objects, but whose application of it was determined solely by looks (and perhaps feel and taste). This concept would apply not only to characteristic tomatoes, but also to synthesized tomato-like objects produced by Kraft laboratories. By contrast, the experiential element in the (visual) concept of something square cannot be enjoyed by someone not capable of operating with, or conforming his judgements to, a rudimentary theory of the world which acts upon him. The point is that there is nothing standing to being square as being tomato-like stands to being a tomato. There is nothing which is both the experiential component of the visual concept of being square and which could also be enjoyed by someone who does not possess all the concepts and theories possessed by someone who has that concept of being square. There is indeed a complex, higher-order property, a sensational property, which the visual field has whenever something is seen as being square — a sensational property which captures the experiential analogues of texture gradients, perspective and so forth. The property could not be less complex

[5] It is a virtue of Quine's latest criterion of observationality that 'This is a tomato' is not counted as an observation sentence. The criterion reads 'An observation sentence is an occasion sentence that the speaker will consistently assent to when his sensory receptors are stimulated in certain ways, and consistently dissent from when they are stimulated in certain other ways' ('Empirical Content', p. 25). 'This is a tomato' fails on the first count when the subject believes that the tomato-like object in front of him is a fool's tomato.

than this: for it is not true that a square material object is normally presented to a properly functioning perceiver in a square' region of his visual field. (That is true only if his line of sight is perpendicular to the object's centre.) But this does not give us something in the case of the visual concept of being square which stands to it as an experience of something tomato-like stands to the concept of a tomato. For any such visual field property, being a purely sensational property, can be instantiated without the subject seeing anything as being any particular shape at all. The higher-order sensational property fails to capture the full experiential component of the visual concept of being square.

All this may suggest that 'tomato' should be excluded as an observational concept because, although possession of the concept of a tomato involves suitable sensitivity of judgements containing that concept to experiences of tomato-like objects, one could have the (unstructured) concept of being tomato-like without having any natural kind concepts, nor the idea of an internal structure determining perceptible properties. But matters are more complex than this. If one immediately generalized this idea into a criterion, then one would be in danger of counting 'tomato' as an observational concept. The problem is that while 'tomato-like' is a perfectly intelligible concept, it is not one which enters the content of our perceptions. We see tomatoes as *tomatoes,* and not as anything weaker. If the representational content of experience is given by what someone would judge, taking that experience at face value, then our ordinary experiences have a content concerning tomatoes, and not tomato-like objects. The fact is that we seem in some respects to be in relation to the concept of a tomato much as the sophisticated scientist is in relation to that of an X-ray tube. Something which looks like a tomato but is not would still be seen by us as a tomato. It may be true that were we to become familiar with many objects which are fool's tomatoes, we would then come to use the concept 'tomato-like', and perhaps it would come to enter the content of our experiences. But it is hard to believe that this remote possibility has to be invoked to establish that 'tomato' is not an observational concept. Can it really be right to say that if we would never come to see things as tomato-like, 'tomato' would after all actually have to be counted as an observational concept?

The result of this complication is that we give only a necessary and not a sufficient condition of observationality of a concept φ if we require this conjuctive property of φ: that (1) there is some concept φ' such that the capacity to have experiences as of something φ', and to display a suitable sensitivity of one's judgements to the occurrence of such experiences, is needed for possession of the concept φ and (2) it would not be possible to have experiences as of something φ' without having the concept φ. The problem was that for all we know, our concept of a tomato may meet (1) and (2), taking 'tomato' as the φ'. We need some additional condition for sufficiency. If we agree that the *only* problem here is that the concept of a tomato is entering the representational content of our experiences — so that the case is analogous to that of the scientist seeing things as X-ray tubes — it would be reasonable to expect that the cognitive role of the natural kind concept which had 'tomato' in the representational content of its experiential component, and the cognitive role of the natural kind concept which had 'tomato-like' there, would be one and the same. What does this mean, and how can we make it precise? Let us say that the concepts φ and φ' *have the same pattern of epistemic possibilities* iff for any Σ, it is epistemically possible that $\Sigma(\varphi)$ iff it is epistemically possible that $\Sigma(\varphi')$. This is a relatively clear sense in which the concepts may have the same cognitive role. To illustrate: the natural kind concept 'tomato' does not have the same pattern of epistemic possibilities as the observational concept 'tomato-like'. It is epistemically possible that something which is tomato-like is not a tomato.

We can now offer a third condition for a concept to be observational: it must not have the same pattern of epistemic possibilities as some concept which *fails* to meet (1) and (2). Even if we are not capable of experiences as of tomato-like things, our concept 'tomato' seems to have the same pattern of epistemic possibilities as the concept 'of the same natural kind as the tomato-like things encountered by my linguistic community', employed by hypothetical beings who are capable of such experiences. But this latter concept clearly does fail to meet (1) and (2), so by the third condition, 'tomato' is not observational. So much for legalistic matters.

This test which has emerged we will call 'the Inseparability Criterion'. It characterizes experience as in a certain way essential to possession of a concept, and possession of the concept as essential to the capacity to have the experience. It would be surprising were the Inseparability Criterion to be a brute fact; a satisfying account should explain why it is that some concepts have the property it isolates. But it does offer some promise that there are divisions of interest for an account of thought in the ways theory and experience are related: the terrain may not be completely irregular.

The Inseparability Criterion is not the only principle which might be suggested for separating the cases of 'square', 'tomato', and the rest. In his characterization of observation sentences, Dummett requires of such a sentence that 'in every case in which the sentence is true, it must be in principle possible that it should be observed to be true'.[6] This would exclude 'That's an X-ray tube' and 'That's a geiger-counter' as observational sentences, for these may be built in unusual ways and theory may be needed for recognizing them. It would exclude, because of the possibility of unusual tomatoes, 'That's a tomato' too. But does the Dummettian requirement exclude too much? Does it allow things too small or too large to be seen to fall under exactly the same concept 'square' under which tables and tiles may fall? For those who do wish to allow that they fall under the very same concepts, as it seems we should, and who also wish to accept Dummett's requirement, the path here forks into two.

The headier path proceeds by taking it that the phrase 'in principle possible that it should be observed to be true' allows us to take account of what we would observe to be square if we were smaller than full stops or bigger than galaxies. But it seems a compelling principle that if we can make sense of such counter-factuals, we must be capable of doing so in virtue of features of our actual employment, at our current size, of the concept of squareness. It is these features which must be fundamental.

The other, more frequently taken, path construes the admission of possibilities in principle to permit appeal to what one can observe using electron microscopes, radio telescopes, and other instruments. Now we earlier said that in an account of what it is to possess the visual concept of squareness, there would be a requirement of sensitivity in appropriate circumstances of judgements containing that concept to experiences in which an object is

---

[6] 'What is a Theory of Meaning? (II)', p. 95.

presented as square. But looking at the visual display unit of an electron microscope or radio telescope would not be amongst those circumstances. There is no difficulty for the thinker in entertaining the possibility that the circumstances of perception are normal, he himself is functioning normally, and yet the objects represented on the screen as being arranged in a square do not in fact form a square. When the scientist looks at the screen, he indeed usually believes that very tiny or very large objects which form a square are represented on the screen as doing so, and conversely. Even if he comes to use the device without any conscious inference, what he learns from it will still rest on such a belief; and the belief has no kind of constitutive or *a priori* status. But the belief has a content which simply takes it for granted that very small or very large objects *can* be arranged in a square: the use of such instruments, as a quite legitimate way of coming to know about the small or the large, simply presupposes rather than explains the possibility of applying in those domains the very same concepts as can be applied observationally. The appeal to the use of instruments is either circular (in the case in which the requisite beliefs are present) or ineffective (in the case in which they are absent). An appeal to instruments is neither of these things when the question is that of establishing the truth of claims about squareness in the very small or very large: but our question has been not one of truth, but of understanding.

We have considered only two ways of understanding 'possibility in principle', and there may be others; but the difficulties which have arisen are instances of a general problem for any such position. In the nature of the case, such positions must consider situations in which, as we actually are, the connection between an experience and an application of the concept in question is not constitutive. This makes it hard to see how the application of the concept in these circumstances can fail to involve theoretical inference.

Someone who accepts the Inseparability Criterion may not incur the problems we just considered, but he has equally to say how *he* is in a position to say that observational concepts can apply to things too small to see. One approach would be to say that subvisible square things satisfy approximately the same set of laws as do perceptible square things. If an apparently solid disc is held in front of a slide projector, and so on the screen small square patches of light appear within the shadow of the disc, it takes no great theoretician to infer that there are holes in the disc too small to see, and that they are square. That is not to say that it is *a priori* true that light behaves in relation to things of observable size in the same way it does to the small or the large: such hypotheses can be overturned and indeed we can imagine reasons for saying that the subvisible holes have a different shape. But in those circumstances, we would have to have a suitable set of laws preserved in the small for whatever shape we took the holes to be. Generally, preservation of a suitable set of laws acts as a bridge, from initial cases in which an observational concept is applied without inference to other cases concerning unobservables, in a way analogous to the bridge from some initial sample of members of a natural kind to very unusual members provided by the relation of being of the same underlying structure.

The second type of attack was on the alleged vacuity of many characerizations of observational concepts. If, with Ryle, theoretical terms are described as those knowledge of whose meaning requires grasp of a theory, then even the simplest sentences and the thoughts expressed by them will be theoretical.[7] It is certainly true that there is no explicit reference to theory in the initial intuitive characterization of observationality given by those sympathetic to the notion. Dummett is not atypical within that class when he writes 'we are . . . concerned to pick out those cases in which an ability to use a given sentence to give a report of observation may reasonably be taken as a knowledge of what has to be the case for that sentence to be true'.[8] The important question is whether, if theory is implicitly involved here, we can isolate the special relations in which observational concepts stand to it.

That theory is implicated even in the simplest case can be made vivid by introducing a Goodmanesque predicate. 'Squound' is to be truly predicated of an object at a time by someone if either he observes it then to be a square or he does not observe it then and it is round. 'Square' is commonly counted as an observation predicate by those who admit the notion of observationality at all, but it does not mean the same as 'squound'. Yet for any object that a person observes, he can truly predicate 'squound' of it iff he

[7] G. Ryle, *Dilemmas* (Cambridge: CUP, 1953), p. 90.
[8] 'What is a Theory of Meaning? (II)', p. 95.

can truly predicate 'square' of it. This is not just an extensional coincidence: it holds in counterfactual conditions too. If any object someone does not actually observe were to be observed by him, he could then truly predicate 'squound' of it iff he could then truly predicate 'square' of it. So it seems essential in explaining the difference involved in understanding the two predicates that we bring in the difference between the way in which it would be established that an object one does not observe, say the table in the next room, is squound and the way in which it would be established that it is square. The ability to employ these different ways, and to judge in accordance with a simple theory of the world, must be mentioned in accounts of what it is to understand the predicates, and this goes beyond what shows up in noninferential responses to observable circumstances. (This is simply one way of making the point, stated by Evans with great clarity, that a state of affairs one observes to obtain is something that can obtain unobserved.[9]) The point here is not that a change in theoretical beliefs about the shape-properties of unobserved objects must alter the observational shape-judgements a thinker makes: on the contrary, that would not be so in all cases. The point is rather that a subject is employing the concept 'square' rather than 'squound' in his judgements only if he is prepared in some circumstances to make judgements that some unobserved object is square, and is in doing so appropriately sensitive to the right evidence – different evidence from that appropriate to judging that an unobserved object is squound. The theory involved here is not any detailed theory about unobserved objects, but the theory that there are material objects and a space, the former distributed in the latter; which space is also occupied by the thinker himself, and the objects in which cause his experiences. Acceptance of this is partially manifested in the thinker's willingness to suppose that an observational concept which he perceives to be instantiated may be instantiated unobserved.

It would be a mistake to suggest that it would be a genuine

---

[9] 'Things Without the Mind', in *Philosophical Subjects* (Oxford: OUP, 1980), ed. Z. van Straaten, pp. 88–9. One needs to be careful in specifying the tie of the child's utterance 'It's φ-ing' with experience which Evans there envisages as being first tight, then loosened; for the type of experience is not literally the same, on the account presented in this book, before and after the acquisition of concepts of the objective spatial world. After that acquisition, the type of experience is one which, because of its representational content, could not be enjoyed without the possession of such concepts.

alternative to these points to say that one can tell whether someone means square rather than squound by asking him whether the extension of the expression in question has an *a priori* dependence upon the situation of observers. To understand the notion of dependence here one has to have grasped the conception that an object may have certain properties whether observed or not. So to check that someone is understanding 'dependence' correctly one must be able to identify some observation-independent notions he employs and check that 'depends' (or whatever is taken to translate it) is applied correctly to them. But to identify such notions was the original problem.

The sense in which someone who is able to judge that unobserved objects fall under observational concepts must be 'judging in accordance with a theory' cannot be that he can state or even that he knows that theory. An explicit formulation of our everyday theory of an objective world would certainly have to use the notion of experience, a sophisticated concept which need not be possessed by one who judges in accordance with the theory. Such a subject needs only to have experiences which are related to the judgements in the same manner as those of someone who does know the theory — someone who, in the way described by many writers, makes sense of these experiences by taking them as produced by objects in a world through which he and they may move. It would be quite indeterminate which theory would be in question if one were to look only at the subject's actual judgements about the objective world. But the theory in accordance with which the subject is operating may be determined not only by his actual judgements but also by the judgements he would make in various counterfactual circumstances in which he has different experiences and different evidence.

The central reason I would offer for saying that the (visual) concept of squareness is observational is that it meets this condition:

It is not epistemically possible for someone who has the concept of squareness that: from all the different angles from which an object may be seen, it is seen as square, his perceptual mechanisms are operating properly, the circumstances of perception (the environment in which the causal processes take place) are normal, the object is constant in shape, and yet that presented object not be square.

This can be generalized to other sense-modalities, with their analogues of the angle from which the object is seen. It is necessary to bring in different angles because even when the other conditions mentioned are met, from one angle alone something which is not square may look square provided it reflects the same pattern of light as would something square. (This possibility is exploited by the Ames demonstrations, in which a highly distorted room is viewed from a position at which it presents the same bundle of light rays to the eye as would be presented by a normal room: from that position the room looks normal.[10]) The suggestion is, then, that the visual concept of a square is a concept of a property whose presence in an object can in normal circumstances be established in precisely that way, of looking from different angles and seeing the object as square. If circumstances are known to be normal, experiences from different angles as of an object as square provide canonical but nonconclusive evidence that it *is* square.

By contrast, consider the concept of the creation of a particle-pair. Is this a concept such that one cannot conceive that one's perceptual mechanisms are working properly, that a streak is from many angles experienced as resulting from such creation, but yet that the streak does not really so result? No: one can conceive that it does not so result, and it is the theoretical connections of the notions of particles and particle creation that allows one to conceive this. These give one a way of thinking of creation of particle pairs on which they are not necessarily epistemically linked with trails seen as the result of such creations.

Observational concepts are then here being distinguished from others in terms of the absence of a certain complex epistemic possibility which is present for nonobservational concepts. It may help to forestall some potential misunderstandings. It is certainly not being asserted that squareness is a secondary quality, explained in terms of its power to produce certain sensations: rather, in an account of an observational concept (a way of thinking of a property), having the concept φ and being capable of experiences as of something φ are treated as coeval, to use Wiggins' excellent term.[11]

[10] For a vivid popular account, see R. L. Gregory, *The Intelligent Eye* (London: Weidenfeld and Nicolson, 1970), pp. 26–31.

[11] See D. Wiggins, *Sameness and Substance* (Oxford: Blackwell, 1980), pp. 49ff. One way of construing Dummett's demand for a full-blooded and not merely a modest theory of meaning ('What is a Theory of Meaning? (I)' in *Mind and Language* (Oxford: OUP,

Nor, again, is appeal being made to the trivial point that it is not possible in any sense that one not be misperceiving in having an experience as of it being that *p,* when in fact it is not true that *p.* That would apply to any *p* whatever, observational or otherwise. The point is not that trivial one because the appeal is to normal circumstances of perception and proper perceptual functioning. These can be investigated and ratified as such, consistently with one's recognition that one's experiences as of X-ray tubes are in fact produced by stage props. This account of observationality also makes no reference to the genesis of a judgement on a particular occasion, the absence of conscious inference not being, on this view, the heart of the matter.

The situation is actually more complex than this. The astute reader will note that any account of perception has to use a notion of the representational content of an experience matching or being made true by the experiencer's environment. But if 'The creation of a particle-pair caused that streak' is part of the representational content of an experience, and matching is required for perception, how could there be any nonobservational concepts by the test of epistemic possibility? For it would be *a priori* that if such an experience is perceptual, the creation of a particle-pair did cause that streak. One answer is that perception and observational concepts have to be characterized simultaneously, and one requires for perception matching only in respect of observational contents. Circularity could then be avoided by this further constraint: that when a perceived object is experienced as falling under a nonobservational concept, there must be some level of representational content at which that experience could be perceptual even though the object does not fall under that nonobservational concept. This classifies 'streak produced by the creation of a particle-pair' as nonobservational. It classifies

1975), ed. S. Guttenplan) is to take it as an endorsement of the requirement that in stating what it is for someone to have the concepts expressed in a given language, one at no point make ineliminable use of notions which presuppose that the language user has those concepts. It might be hoped that this requirement could at least be met for observation sentences. Dummett's own account of observationality does seem to meet it. The epistemic possibility criterion I have stated does not seem to meet it, since experience as of something φ and possession of the concept are said to be coeval; but it does not rule out the possibility that it could be met. It would be met if one could in addition supply an account of what it is for an experience to have a certain representational content without appealing to the content of other psychological states ineliminably. I do not know whether this can be achieved.

ordinary shape concepts of physical objects as observational. For if components of an experiencer's representational content containing them are false, there is no more primitive level of representational content which could be true. This constraint gives one reason why, despite the fact that there are experiences whose representational content must be given using the concept of causation (experiences of the type investigated by Michotte[12]), causation is not an observational concept.

How does the epistemic possibility criterion explain the Inseparability Criterion? We think of the property of being square as the property such that it is not possible that something fail to have it in the circumstances of the above displayed condition: or more accurately, our judgements are as if we consciously followed this characterization of the concept. This explains the inseparability of possession of the visual concept of being square from experience, given the role of experience in the displayed condition. Similarly, the experiential component of possession of the concept is a type of experience the capacity to have which requires grasp of all the theories required for grasping the concept 'square' because the type of experience mentioned in the displayed condition is an experience as of something falling under the very concept 'square' in question.

Those familiar with Wright's definition of the concept 'is a sentence capable of actual verification' will note that the present attempts to explain observationality by an epistemic possibility criterion are similar in spirit to that definition.[13] Wright suggests that in the case of a sentence which is capable of actual verification, if we first, as a result of some investigation, believe in its truth, and later grounds -call that belief into question, those later grounds must also rationally make us question the holding of the conditions presupposed as true in following the initial investigative procedure. But Wright's test and the epistemic possibility test give different answers at some points. Wright's criterion seems to include as capable of actual verification hypotheses about the behaviour of subvisible particles, on a particular occasion where these hypotheses are confirmed by some experimental result: that the experimental apparatus works in a certain way is a condition presupposed in the investigative procedure. His criterion also

---

[12] *The Perception of Causality* (New York: Basic Books, 1963).
[13] C. Wright, 'Strict Finitism', *Synthese* 51 (1982), 203–82.

counts some past-tense sentences as capable of actual verification. When a past-tense judgement is caused by an apparent memory one presupposes that one's memory mechanisms are working properly, as one does also for one's perceptual mechanisms in the case of present-tense perceptual judgements. I have been concerned with observational concepts, rather than complete thoughts, and have made use of properties of demonstrative perceptual judgements in which they occur. One reason for this approach is that it is constitutive of possession of an observational concept that one be capable of employing such demonstrative modes of presentation of objects in combination with the observational concept. But no type of mode of presentation of objects made available by memory seems connected in the same strict way with the possession of observational concepts. Certainly the capacity to have memory images and to employ modes of presentation of objects made available by them is not essential. Nevertheless, these divergences from Wright's account ought not to be overemphasized: it may well be that if the concept of experience were added in the right way to his criterion, these differences would vanish.

On the criterion we suggested, observationality is not relative to the sophistication of the observer, nor to the stage of development of scientific knowledge and technology, nor to one's general philosophy of science. Smart once wrote: 'If we keep to a realistic philosophy of science there is no difficulty about saying that when looking at a milliammeter we may directly observe that the current through it is 5 milliamperes. The milliammeter functions as an extension of our ordinary senses.'[14] Smart agrees that we employ a theory we know in making such direct observations of the current but this, he says, is analgous to the way in which the brain makes computations of distance of seen objects from (he says) the convergence of the eyes. Yet from the point of view of the subject himself, the cases seem quite different. To see objects as at a certain rough distance from himself, the subject need not have the concepts of convergence, corresponding points on the retinas, and so forth. Even if he does have them, they will not give a true analogue of the epistemic possibility which obtains for the

---

[14]J. J. C. Smart, *Between Science and Philosophy* (New York: Random House, 1969), p. 136.

nonobservational concept of electric current — that he is perceiving properly, but it is not current which is causing the pointer to move. For something to be literally and not just figuratively an extension of one's senses, there would have to be a way φ of thinking of the physical property λx [there is current flowing through x] such that it is not epistemically possible that in normal circumstances (etc.) suitable experiences as of a φ thing occur yet no current be flowing in the perceived object. It is no part of my position that such concepts are impossible: my position is just that such concepts are not ours. They would occupy different places from ours in the network of epistemic possibilities. Better instruments, however powerful, would never by themselves give us those new concepts.

I close this chapter with a conjecture about observationality. The conjecture is that no one could have the conception of a spatial world in which he is located unless he has at least some spatial observational concepts.

This conjecture may seem plausible in its exclusion of an allegedly purely theoretical conception of a spatial world which is also thought of as the spatial world in which one is oneself located. It seems that any theoretical concept, however *recherché*, is a mode of presentation which makes some connection, however indirect, with observational concepts, even if only by some complex relation of a theoretical kind to some observational notions. This claim is very mild, and does not exclude the fact that the greatest ingenuity and depth of thought may be needed to devise observational tests of hypotheses involving theoretical concepts. But what of the other consequences of the conjecture?

Can we not, as against the conjecture, conceive of someone who consciously works out the spatial significance of his various sensations, but who has no observational concepts which enter the content of his experiences? Here we have to guard against a certain illusion. Let us consider again the subject equipped with a tactile–vision substitution device.[15] One congenitally blind subject who was equipped with such a device did actually at first have consistently to work out the spatial significance of changes in his new sensations. So why, it may be asked, should not such conscious inference and speculation about the spatial significance

[15]See Chapter 1, p. 15 above.

of his sensations not be present in someone with only one sense-modality? Certainly that possibility would refute the conjecture. But to infer that it is a possibility from the TVSS case would be a *non sequitur*. The blind subject using the TVSS has a way of thinking of spatial properties and relations given him by his tactual experiences, experiences which have a (tactual) observational representational content. If we totally remove (in thought) this and other senses before equipping a being with a TVSS, what way of thinking of spatial properties and relations is he supposed to employ in the conjectures he is envisaged as forming and testing about the objective spatial significance of his sensations? There seems to be no way of thinking of them left to him. Someone can work out the spatial significance of some of his sensations, but only if he has spatial observational concepts in some other sense-modality.[16]

[16] It seems to follow from these views that a being not capable of having experiences could not understand scientific theories, and *a fortiori* could not engage in scientific research. This conclusion is in conflict with Feyerabend's views as stated in 'Science Without Experience' (*Journal of Philosophy* 66 (1969), 791–4). But though 'experience' occurs in his title, many of Feyerabend's arguments are concerned to establish the conclusion that 'sensations' play no essential role in coming to know or in understanding scientific theories. If 'sensation' here means 'experience with no representational properties', it is not in conflict with what I have said. But none of Feyerabend's arguments establish that experiences *with* representational properties are inessential to scientific understanding. Feyerabend emphasizes that there are ways of coming to believe propositions (and perhaps even to know them in suitable circumstances) which do not require the occurrence of experiences. He cites subliminal learning, post-hypnotic suggestion and latent learning. But it does not suffice to show experience to be inessential to scientific knowledge that on a particular occasion no relevant experience occurs and yet still something is learned: for it may be that it is a necessary condition for entertaining and grasping the content of what is learned that the learner be capable of having and responding suitably to experiences of a certain type.

5

Demonstrative Content I

Why is the thought that it is now three o'clock so much more informative than the thoughts that now is now or that three o'clock is three o'clock? What am I thinking when I judge that I am Christopher Peacocke? Why did Descartes have to state the *Cogito* in the first person and not in the third?

These are the sorts of puzzle one would like to have answered by a theory of demonstrative and indexical thought: and they are questions which partially motivate the discussion of demonstrative content in this chapter and the next. But besides their intrinsic interest, questions of demonstrative content are also continuous with the previous topics of this book. It is hard to conceive of a creature which satisfies the conditions of the Basic Case but which is incapable of having attitudes to demonstrative thoughts about objects in its immediate environment. In the discussion of observational concepts, too, we found ourselves attempting to give an account which made reference to such concepts as applied to objects demonstratively presented in perception.

Our fundamental question here and in the next chapter is this: what is it to be capable of having propositional attitudes to thoughts which contain demonstrative modes of presentation ('demonstrative m.p.'s') amongst their constituents? The question is couched in Fregean terminology. I shall use the word 'thought', in occurrences in which it would otherwise be ambiguous, only for the content of an attitude, and not for the mental occurrence or state which has that content. Thoughts will also be taken as structured entities; the phrase 'mode of presentation' will be used relatively non-committally for whatever is a constituent of such thoughts.

The general question 'What is it to have attitudes to demonstrative thoughts?' is not intrinsically linguistic. It is a substantive claim that a being cannot employ in thought some demonstrative m.p. without also having in his vocabulary some symbol which expresses that m.p.; and the account I shall finally suggest seems clearly to leave room for someone to have attitudes to demonstrative thoughts without having the means to express them linguistically.

There is also a second respect in which the question is not intrinsically linguistic. There is no antecedent presumption that the class of demonstrative m.p.'s is either identical with or strictly includes the class of senses of possible utterances of indexical expressions of English. It is, for example, not clear that the word 'tomorrow' means anything other than 'the day following today'; and if it does mean that, utterances of 'tomorrow' have a mixed descriptive–demonstrative sense. With such a mixed sense, an utterance today of the word 'tomorrow' would express a thought containing a demonstrative m.p. of today, but would present tomorrow only descriptively, as the day following today. Yet even if the class of indexical expressions of English were to determine the class of demonstrative m.p.'s, one would want a theoretically more informative characterization. There certainly could exist an expression α which on any occasion of utterance refers to the utterer's paternal grandfather. On a particular occasion, this word α would express a complex sense of the form 'my paternal grandfather'; this sense would indeed contain a demonstrative m.p. of the utterer, but not of the utterer's grandfather, who would only be presented descriptively. Even if the English expressions were to fix the class of demonstrative m.p.'s, we should still want to know what feature their senses possess which is not possessed by the hypothetical α. A good theory of demonstrative thought should answer this question.

A good theory of demonstrative thought ought also to explain the immensely rich variety of phenomena displayed by demonstrative m.p.'s. These phenomena, now well documented in the literature, fall into two broad classes. The first class contains those phenomena displayed by all demonstrative m.p.'s: it includes the irreducibility of demonstrative to purely descriptive thought and what is sometimes called, following Shoemaker, the immunity to error through misidentification of certain demonstrative thoughts.[1] The

---

[1] '. . . to say that a statement "a is φ" is subject to error through misidentification relative to the term "a" means that the following is possible: the speaker knows some particular thing to be φ, but makes the mistake of asserting "a is φ" because, and only because, he mistakenly thinks that the thing he knows to be φ is what a refers to.' 'Self-Reference and Self-Awareness', *Journal of Philosophy* 65 (1968), 555–67, at p. 557.

second class contains phenomena special to particular demonstrative types, such as the occurrence of m.p.'s of the first-person and present-tense types in the Cartesian thoughts which are the strongest candidates for being infallibly known. Phenomena of this second class ought to be explained by a general account of demonstrative thought specialized to what is distinctive of the particular type displaying the phenomenon.

In this chapter I shall outline a general conception of content, and develop an account of demonstrative thought which is guided by that general conception. I will argue that this account can solve some of our initial puzzles about particular demonstratives. It will not, however, be until the next chapter that I provide a general criterion for a way of thinking to be demonstrative.

There is one piece of terminology it is helpful to have right at the outset. In discussing demonstratives, one often needs to make a distinction of level which is inapplicable when the topic is reference by pure definite descriptions. Suppose Peter thinks 'I am hungry' and Paul thinks 'I am hungry'. Since we are following the Fregean model, the modes of presentation they each express by 'I' must be different: for they determine different objects, Peter and Paul respectively. But of course when they think these thoughts, Peter and Paul think of themselves in the same *type* of way. It is this type ,which is denoted by '[self]'. The constituent of all Peter's first-person thoughts is called a token mode of presentation; it can be taken to consist of the type [self] indexed by Peter, that person himself. This token m.p. will be denoted by '[self$_{Peter}$]'. So it is token m.p.'s which are constituents of thoughts and which pick out particular objects. But one should not be misled by the label 'token': there is nothing relevantly unrepeatable about [self$_{Peter}$]. On many different occasions, Peter may have attitudes to thoughts which contain it as a constituent. Similarly '[now]' refers to the present-tense type. If you and I both think 'It is cold in here' at the same time t, the token m.p. [now$_t$] is a constituent of the thought which we both judge.[2]

[2]This terminology is taken from my paper 'Demonstrative Thought and Psychological Explanation', *Synthese* 49 (1981), 187–217. The account in these chapters supplements the account in that paper in that it attempts to provide substantive theories of particular demonstrative types which were there simply taken as primitive; but the present account could be true and many of the claims in the earlier piece false (and conversely, for that matter). There is no dependence upon the earlier account.

An Evidential Approach: Constitutive Role

The approach to demonstrative thought to be adopted here is guided by the view that a theory of Fregean thoughts must be at least a theory of evidence or grounds for judging those thoughts. Fregean thoughts are individuated by considerations of cognitive significance. If a pair of thoughts differ in the essential ways they can come to be known, it will be possible for a thinker rationally to believe one and not the other: so the thoughts must be distinct. As Dummett writes:

a difference in the possible grounds for one and [another] . . . belief, or in the mode of this and that item of knowledge, entails a difference in the objects of belief or knowledge . . . Frege's conception of a thought as a possible object of knowledge or belief . . . was surrounded by doctrines which forced this conclusion on us.[3]

In the development of an evidential approach to demonstrative thought, epistemology and the theory of thoughts will inevitably be intertwined.

Let us begin to implement such an evidential approach. What positive account can be given of the type of m.p. under which someone x thinks of himself when he judges that he was in New York, i.e., that [self$_x$] was in New York, on the basis of his memory images of that city? We need an account on which it is the same first-person m.p. which features in his thought 'I was in New York' whether or not it is based on personal memory images, and the same again as that which features in his thoughts 'I am hungry', 'My legs are crossed', and 'I will be in Oxford next year'.

There is some initial plausibility in the claim that when someone thinks of himself in the [self] type of way, his way of thinking of himself is specified by the mixed descriptive–demonstrative 'the person who has *these* conscious states', where the demonstrative picks out his token conscious states at the time of thinking. If this idea is to be defended, we shall need to draw a distinction between two ways in which a description may determine an m.p. It may do

---

[3] 'What is a Theory of Meaning? (II)', at p. 134. I should perhaps add that though I shall be developing an account which presupposes the correctness of an evidential theory of content, I believe that in the cases with which I shall be concerned, an evidential and a truth conditional theory of content are not only consistent but that properly understood, each determines the other. I hope to argue for this belief elsewhere.

so simply by giving the content of an m.p., as it does with descriptive m.p.'s. 'The person who has these conscious states' certainly does not give the content of the [self] m.p. Someone can have first-person thoughts without having the intellectual sophistication actually to think about his own experiences and thoughts, either demonstratively or in any other way. But giving the content is not the only means by which a description can determine an m.p. It can also specify what I shall call the *constitutive role* of an m.p. In order to explain this notion we need to step back and consider m.p.'s more generally.

I suggest that associated with each type of demonstrative m.p. is a kind of evidence which disposes a thinker to judge thoughts containing constituents of that type. With perceptual types is associated evidence concerning the properties of the object which causes, in the way required for perception, the properties of the region of the visual field in which the object is presented; with [self] is associated evidence concerning the person who has the token experiences and thoughts which the thinker in fact has; with memory-image types is associated evidence concerning the thing which causes, in the way required for memory, a particular feature of that image. It is constitutive of a token m.p. being of a given type that judgements containing that token be sensitive to evidence of the kind associated with that type. The reader might be tempted to be more specific than this, and say that what is distinctive of each type is a means of coming to believe a certain kind of thought with a constituent of the type: thus sensitivity to perceptual experiences of present-tense observational judgements would be distinctive of perceptual types, sensitivity to memory images of memory demonstratives, and so forth. But though such sensitivities may well have to be a consequence of any good account of such demonstrative types, they could not themselves supply a general account. For perceptual types of demonstrative can feature in past- and future-tense thoughts, and memory types in present- and future-tense thoughts. Any general account of a type must be applicable to all the thoughts of which a token of that type may be a constituent. In associating a kind of evidence with a type, we do not place any restrictions on the range of thoughts to which the account applies.

The constitutive role of a demonstrative type will have three components: a sortal concept,[4] some reference to a psychological

---

[4]Or at least something that fixes the temporal and spatial identity conditions of the object relevant to the thought in which the demonstrative occurs.

state of a thinker, and some relation between them (a partially causal relation for perceptual m.p.'s). All three components play a distinctive role in the conditions under which the thinker is prepared to withdraw or take as confirmed the judgement of a thought containing the m.p. in whose constitutive role they feature. If our thinker judges of a perceptually presented object 'that bowl was made in China', he will probably withdraw the judgement if he walks up to it, examines its underside, and reads 'Made in Japan'. If his perceptions over time from first seeing the bowl were different, and he saw a new bowl take the place of the old one on the stand, there would not necessarily be any revision of the original judgement after examination of the second bowl. The thinker does not need to possess the concept of a visual m.p. or the concept of properties of the visual field to react differently in the two cases. He just needs to respond differently to sequences of perceptions which are on different sides of the boundary between those sequences which present a bowl which is obviously identical with the one presented in a certain way in perception, and those which do not present such an identical bowl. A distinctive role is played here not only by the property of being presented in a certain region of the visual field, but also by the sortal *bowl*.

How are we to specify these patterns of evidential sensitivity? Ideally we would provide a direct, fully explicit characterization of the pattern of evidential sensitivity of thoughts containing demonstratives of a given type. This would consist of something which, for a given demonstrative type Δ and concept φ, specifies directly a function from sequences of perceptions, beliefs, and memories to thoughts of the form '$[\Delta_x]$ is φ' (tense omitted). Even in the simplest cases, such a function must be of formidable complexity. Consider the present-tense, observational judgement 'That (perceptually presented) lump is cubic in shape'. The positive evidence for such a judgement would have to include the actual or possible occurrence of perceptions as of something cubic from different angles (or experiences as of something with a square cross section in special cases). To confirm that these evidential conditions are met involves an array of simple but still theoretical assumptions, which have somehow to be borne out by experience. Amongst these is the assumption that in certain circumstances the subject has changed location and in such a way that he is still perceiving the same object. This in turn would have to be confirmed at least in part by his changing experience of *other* objects as his spatial relations to them vary. How these experiences will vary in turn depends on the shapes of those other objects: and the thoughts that they have certain shapes are thoughts of the same kind as the original thought whose confirmation is in question. This suggests, unsurprisingly, that one can only confirm several such thoughts simultaneously. Another simple theoretical assumption involved in such confirmation is that one can check how a thing would have looked earlier from a particular angle by later moving to that angle. This involves some hypothesis about the stability of shape over time, and again some simple use of a criterion of identity over time. Clearly, one could continue in this vein.

We do not at present have any such direct description of evidential patterns, and if we are to obtain any illumination about demonstrative thought by considering their evidential patterns, those patterns will have to be characterized in some other way. But as I agree that a direct description is the ideal, when in what follows some claim can be justified on the basis of what we do know of the direct description of an evidential pattern, I will appeal to the direct characterization.

The indirect descriptions of evidential sensitivity I will use are based on this idea: the pattern of evidential sensitivity displayed in the use of a demonstrative m.p. may be the *same* as some part of the pattern of evidential sensitivity displayed by someone using more sophisticated concepts, concepts not necessarily possessed by someone using the demonstrative m.p. This is what I meant when I said that the first-person m.p. has a constitutive role given by 'the person who has *these* conscious states'. Here is a more precise statement. A partially descriptive m.p. 'the object which is C' specifies the constitutive role of a type iff (a) any family of perceptions, beliefs, and memories which would cause someone to judge a thought of the form '$[\Delta_x]$ is φ' would also cause someone with the requisite concepts to judge 'the object which is C is φ', and (b) any family perceptions, beliefs, and memories which would cause someone with the requisite concepts to judge 'the object which is C is φ' would also cause him to judge '$[\Delta_x]$ is φ'. Here we must add the qualifications that enjoyment of the families of states in (b) does not require the possession of concepts not necessarily possessed in employing Δ, and that this family is the subject's total informational state at the time.[5] Someone can display the same pattern of evidential sensitivity as is displayed by another person in exercising more sophisticated concepts, without necessarily possessing those more sophisticated concepts. Thus in the example of the person judging 'that (perceptually presented) bowl is Chinese', there was a pattern of evidential sensitivity to the properties of a particular region of the visual field, a sensitivity which would also be displayed by someone employing the more sophisticated m.p. 'the bowl responsible, in the way required for perception, for the experience as of a bowl in *that* region of my visual field'. Similarly, the constitutive role of the pure present-tense type [now] is plausibly 'the time *this* attitude (thinking, belief, intention, etc.) occurs': this is so because the subject is disposed to judge a thought '$\varphi([now_i])$' in the same circumstances (with the above qualifications) in which someone would be prepared to judge that the time at which that judgement is made is φ. Here the second judgement makes reference to the first: it is not self-referential.[6] Let us say that in these circumstances the subject *has evidence** that the time that attitude occurs is φ: this will prove a convenient abbreviation in what follows. Evidence* is wider than evidence both in that it includes for instance experiences which may cause judgements and in that, as introduced, someone may have evidence* that p without having all the concepts from which the thought that p is built up.

We can now formulate the following *Sensitivity Principle*. Where 'the object that is C' specifies the constitutive role associated with the type of m.p. Δ for a given thinker at a given time,

> It is *a priori* and necessary that the thinker is disposed at that time to judge a thought of the form '$\varphi([\Delta_x])$' in the presence of evidence* that the thing which is C is φ.

(Here 'C' is a schematic letter.) Constitutive role is defined by the place of C in the Sensitivity Principle: the constitutive role of the aribrary type of m.p. Δ for a given person and time is whatever meets the condition on C in the Sensitivity Principle.

[5] These two qualifications are seen to be necessary when one reflects that the more sophisticated person might be reliably told something about his experiences, information not necessarily accessible to someone exercising perceptual m.p.'s. (Here I am indebted to discussion with Stephen Schiffer.)

[6] There are further complexities here, discussed a few paragraphs below.

I have written 'the' constitutive role; but nothing in the logical form of the Sensitivity Principle justifies the implication of uniqueness. So what does justify it? We need not worry about nonuniqueness within a class of descriptions of the form 'the thing which is C' if all the descriptions are uniformatively equivalent, for our concern is always going to be with the sense of the description. Suppose there are two descriptions 'the thing which is C' and 'the thing which is C'' which seem to be candidates for the constitutive role of a demonstrative type Δ, and that a thought of the form '[Δ_x] = the thing which is C' is uninformative, while a thought of the form '[Δ_x] = the thing which is C'' is informative: then 'the thing which is C' will be taken as the specification of constitutive role. But what of a case in which there are two descriptions which specify the constitutive role of a type and which are not *a priori* equivalent? But it is questionable whether any coherent demonstrative type could be like this. For if the two descriptions, 'the thing which is C' and 'the thing which is C'', say, are not *a priori* equivalent, then there will be some epistemically possible circumstances in which they are not satisfied by the same thing. In the epistemically possible circumstances in which the thing that is C is φ and the thing which is C' is not φ, is a thought of the form '[Δ_x] is φ', where Δ is the type in question, to be judged true or not? It seems impossible to answer the question. Two different sufficient conditions have been given for judging the thought, and it is not *a priori* that they coincide. There is not a unitary, single demonstrative type here. This point noted, I shall continue to speak of the constitutive role of a demonstrative type.

There are some possible misunderstandings of the intended function of constitutive roles in what follows which are worth mentioning. One such misunderstanding is the view that use of the apparatus of constitutive roles commits one to the view that demonstrative m.p.'s are really a disguised form of partially descriptive m.p.'s. But there is no such commitment: in fact in the next chapter, we will attempt to give a criterion for an m.p. to be genuinely demonstrative, and will do so by appeal to the special properties of certain constitutive roles. A related possible misunderstanding is that constitutive role is what guides a thinker in reaching judgements whose contents contain the m.p. which has that constitutive role. On the above means of introducing the notion, constitutive role is simply an indirect means of describing a pattern of evidential sensitivity, a pattern which will always have a more direct description. Someone's judgements can display the evidential pattern corresponding to a particular constitutive role without that role itself even entering his thoughts. The point of introducing constitutive roles is to illuminate certain features of demonstrative thought: the Cartesian phenomena, the distinctive properties of demonstrative as opposed to descriptive thought, immunity to error through misidentification – and in general any cognitive phenomenon distinctively tied to demonstrative thought. It is in these tasks that constitutive roles will be employed below.

Since I have agreed that direct descriptions of patterns of evidential sensitivity are always fundamental, these cognitive phenomena must ultimately be grounded (if the evidential conception of content is right) in properties formulable in terms of that direct description: I certainly hope that someone can improve on the account to be given here, by explaining both constitutive role and the phenomena it illuminates in terms of that more fundamental level. But constitutive role can still take us some distance. I will be making claims of this form: any m.p. whose pattern of evidential sensitivity has a certain constitutive role will also have certain further cognitive features. The converse claim will not be true. The constitutive role of an m.p. depends upon the character of *all* the thoughts in which it occurs, whereas the cognitive phenomena in question relate to a more limited class. There is a limited parallel to this general approach in the sort of illumination one obtains when a complex inference pattern someone accepts is shown to be a consequence of several simple principles to which the operators in the inference conform. We still enjoy this illumination even if those who employ the inference pattern have never explicitly formulated the several simpler principles. Those simpler principles still determine conditions to which their judgements, when correctly related to their other judgements, conform. (Recognition of this intermediate level of illumination does not exclude a Wittgensteinian account of logical inference: such an account is a theory of what the illumination is illumination about.)

The Sensitivity Principle uses a notion of evidence. Appeal to an undifferentiated notion of evidence in giving a theory of any sort of mode of presentation would be an unpromising strategy: for it seems to be true that anything can be evidence for a given thought in some circumstances or other, while virtually nothing can be evidence for it in all circumstances. But these truths are consistent with the existence of *canonical* evidence for a thought. A perception, a memory or a piece of information of a certain type (or a particular type of set of these) is canonical evidence for the thought that p iff it is constitutive of the thought that p that a thinker takes states or information of that type as *prima facie* evidence justifying the judgement that p. Again there is a partial parallel with properties of the logical constants. A conjunctive thought, for instance, may be inferred from a premise of any form provided suitable auxiliary premises are available; but it does not follow there are not canonical principles governing conjunction and other operators, principles such that any valid argument must be verifiable as such by using these principles.

The parallel is, however, partial because canonical evidence need not be conclusive evidence: the dispositions to judgement mentioned in the Sensitivity Principle must match this fact. The designation of some evidence as canonical does not preclude the recognition of differences between thinkers employing the same concepts in respect of inductive boldness. Such differences can be present either because some of the canonical evidence is not conclusive, or because there are differences in inductive policies when assessing links between non-canonical and canonical evidence. In these general formulations of the concept there is also no restriction on the form that might be taken by a specification of canonical evidence for a given type of thought. The canonical evidence could, for instance, be specified in terms of the existence of various other truths which conform to the pattern determined by a certain form of theory; so a specification of canonical evidence may have a holistic character. Generally, one can think of an account of canonical evidence for a certain type of thought as an indispensable part of what one would need if one were enquiring whether a particular person does indeed possess attitudes to thoughts of that type.[7]

[7] This last formulation with its reference to manifestation clearly raises very sharply the question of realism in Dummett's sense (see 'What is a Theory of Meaning? (II)'). But as far as I can see, the claims of this chapter are neutral with repect to antirealism, for two reasons. (i) Even if some demonstration could be given that realism is correct, it is plausible that canonical evidence must remain part of an account of sense, and that is all that is needed for the explanation I will try to give of the phenomena involving demonstratives. (ii) There also seems to be no commitment in the theory given below to construing the concepts used in specifications of canonical evidence realistically nor to construing them antirealistically.

The requirement that the evidence be canonical affects the range of considerations relevant to any particular suggestion about the constitutive role of a demonstrative type. Even when we do possess the concept of conscious states and are capable of demonstrative thoughts about our own conscious states, the thought 'the person with these conscious states is φ' is not likely to be the first thing we think of when asked what we would need to establish 'I'm φ'. But what we first think of in answering this question may be determined by a great deal of collateral information, including identities. Constitutive role is meant to capture what is essential to the evidential pattern of first-person thoughts even when the collateral information is absent. When the thinker is suffering from amnesia and has just woken up in hospital after an accident, he will not find so far-fetched the idea that to establish 'I'm thus-and-so' he needs to establish 'the person with these conscious states is thus-and-so'.[8] (We return later to the issue of whether the first-person m.p. and 'the person with these conscious states' are really as tightly linked as we have claimed.)

An account of sense which makes reference to canonical evidence can respect the structure of thoughts. Consider thoughts of the form $\emptyset[\varphi(\tau)]$, where $\emptyset$ is a temporal operator, φ some concept and τ an m.p. of an individual. For each τ, an account must be given of its contribution to canonical evidence which can combine with the account for an arbitrary φ and arbitrary $\emptyset$. Symmetrically, there will be in such an account an implicit account of how the canonical

---

[8] Note that if concepts are individuated by reference to canonical evidence, it is not only collateral beliefs which must be set aside as irrelevant to possession of the concept itself. The same applies to prototypes, in the sense investigated by Rosch (see 'Classification of real-world objects', reprinted in *Thinking: Readings in Cognitive Science*, ed. P. Johnson-Laird and P. Wason (Cambridge: CUP, 1977)). For all its importance in empirical psychology, a prototype cannot be regarded as essential to a concept: for a concept can be fixed, but the prototype which a given thinker associates with it can vary. As has often been noted, the prototype commonly associated with the concept 'grandmother' in our society (white-haired, old, frail) would not be the same as that commonly associated with it in a strongly matriarchal society in which women had children when very young— there the prototype would be of a powerful, middle-aged individual. But canonical evidence that someone is a grandmother— that she is the mother of a parent— would be the same in the two societies. An evidentially-based account of concepts which uses a notion of canonical evidence would thus be entirely consonant with, and help to explain, Dennett's point that difference of (e.g.) reaction-times is not sufficient to establish that two subjects do not have the same beliefs, built from the very same concepts: see D. Dennett, *Brainstorms* (Montgomery, Vt.: Bradford Books, 1978), p. 105.

evidence for a given concept can combine with an arbitrary τ and $\emptyset$; and similarly for each given operator $\emptyset$.

We can distinguish between those constitutive roles which are *original* and those which are not. An original constitutive role for a type is one which mentions only those states and events which would be quantified over in the direct account of canonical evidential sensitivity for that type. The constitutive role 'the person who has these conscious states' of the first-person type is plausibly original. 'The time that attitude is possessed' for the present-tense type, where 'that attitude' refers to a particular present-tense attitude, is not an original constitutive role: the direct account of the canonical evidence for judging a content can hardly presuppose that one has already judged it. In general, a direct account of the pattern of evidential sensitivity for judgements to the effect that so-and-so is now the case will not always mention judgements and beliefs; rather, other states (experiences and so forth) will be mentioned, and in suitable circumstances a judgement or belief will be made after these other, often non-judgemental, factors have been taken into account. It is true that whenever a reflective person judges '*A* holds now', he will be prepared to judge '*A* holds at the time at which that (former) judgement is made'; but this is a consequence of the direct account of evidential role, and not a component of it.[9] The feature of the direct account of evidential sensitivity which the description 'the time of occurrence of this particular attitude' reflects is rather this: a judgement that such-and-such is the case now possesses the feature that the canonical evidence for its content is evidence about the state of the world at the time at which that judgement is made.

Thus, to summarize the general structure so far: what is distinctive of a given demonstrative type is the pattern of evidence or prior states to the holding of which judgements containing tokens of that type must be sensitive; and the constitutive role associated with a given type is intended to capture this complex pattern of evidential sensitivity.

---

[9]Compare Russell's point in this passage: ' "This" is a proper name applied to the object to which I am now attending. If it be asked how I come to select this object, the answer is that, by hypothesis, I am selecting it, since it is the object of my attention. "This" is not waiting to be defined by the property of being given, but is given; first it is actually given, and then reflection shows that it is "that which is given".' ('On the Nature of Acquaintance', reprinted in *Logic and Knowledge* (London: Allen and Unwin, 1956), ed. R. C. Marsh, at p. 168.

Let us return to the idea that the constitutive role of [self] is given by 'the person who has these experiences and thoughts'. There are two possible misunderstandings to be avoided here. The first can be introduced by considering a remark made by Chisholm. He notes Anscombe's view, which we will touch upon again below, that 'I am this thing here' means 'the thing here is the person of whose action *this idea* of action is an idea (&c.)'.[10] Chisholm then comments:

> She thus attempts to explicate *her* use of the first-person pronoun in terms of 'this'. It is clear, however, that she cannot explicate *my* use – or your use – of the first-person pronoun in this way.[11]

Can a parallel objection be made to what we have so far said about constitutive role? Implicit in what we have said is a distinction between *generalized* and *particularized* constitutive roles associated with a given demonstrative type. The particularized constitutive role of [self] for a given thinker at a given time is determined by taking his conscious states at that time and forming the mixed descriptive–demonstrative 'the person with these conscious states'. (This last demonstrative 'these conscious states' is one which can be used to refer to *his* conscious states only by the given thinker.) The generalized role of a given type such as [self] may be said to be the function from thinkers and times to the associated particularized constitutive roles for that type. The different particularized consitutive roles for [self] for the thinkers Chisholm and Anscombe are determined by a uniform recipe, the recipe which in fact fixes the generalized constitutive role for [self]; the same applies to Chisholm's thoughts of himself at two different times. (Anscombe could of course make a corresponding reply to Chisholm.) There also seems to be a failure to distinguish generalized from particularized levels in this passage from Husserl:

> The word I names a different person from case to case, and does so by way of an ever altering meaning. What its meaning is at the moment, can be gleaned only from the living utterance and the intuitive circumstances which surround it . . . In solitary speech the meaning of 'I' is essentially realized in the immediate idea of one's own personality . . . Each man has

[10] 'The First Person' in *Mind and Language: The Wolfson Lectures, 1974* (Oxford: OUP, 1975), p. 61.

[11] R. Chisholm, *The First Person* (Brighton: Harvester, 1981), p. 46.

his own I-presentation . . . and that is why the word's meaning differs from person to person.[12]

The second possible misunderstanding may be produced by a whiff of a bundle theory of the self carried by those suggestions on constitutive role. Any such olfactory impression should be disregarded. What I have said is neutral on the correctness of some bundle theory of the self. It is neutral because it is part of a theory of a distinctive way of thinking of persons, and not of persons themselves nor of their nature and principles of individuation.[13]

The present account of the constitutive role of [self] can explain why the Cartesian thoughts about which we are arguably infallible have a distinctively first-person character. They are thoughts like '*I* am in pain', '*I* have an experience as of a tree'. From the Sensitivity Principle and the particularized constitutive role for [self], we have that

someone x is disposed to judge that $\varphi([self_x])$ in the presence of evidence that the person with *these* conscious states is φ.

Suppose x is in pain, and that pain must be experienced as pain. Then

x is disposed to judge that $[self_x]$ is φ in the presence of evidence* that the person with these conscious states, including this pain state, is φ.

Substituting 'pain' for 'φ', we get: to be disposed to judge he's in pain, the subject simply requires evidence* that the person with these conscious states, including this pain, is in pain — and this evidence* he has. The particularized constitutive role of [self] plays a crucial role in this argument. One cannot similarly give a sound

[12] *Logical Investigations* (London: Routledge, 1970), pp. 315–16.

[13] Two further caveats: (i) if an expression is used in a language which for present-tense sentences coincides in sense with our 'I', but which has no occurrences in past- or future-tense sentences, it may be excess of content to attribute to it the constitutive role involving the concept of a person which we assign to [self]. (ii) In a world with fission and fusion of persons, one may want to weaken the constitutive role of [self] in the past-tense throught '[self] was φ' to 'some person who bears the relations which matter in ordinary cases of personal identity to the presently existing person with these conscious states' — and analogously for the future.

argument for the conclusion that the subject who is in pain must have a disposition to judge that the person meeting some descriptive condition, or looking thus-and-so, is in pain; for he does not, simply by being in pain, have evidence* that the person meeting that descriptive condition, or looking thus-and-so, is in pain. Thus the possession by the first-person m.p. of the constitutive role 'the person who has *these* experiences' can explain why it is that in first-person present-tense ascriptions of conscious states, one does not have to apply any tests of identity to check that the person in pain is oneself.[14] Analogous arguments could also be given for the occurrence of the pure present-tense [now] in the apparently infallible self-ascriptions of conscious states as opposed to m.p.'s like '3 p.m. on 21 February 1981'. Here too there is no question of having to check that the time at which one is in pain is indeed the present.

The point that in making such judgements tests of personal identity are unnecessary could be made by appealing to a direct characterization of patterns of evidential sensitivity. A direct characterization should include or entail this point: that if anyone x has the concept φ, where φ is a concept of a conscious psychological state, then if x falls under φ, x is disposed to judge that [self$_x$] is φ (that *he* is φ) if the question arises in thought. This seems to be constitutive of possession of the concepts of oneself and of a conscious psychological state. But it is neither constitutive nor even true that if someone x has the concept φ, then if the F falls under φ, x must be prepared to judge that the F is φ — not even if he is the F.

This account of the constitutive role of [self] should make it unsurprising that any given person x is the only person who can think of x under the m.p. [self$_x$]. (Another person y can think of himself y under the m.p. [self$_y$], and can think *about* the m.p. [self$_x$], but he cannot employ [self$_x$] to think about x under an m.p. of the first-person type.) For any given particular token conscious states and thoughts a thinker enjoys, only he and no one else has those particular token states and thoughts (and this is not a contingent fact). So he alone can make demonstrative reference in thought to them in ways someone is capable of making such reference in virtue of having those particular states. No one can think of another's

[14] L. Wittgenstein, *Philosophical Investigations* (Blackwell: Oxford, 1958), sections 404–11; and P. F. Strawson, *The Bounds of Sense* (Methuen: London, 1966), pp. 162–74.

states demonstratively where the demonstrative way is dependent upon being in those conscious states. To say this is not to be committed in any objectionable sense to the privacy of another's sensations and conscious thoughts: it is quite consistent with these claims about the constitutive role of [self] that one can on occasion know what type of experience and what thoughts another is having. All that is entailed is that one cannot think of the other's conscious states in the particular ways in which that other person can think of them.

Consider the thought 'I am the person with these conscious states and experiences', where the demonstrative reference is to one's own current conscious states and experiences. This is not a great discovery, on a par with the discovery that Hesperus is Phosphorus or that genes are DNA molecules; but on the other hand, it does not seem quite as trivial as the thought that I am me or that the person with these experiences is the person with these experiences. This is true even for the thinker who does have the concept of conscious experience, and who is capable of making demonstrative reference to his own experiences. Yet is it not a consequence of the theory I have been promoting that 'I am the person with these experiences' is just as trivial as these latter cases? For the m.p.'s employed on each side of the identity possess, I have claimed, the same constitutive role, the same pattern of evidential sensitivity, and precisely this I have said determines the m.p.

The fact that 'I am the person with these conscious states' is not utterly trivial can be explained by invoking a distinction between *exercising* an ability and *describing* that same ability. When someone employs an m.p. of the type [self] in his thoughts, he has the ability to make various judgements as a result of his enjoyment of suitable experiences. He will, for instance, be prepared to judge 'I am standing on a hill' when he has a suitable visual experience and does not take conditions of perception to be abnormal. But before he is prepared to judge 'the person with these experiences is standing on a hill', he has to think about the visual experience he is enjoying, and to reflect that in the context of his other attitudes, it is equally reasonable for him to judge 'the person with these experiences is standing on a hill'. Similarly, in the general case, to establish that in any circumstances in which one would be prepared to judge 'I am thus-and-so', one would be prepared to judge 'the person with these conscious states and experiences is thus-and-so', and conversely, one has to reflect upon and describe the abilities that one normally exercises unreflectively in making first-person judgements. It is the fact that a thinker may not have carried out this reflection, or remembered its results, that makes the thought 'I am the person with these conscious states' not entirely trivial, even for the thinker who has the concept of conscious states. It is not that there are no abilities required of a thinker who is able to employ the m.p.'s in 'the person with these conscious states and experiences': on the contrary, there will be all the abilities required of one who can use definite descriptions and make reference to his own experiences in thought. The point is not any absence of abilities in the latter case, but the fact that it takes a little thought to discover what the relation of those abilities is to the abilities necessarily employed by someone using the first-person m.p. Exactly parallel remarks could be made about the identity, concerning a dog perceptually presented in a visual experience, 'that dog (so presented) is the dog causing, in the way required for perception, the properties of this region of my visual field'.

A competing account of the marginal informativeness of 'I am the person with these conscious states' might be suggested. It might be said that though [self] and 'the person with these conscious states' have the same constitutive role, [self] has canonical but nonconclusive evidential conditions which are not shared by 'the person with these conscious states'. It is certainly true that some concepts have canonical but nonconclusive conditions of application. A clear case is provided by the relation of an instance of a universal quantification to the universal quantification itself: the truth of an instance is nonconclusive evidence, but it is constitutive in the sense that a sentence of which a putative instance is not taken as partial confirmation, to however small an extent, cannot properly be interpreted as a universal quantification. In this example, however, as in many if not all others, the evidential condition is one which is entailed by the holding of the condition for which it is evidence. It is a question whether there are or can be, as this rival suggestion requires, any examples of canonical, nonconclusive evidential conditions which are not so entailed. There are reasons for doubting the coherence of the idea that there could be such conditions; for if the evidence is nonconclusive and not entailed, why should not a thinker's using the condition as evidence simply be taken as a manifestation of a belief that the condition is evidence for the obtaining of a certain state of affairs? As against this, it may be said that the account we gave of observational concepts itself employed nonconclusive canonical evidential conditions. For was not the occurrence of an experience as of something φ a nonconclusive but canonical condition for the application by a thinker of the concept φ? But this would be a mistaken interpretation. It was not possible (not even epistemically possible) for an observational concept φ that an object of perceptible size, and which in normal circumstances (etc.) produced an experience as of something φ, not be a φ thing. If the thinker takes conditions to be normal (etc.) then the occurrence of an experience as of something φ will be entailed on this account by all that he believes. The case will be analogous to that of the universal quantification and its instance. If, on the other hand, conditions are not taken to be normal, the occurrence of the experience is in no way canonical evidence.

Even if these points are taken, room is still left for the possibility that one should treat [self] in a way analogous to that in which observational concepts are treated. A visual experience which makes one willing to judge 'I am standing on a hill' would be regarded as bearing comparable relations to the m.p. [self] as those borne by an experience as of something square to the visual concept of a square.

There are several obstacles to adopting such a view. The first is that it seems far from providing an explanation of the essential occurrence of the first-person m.p. in the Cartesian indubitable thoughts 'I am in pain' and the rest. Second, a subject's optic nerve may receive its input from a distant television camera. He may be genuinely perceiving the distant scene. But those components of the representational content of his experience which concern the perceived objects' spatial relations to him may well be false; and he can know them to be false if he knows of his link to the camera. This falsity need not be something which shows up as the camera changes its angle on the distant perceived objects; the case is not quite analogous to observational concepts. In defence of a qualified form of the view it may be replied that we allow the subject's thought 'These objects (perceptually presented) do not really bear to me the relations my experience represents them as bearing' to be true; but this is because the weight of his other perceptions with biological eyes locates him far away from this scene. The qualified view would appeal to weighting principles. This, though, sounds a plausible account not of the nature of [self], but rather of the principles that, for each thinker, determine which place is his location. A thinker in unusual circumstances[15] may coherently wonder whether these principles determine any place as his location. This, however, is not yet to wonder whether perhaps he does not exist. (Some of these issues are pursued further in Chapter 6, in the section 'A Comparison'.)

There are many conceivable demonstrative ways of thinking which receive no unambiguous expression in English. We can, for instance, introduce a set of perceptually-based demonstrative types of ways of thinking of a place. These types could be referred to by terms of the form '[This ^{T} place]'. Here T is a kind of experience. In an experience as of objects around oneself, the objects are represented as standing in various particular spatial relations to oneself. The place x (if any) which is presented in the type of way [this ^{T} place] in relation to the token experience of kind T is the place x (if any) which stands in these particular spatial relations to the objects presented in the experience.[16] If such a place exists, it is a place in public, physical space. In normal circumstances a token of such a type of m.p. will present the location of the perceiver's head. This use of '[this ^{T} place]' and of correspondingly indexed types is purely stipulative, and is not intended to explain the sense of an expression already existing in English. If on a particular occasion an experience of a given type is a total hallucination, there will for the thinker then be no token of the corresponding type of m.p. There may still be no token even when no apparent object presented by the experience is hallucinatory. This will be the case if, because of some arrangement of mirrors, while the objects in the left of the thinker's visual field are in their normal position relative to him, those in the right are behind him. In unusual circumstances a token of this invented type can present other places. If your visual cortex is connected to the optic nerve of another person, your tokens of the type [this ^{T} place] will refer to the location of that other person's head. When Dennett was on his mission to retrieve a nuclear device from underneath Tulsa, Oklahoma, while his brain remained

---

[15] 'Where Am I', in Dennett's *Brainstorms*.

[16] It would be possible explicitly to introduce a token experience e of the kind T into the notation and write '[This $^{T, e}$ place]' for a type of m.p. and '[this $^{T, e}_x$ place]' for a token of that type.

behind in Houston, he may have had a thought of the form
'[this ^{T} place] is dark and dangerous': in this thought he referred to a
place in Oklahoma, not Houston.[17] One could similarly introduce
a perceptually-based temporal indexical [this ^{T} time], for a way of
thinking of times. If someone has an experience of type T, the time
presented in a token of the type [this ^{T} time] will be the time (if any)
at which the events (if any) presented in the experience occurred.
Similarly when M is a kind of memory image, we could introduce
the type [that ^{M} place]. In a memory image as of objects around
oneself, the objects are represented as standing in various particular
spatial relations to oneself. The place x (if any) which is presented in
the type of way [this ^{M} place] in relation to a given token memory
image of kind M is the place (if any) which stood at the time of the
remembered encounter in these particular spatial relations to the
objects presented in the memory image.

The demonstrative [this ^{T} place] also prompts an objection to
what we have said about [self]: [this ^{T} place] does not give the sense
of the English word 'here', for one can wonder 'What is going on
here?' while not perceiving anything at the place referred to by 'here'.
Could it not be, then, that the correct account of the first-person m.p.
stands to an m.p. with the constitutuve role 'the person with these
conscious states' as the sense of 'here' stands to [this ^{T} place]?[18]
The analogy here is not perfect. For we have seen that one can
make sense of the supposition that [this ^{T} place] is not here,
whereas it does not appear possible to make sense of the supposition
that I am not the person with these conscious states. Nevertheless,
the suggestion can reasonably be construed as requiring something
more dispositional. Though it is true that whenever someone is
consciously thinking, there will be conscious states which are picked
out in the phrase 'the person with these conscious states', not all
attitudes which have first-person contents require the occurrence of
events in consciousness. Belief, for instance, does not. Suppose
someone believes he was born in London. Then we can make the
dispositional claim that were he to have some conscious experiences
or thoughts, he would revise that belief in the presence of evidence*
that the person with those conscious states was not born in London.
There may be a parallel with a belief possessed while no memory
image occurs to someone, that that Greek island was sunny. Such a

---

[17] 'Where Am I?'.

[18] I am indebted to John McDowell for raising this question.

belief could be intelligibly attributed if the subject has a reliable ability to recall in a memory image that Greek island, even if no image occurs at the time at which the belief is said to be possessed.

Does a specification of its constitutive role fully determine the first-person m.p., or is some crucial feature omitted? Perry has emphasized that there is a link between the first-person m.p. and action.[19] If Ivan Tovar has the first-person belief that he is heir to a large fortune, we will expect him to take steps to claim it. If he believes only that Ivan Tovar is heir to a large fortune, and fails to believe that he is Ivan Tovar, we will not expect him to take such steps. It seems undeniable that Perry is right in thinking that there is some such link. So what is its relation to constitutive role?

We expect Tovar to act when he has the first-person belief because we have a background expectation that he wants wealth: if we were to believe either that he does not want wealth, or that such desires do not lead him to form intentions to act, we would not anticipate action.[20] If a first-person belief does not lead someone to form any new first-person present-tense intentions or decisions, we do not expect it to lead to any new actions; while on the other hand, we expect to lead to new actions any new belief, such as 'Today is the last day of the exhibition', whether first-person or not, which leads, in the context of other attitudes, to the formation of a new first-person present-tense decision or intention. Thus the crucial point which we need to consider is the occurrence of the first person in present-tense intentions (or more strictly, intentions concerning the immediate future: henceforth this nicety is ignored).

The well-entrenched principle on which we rely in explaining actions is roughly this: if someone at a given time intends that he φ's at that time, he tries to φ at that same time – i.e.

$$(\forall x \forall t (x \text{ intends at } t \text{ that } [self_x] \; \varphi \text{ at } [now_t] \supset x \text{ tries to } \varphi \text{ at } t)).$$

There are two different positions one might take on the relation of this principle and intentional action in general to the first-person type [self]. Position (1) holds that if this principle is not explicitly included in an account of what it is to employ the first-person m.p.

---

[19] 'Frege on Demonstratives', *Philosophical Review* 86 (1977), 474–97.

[20] Perry is of course well aware of this: in 'The Problem of the Essential Indexical', *Noûs* 13, 3–21, the link with action is restricted to those with certain motivations—'goodhearted people' and 'responsible professors'.

in thought, then that account will at best fail to determine uniquely the first-person m.p.: the account will be satisfied by more than one type of m.p. Position (1) would apply to the account of [self] in terms of constitutive role, since that account appeals only to evidential sensitivity, and certainly does not explicitly mention the relation of [self] to intentional action. Position (2) holds that a specification of an m.p.'s constitutive role does uniquely fix that m.p. It need not be a claim of this second position that we can conceive of beings capable of first-person thought who are incapable of forming intentions. The claim is only that however central intention may be to the possession of psychological states with content, an account of intention will be able to draw upon an independent account of the first-person m.p.

Not surprisingly, then, I will defend Position (2). There are two related objections to Position (1). According to Position (1), constitutive role fails to determine m.p. So there ought if it is correct to be an example of a pair of m.p.'s which have the same constitutive role but are yet distinct. It is hard to think of any such cases. The second objection to Position (1) is an objection of principle which suggests that the lack of obvious examples is not a failure of imagination. We earlier endorsed the view that a difference of constitutive roles of, say, τ and ς is sufficient for the distinctness of the thoughts that τ is φ and that ς is φ. But it seems equally compelling that the sameness of their constitutive roles is sufficient for sameness of the thoughts that τ is φ and that ς is φ (for any φ). If judgement of the thoughts that τ is φ and that ς is φ are sensitive in exactly the same circumstances to the same evidence, how can a thinker rationally judge the one and withold judgement on the other? Yet this is what Position (1) has to allow. It might be replied on behalf of Position (1) that although one could not judge the one thought without judging the other, it could still be that one could intend one thought without intending the other. But this again is not as intelligible as it may seem: how can one have the one intention without the other if for the thinker, in all conceivable circumstances, the evidence that the one intention has been fulfilled is evidence that the other has been fulfilled? For these reasons I conclude that Position (2) and not Position (1) is correct, and that the genuine links between first-person thought and action do not mean that [self] is not fully determined by its constitutive role.

But this still leaves an unanswered question. *Why* is it that the m.p. which has the constitutive role of [self] also has this special connection with action? The special action property which [self] has is this: it is the unique m.p. Δ of a person such that no intentional action on the part of an agent occurs unless he has some intention of the form '[Δ_i] is φ'. In acting, someone may intend that a perceptually presented person speak to him; but [self] is the only m.p. such that necessarily in every case of intentional action the agent has an intention that the person thus presented be such-and-such. (The only other m.p. which has to occur in every such case is an m.p. of a time, [now] or 'the time immediately following [now]'.)

Suppose someone intends to bring about a particular state of affairs. If he thinks of that state of affairs as he himself being thus-and-so, the content of his intention certainly contains the first-person m.p. If he does not so think of it, he must nevertheless intend that state of affairs to result from some action of his. So he will intend that he perform certain actions to bring about that state of affairs; and again there is an intention with a first-person content. It is, then, in the nature of intention for there to be a first-person content somewhere in any plan of action. This argument is quite neutral on the nature of first-person thought, since it does not appeal to any theory of the first-person m.p. Intention is of course hardly unique in having a distinctive tie with the first person; it is equally in the nature of the emotion of guilt to have a first-person content at some point.

Constitutive roles do contain demonstratives. Were they to contain demonstratives of the type for which a constitutive role was being specified, the account would be uninformative. Suppose, for instance, that the constitutive role 'the thing that is C' of a perceptual m.p. contained a demonstrative perceptual m.p. In saying that this is the constitutive role of that type, we would be saying that the pattern of canonical evidential sensitivity for that type is the same as some fragment of the pattern for 'the thing that is C' for a sophisticated thinker. But what pattern is that? If 'the thing that is C' again contains a perceptual demonstrative, then it would succeed in informing us of the pattern of canonical evidential sensitivity only if it were redundant: it would tell us something of such patterns only if we already knew the patterns of demonstrative perceptual types.

In fact the demonstratives in constitutive roles are all of a special kind: they are all demonstratives referring to the thinker's current conscious states — experiences and thoughts. When you think demonstratively of a particular current token conscious state, you are able to think of this state without needing to think of it in any way other than that given by its type; you are able to think of such a state simply by being in it. It is tempting to express this point by saying that one can think of one's current conscious states without thinking of them under any mode of presentation at all. But if m.p.'s are simply introduced as constituents of thoughts, and thoughts are individuated by the two Fregean requirements that they have unrelativized truth values and are the content of propositional attitudes, that temptation has to be resisted. There are certainly distinctive patterns of cognitive significance associated with conscious states demonstratively thought about, as indeed there are with anything else which may be so thought about. On such a Fregean conception of thoughts and m.p.'s, these patterns need explanation by m.p.'s. One might insist in some special case on putting only the object into the thought — in the case of experiences, oneself or the present — but facts about cognitive significance still need explanation. So after such a decision, somewhere else in a theory these facts must be explained, and whatever does the explanation will be doing the explanatory work definitive of an m.p. Resisting the temptation to say that the experience is thought of without being thought of in any particular way is however consistent with drawing distinctions between different kinds of m.p. The only notion of an m.p. of a token experience one needs when it is thought of demonstrative by its possessor is that given by its intrinsic properties — what it is like to have an experience of its type. We do not need any richer notion.

The classical, and in other cases irresistible, arguments for a richer notion of m.p. do not apply to a thinker's current experiences when thought of demonstratively. It seems that if e and e' are distinct current token psychological states, then it is an uninformative thought that they are distinct, when demonstratively presented: it is not news that that pain in my toe is distinct from this token visual experience. In a similar sense, if e and e' are identical, it seems uninformative that they are. These points apply of course only to ways of thinking of a conscious state which one can exercise simply in virtue of being in that state. In examining your own brain with a cerebroscope you may be visually presented with a physical event which, if the identity theory is correct, could be a pain; and the identity 'this event (visually presented) is this pain' is informative. But the visual m.p. of the event is not one you are capable of using to think of that pain solely because you have that pain.[21]

Here there are two points of contact with Russell's views. One is that all of the supposed things with which Russell held a thinker to be acquainted are things whose identity or distinctness would be held to be obvious to that thinker — sense-data and the rest; and these are precisely the objects corresponding to singular-term position which Russell would include as constituents of propositions, constituents unaccompanied there by any m.p. But although this may mitigate the natural Fregean criticism of Russell's conception of a proposition, it cannot exonerate Russell, even if we accepted his epistemology. For (as far as I know) he did not appeal to obviousness in arguing for the legitimacy of taking the objects of acquaintance as the constituents of propositions; and in his popular, unofficial exposition when he spoke of physical objects as propositional constituents, he added no riders or qualifications concerning obviousness. The second point of contact more generally is with his view that physical objects are thought of in perception under the mixed descriptive–demonstrative mode 'the physical object which causes these sense-data'. The present account cannot literally confirm this, for we have taken it that perceptual m.p.'s are genuine demonstrative m.p.'s of the perceived object itself. Nevertheless, the mixed mode that Russell gives is not entirely irrelevant — at least if we replace 'sense-data' by 'experience': Russell has mistaken a plausible specification of constitutive role for the *content* of the m.p. We will return to Russell's views in a later chapter.

Although constitutive roles are not then straightforwardly circular, there is another respect in which this account of them is not eliminative. The perceptions, beliefs, and memories which would be canonical evidence for a judgement 'that chair (perceptually presented) is φ' will certainly include experiences which have a propositional representational content which itself is built up from perceptual demonstrative m.p.'s of objects. My current visual

---

[21] Could perhaps an identity between demonstratively presented current token experiences be informative because both are identical with some physical event? But how could we come reasonably to believe that this visual experience (token) is this tickle? It seems obvious that either one could exist without the other existing, and that any identity theory which denies this must be rejected.

experience, for example, represents this hand (perceptually presented) as moving. This interdependence of the content of experience and of judgement seems inescapable: for on the one hand, no experience can have the content 'that F (perceptually presented) is thus-and-so' unless the experiencer is capable of using the same m.p. 'that F' in judgements, while on the other, one can hardly employ such a perceptual m.p. in judgements unless one is capable of perceiving Fs. What we have here is a phenomenon which shows that the account of the content of judgements cannot be selfcontained in the sense of not needing to make reference, either directly or indirectly by means of some analysis of the notion, to the content of other psychological attitudes. Such interdependence does not exclude (and does not entail) the existence of some reductive account that simultaneously explains what it is for judgements and experiences to have particular contents.

There is another circularity issue here. We said that the constitutive role of the first-person m.p. is given by 'the person who has these conscious states'. But it is a necessary condition of being a person that one be capable of having attitudes to first-person thoughts. Constitutive role was meant to give an indirect specification of a pattern of evidential sensitivity, and thus to specify what it is for something to be the first person m.p. But if the specification of constitutive role just uses the notion of a person, and so ultimately rests on some understanding of the first-person m.p., how have we advanced our understanding?

But it is not all aspects of the concept of a person that we need in stating constitutive role. Consider someone who can make first-person present-tense judgements about his own experiences and other conscious states, those judgements which seem to involve no application of criteria of identity. There are other abilities someone must have if he is to be employing the first-person m.p. in his thoughts. He must be capable of displaying some grasp of the synchronic and diachronic identity conditions of persons in his judgements about himself. The person we imagined must be able to respond to suitable evidence with past- and future-tense judgements about himself; he must also, with sufficient explanation, be able to make sense of the possibility that he is not the person who is in front of the objects which are presented in his experience as being in front of him (when, for instance, his visual cortex is connected to someone else's retina). It is mastery of these identity conditions at a time and over time which matters in the specification of constitutive role. There does not seem to be any dependence here on the first-person m.p. we were out to explain.

But does this really meet the objection? Suppose the question arises for the thinker whether he is identical with the thing x which was F at t. If x is not a person at t, the thinker certainly is not identical with x; and if x cannot at t employ the first-person m.p. in his thoughts, x (if it exists at all then) is not a person then. The thinker must be able to exclude the possibility that this is not the case; so does not the circularity remain? The answer must be that what is required is that x be able at t to make present-, past- and future-tense judgements containing the first-person m.p. employing those same synchronic and diachronic identity conditions. What we have here is not a circularity, but rather some requirement analogous to a closure property: in any case in which a thinker is prepared to judge that he is identical with the thing which is F at t, he must take into account evidence* that x then has those same abilities we mentioned to make first-person judgements in which he displays a grasp of the identity conditions of persons at and over time.[22] The fact is that the general concept of a person and the first-person type [self] are interlocking and inseparable notions. An elucidation of either one must needs make use of the other.

Special Objects, Special Senses, or Special Reference Rules?

I have distinguished a theory of a mode of presentation of an object from a theory of the nature of the object presented; and I have tried to explain some epistemological phenomena in terms of accounts of the former, not of the latter, kind. This approach stands in contrast with a possibility explored by Robert Nozick in his book *Philosophical Explanations*. Of the possibility, he writes that he is 'driven to entertain it (but not quite to endorsing it yet)'.[23]

Nozick suggests that 'the I is delineated, is synthesized around

[22] A different objection would be: 'Since the identity conditions for token experiences and thoughts make reference to the identity conditions for persons, one cannot think of such a token state without independently identifying in one's thought its possessor.' I attempt to answer this objection in the section of the next chapter entitled 'A Comparison'.

[23] (Cambridge, Mass.: Harvard UP, 1981), p. 87.

. . . [the] act of reflexive self-referring. An entity is synthesized around the reflective act and it is the ''I'' of that act'.[24] The details of what he means by 'synthesis' are not important for present purposes. What matters for us is his further claim that 'Only a theory of such a synthesized self can explain why, when we reflexively self-refer, we know it is *ourselves* to which we refer'.[25] He calls this knowledge immune to error through misidentification in Shoemaker's sense. Nozick is then here making a claim to the effect that an epistemological fact can be explained, and in fact explained only, by a particular account of the nature of the object thought about, rather than the way in which it is thought about.

There is an ambiguity in what is being said to be explained here. Is it for each person a conditional he knows, or is it a conditional only the consequent of which concerns his knowledge? The first case is

I know: if I say 'I', then the utterance of 'I' refers to me

while the second is

If I say 'I', then: I know the utterance of 'I' refers to me.

The latter is not a genuine datum in need of explanation, since it is not generally true. An utterance can occur and I be its producer without my knowing that I am its producer. I and my twin brother may both be in the same room, and both of us may try to utter the same sentence. If the vocal cords of one of the two of us are inoperative — we do not know which — and the normal forms of feedback which would tell one of us that he and not the other had produced the utterance have been severed, then neither of us will know whether he issued the utterance: but one of us did.[26]

In the first case, that in which the datum is construed as being that I know that *if* I say 'I', that utterance of 'I' refers to me, it seems that my belief that the utterance refers to me rests on two other beliefs I have, viz.:

[24] Ibid.
[25] p. 90.
[26] Earlier passages in *Philosophical Explanations* make it clear that Nozick is well aware of the possibility of such examples: so this second case should probably be rejected as an interpretation of his text.

The producer of utterance *u* of 'I' = me
Any utterance of 'I' refers to its producer.

From these two it follows that the utterance *u* of 'I' refers to me. Any account which allows a speaker to know these two premises will be capable of accounting for the first datum.

Nozick rightly contrasts one's knowledge that one is referring to oneself when one knows one has uttered 'I', with Oedipus' failure to know that he refers to himself when he utters 'the murderer of Laius'. This difference is present because although Oedipus knows

The producer of utterance *u* of 'the murderer of Laius' = me

(as thought by him), and also knows

Any utterance of 'the murderer of Laius' refers to the murderer of Laius,

he does not have the belief in the identity 'the murderer of Laius = me'; and so he is in no position to conclude that

The utterance *u* of 'the murderer of Laius' refers to me.

So we have the contrast between the first- and third-person cases without appeal to a theory of the synthesized self if we can explain the availability and content of the premises in the first-person case without appeal to such a theory.

Nozick does indeed raise the question of what it is for me to know that it was I who produced a certain utterance.[27] This in turn bears two different interpretations: the question may be 'What is it to know rather than to believe it?' or it may be 'What is the nature of the content, whether known or believed, "I produced that utterance"?'. Nozick seems rightly to be concerned with the second. The first question seems not to raise issues special to self-reference which are not equally raised by such questions as 'How can I know that it was I and not someone else who blew the candle out then?'. The second question is, however, at least offered an answer by the evidentially-based account of content we have been

[27] pp. 79–81.

trying to give. The content 'I produced that utterance' is one which is judged true when the question arises in the presence of evidence* that the person with these (the thinker's) conscious states produced that utterance. Nozick emphasizes that it is not sufficient for my judging that I produced that utterance that I know that *some* utterance of 'I produced that utterance' is true and that I understand English. But this would equally be explained on the evidentially-based theory: these conditions do not give one evidence* that the person with these conscious states and events produced that utterance, and it is for this reason that they do not put one in a position to judge that one produced the utterance oneself.

It may be helpful here to compare the first person with the present tense. It is equally a datum that I know that any current utterance of 'now' refers to now, the present moment. I can know this because I know that, for any such utterance u,

> The time of utterance u of 'now' = now
> Any utterance of 'now' refers to its time of utterance.

From these it follows that the utterance u of 'now' refers to now, the present moment. It does not seem that we need a theory of times as synthesized around acts of reference in either language or thought in order to explain these contents or my knowledge of them.

As we hinted, it is hard to see how Nozick's own theory can explain the datum he says it does, since the datum concerns what can be known, while the theory is not a theory of m.p.'s. Since an object can only be thought about in some particular way, the datum and the account of synthesized selves pass one another by. Perhaps, then, we simply ought to reconstrue Nozick's account as an account of m.p.'s. Is the first-person way of thinking somehow given by the sense of 'the producer of this act of reflexive self-reference'? The first question here is how the act is presented in this complex m.p. It cannot be a perceptual m.p.: from the examples already given, it is easy to see how it can be informative to think 'That act of reflexive self-reference is *mine*'. But a perceptual m.p. may not be the only way of thinking of an act of reference to oneself. There may also be an action-based way, whose constitutive role is 'the act produced by *this* attempt, or trying to speak'. That this act, if it exists, is one's own is indeed not informative. But it also brings the theory much closer to our own account of the constitutive role of the first person, since tryings or attempts at intentional action will be amongst the thinker's conscious states. When we adapt the theory further to accommodate uses of the first-person m.p. in thinking as well as in language, it is not clear that the result would be any different from our earlier suggestions on the constitutive role for the first person.

This is an appropriate point at which to add some remarks on the English first-person pronoun. Consider this passage from Barwise and Perry:

> Let us begin with the word *I*. A reasonable thing to say about this expression is that, whenever it is used by a speaker of English, it stands for, or designates, that person. We think that this is all there is to know about the meaning of *I* in English and that it serves as a paradigm rule for meaning.[28]

The claim that this is all there is to know about the meaning of 'I' in English seems plausible; but is it not in contradiction with the theory we have been developing? Would it not be more in line with the evidentially-based theory of sense to say that any account of 'I' which omits the fact that it is used in English to express the first-person m.p., whose constitutive role has exercised us so much, is incomplete? Certainly in earlier work, I myself suggested, as an axiom in a meaning theory for a fragment of English containing 'I', the principle that any utterer x of 'I' expresses the m.p. $[\text{self}_x]$.[29]

These points would not, however, show that Barwise and Perry are wrong. For the question we need to consider is this: does the rule giving the reference of 'I' on any occasion of its utterance in fact *determine* the m.p. expressed on any occasion? One way we can investigate this issue is to invent a hypothetical expression E, which we stipulate is to be governed by the rule (R):

(R) Any utterance of E refers to its producer.

We can now ask: are there any arguments we can give for saying that E as governed by such a rule would also express on any occasion of its utterance the first-person m.p. of the utterer?

If someone understands such an expression E, he will be disposed to judge that

---

[28] 'Situations and Attitudes', *Journal of Philosophy* 78 (1981), at p. 670.

[29] 'Demonstrative Thought and Psychological Explanation'.

Any utterance of E Smith produces refers to Smith;
Any utterance of E I produce refers to me;

and generally for any x, he will be disposed to judge that

Any utterance of E which x produces refers to x.

Someone who understands this language containing E is, simply in virtue of understanding it, in a position to know that when *he* utters 'E is thus-and-so', he is referring to himself (here he thinks of himself in the first-person way). It is not by contrast true that simply in virtue of understanding the language, he is in a position to know that when he utters 'E is thus-and-so', he is referring to Smith, not even if he is Smith — since he can understand the language without knowing whether or not he is Smith.

Now it is under the speaker's intentional control whether or not he utters 'E is thus-and-so'; others take it for granted that it is, and take it for granted that they all take it for granted. So if an utterance by Smith of 'E is thus-and-so' is regarded as sincere, it will be taken to express a first-person belief of Smith's; for Smith issued the utterance intentionally, knows that he produced that utterance, and, understanding the language, knows that he was referring to himself in doing so. But if Smith does not know that he is Smith, there will be no parallel argument to show that he knows that this utterance he intentionally produced refers to Smith. We seem to have, then, a reason for thinking that any expression governed by a rule like (R) will be taken when uttered as an expression of the first-person way of thinking. The argument rests on the fact that it is commonly known that each person usually knows of the utterances he intentionally produces that it is indeed he who is producing them.

The position I am endorsing, then, is one according to which: (a) Barwise and Perry are right in thinking that the reference rule for 'I' fully determines its meaning in English; (b) The first-person way of thinking or mode of presentation exists and it is important for understanding 'I' that one realize that this word is used to express thoughts containing m.p.'s of this type; (c) Points (a) and (b) are compatible because there is an argument that in this case the reference rule determines what m.p. is expressed. If this is indeed a possible position, it would be a *non sequitur* to argue from the fact that one cannot think of two different expressions with different meanings which are both governed by a reference rule like (R) to the conclusion that there is no need to make reference at any point to a first-person mode of presentation in giving an account of what is involved in understanding 'I' in English. It would equally be a *non sequitur* to argue from the same premise to the conclusion that the Cartesian phenomena we describe using 'I' can be fully explained in terms of the reference rule for 'I', without any need to appeal to the special properties of the first-person m.p. Both moves are incorrect because they ignore the possibility of the intermediate position (a)–(c). A word with a reference rule like (R) is indeed linked with the Cartesian and other distinctive first-person phenomena, but it is so because any such word will be used to express the first-person way of thinking.

Identificational Basicness

It is a point often made that some demonstrative thoughts about an object rest on no further identification of that object. What precisely should be meant by this? And can the evidential account explain the intended phenomena? We must take the former question first, and we will begin with some examples.

Suppose you are travelling in Europe. Having previously studied some maps showing annual average levels of rainfall, you come to have the belief 'This is the wettest place in Europe'. You also see what you take to be a busy café at this same place, and you come to believe 'There is a café at the wettest place in Europe'. This latter belief rests upon your former belief, the belief in the identity 'This is the wettest place in Europe'. Your beliefs 'There is a café here' and 'This café is busy', on the other hand, do not rest on that or any other identity belief. We can generalize the notions illustrated here in a definition. Let us say that someone's belief $F(r)$ rests on no identity concerning r iff there is no mode of presentation s such that his belief that $F(r)$ rests on his beliefs

$$r = s$$

and

$$F(s).$$

If someone consciously infers $F(r)$ from $F(s)$ and $r = s$, that is sufficient for his belief $F(r)$ to rest on an identity concerning r; but it is not necessary. What is necessary and sufficient is that some beliefs $r = s$ and $F(s)$ causally sustain his belief that $F(r)$, and do so because $F(r)$ follows by identity-elimination from those first two beliefs. Thus if someone's belief that $F(r)$ does rest on an identity concerning r, then (overdetermination and failsafe mechanisms aside) there is some belief $r = s$ he has and if he abandoned this belief, he would also abandon the belief that $F(r)$.

The concept of a belief resting upon an identity is relativized, to a person and a time. But we will want to say something general and unrelativized about the m.p.'s that can feature in empirical beliefs which do not rest upon identities. To this end we can introduce the notion of a kind of m.p. being *identificationally basic*. A kind K of m.p. is identificationally basic iff there is a range of concepts φ and a way of coming to know empirical thoughts of the form $\varphi(r)$, where r is of kind K, such that when known in this way, the belief that $\varphi(r)$ rests on no other beliefs. (This will be refined later.) In particular, then, such a belief that $\varphi(r)$ will rest on no identities concerning r. Thus perceptual demonstrative m.p.'s are plausibly identificationally basic because perception provides a way of coming to know that a perceptually presented object has some observationally determinable property without relying on any other beliefs about the world around one — in particular without relying on any identity belief concerning the perceptually presented object. There was such an absence of reliance on any identity belief in the simple example in which you come to believe 'This café is busy'. The descriptive m.p. 'the wettest place in Europe' does not, as things actually are, seem to belong to any identificationally basic kind. In the next chapter I shall be arguing that there are reasons for thinking that it will always be the case that any type of demonstrative m.p. is identificationally basic.

Suppose you believe $F(r)$, where r belongs to some identificationally basic kind, and that you have come to believe it in a way in virtue of which that kind is identificationally basic — for instance, as a result of your visual experience you come to believe of a man perceptually presented to you that he is bald, under a visual m.p. In such a case, Shoemaker would say that your belief is immune to error through misidentification relative to 'that man'. But we could equally speak here of immunity to *correctness* through identification:

the belief simply does not rest on an identity belief at all. Now suppose you believe that that (visually presented) man is the manager, and so judge that the manager is bald. There is a weak sense in which it will be an epistemic possibility for you that though that man is bald, the manager is not – since it is epistemically possible that that man is not the manager. The sense is given by the fact that some but not others of your beliefs could be false in such a way that though you know that that perceptually presented man is bald, you do not know the manager to be bald. By contrast, in a corresponding sense there is no m.p. τ such that it is epistemically possible for you that though τ is bald, that man (visually presented) is not. There is no such corresponding epistemic possibility. Now of course the distinctness of the m.p.'s 'that man' and 'the manager' already follows from Frege's test of cognitive significance, the identity 'that man is the manager' being potentially informative. But the distinctness of the m.p.'s 'that man' and 'the manager' does not guarantee that there is not what we just called 'the corresponding epistemic possibility', i.e. that there is no one such that it is epistemically possible that though he is bald, that man is not bald. 'The manager' and 'the owner' are distinct m.p.'s, but neither is identificationally basic.

Now is the lack of a corresponding epistemic possibility merely a fact about your possibly idiosyncratic cognitive structures, or is it rather a property of the very m.p.'s you employ in your thoughts? We have a strong intuition that in the example of a perceptual type of m.p. this lack of a corresponding epistemic possibility is not something idiosyncratic. Here we need to distinguish those types which are identificationally basic from those which are *constitutively* so. A constitutively identificationally basic type K is (i) identificationally basic and (ii) possession of a certain way of coming to know propositions of the form $\varphi(r)$ which makes K identificationally basic is partially constitutive of the ability to think thoughts containing m.p.'s of the type K. That is, failure to employ this way of coming to know them implies that the thinker would not possess the type K in his conceptual repertoire. It is when identificational basicness is constitutive that it is a feature of the type of m.p. itself, and not something idiosyncratic. In the example we just considered, it is plausible that it is constitutive: what makes a judgement 'that (perceptually presented) man is bald' have the content it does is in part that a thinker is disposed to make the judgement when a man presented in perception looks bald, and the thinker needs special reasons — for instance a belief that he may be hallucinating, that the presented man has been made up to act in a film, etc., before withholding the judgement in these circumstances.[30]

The idea of the identificationally basic needs one more refinement. Imagine a timid man who is not prepared to judge that a perceptually presented object has an observational property without first making the judgement, on the basis of evidence, that he is not hallucinating. From what has been said so far, it follows that this man's belief that that pencil has a sharp point, caused in part by his visual experience as of a sharp pencil, rests on another belief — the belief that he is not hallucinating. But if we are going to develop an account on which demonstrative types of m.p. are constitutively identificationally basic, then this bodes ill. For there seems no good reason to say that this timid man is not employing the very same constituents in the thoughts which he judges true as are employed by the less timid. We can say this: a belief is *derivative* iff it rests on beliefs other than beliefs concerning the perceptions, memories, abilities, and so forth, the occurrence or the result of the exercise of which are canonical evidence for making the judgement. So a judgement may rest on the thinker's belief that he is not hallucinating whilst still not being a derivative judgement. The official account of the identificational basicness of a type of m.p. now becomes this: it is required that there be a range of concepts and a way of coming to know empirical thoughts of the form $\varphi(r)$, where r is of the given type, such that when known in this way, the belief that $\varphi(r)$ is not derivative.

The fact that certain observational judgements about perceptually presented objects are identificationally basic follows from the evidential account we outlined. Consider a judgement of the form 'that (perceptually presented) box is cubic', based in quite ordinary circumstances on a visual perception as of a cubic box. This way of coming to know that thought together with the m.p.'s composing the thought guarantee that it is *one and the same thing* which is both identical with that perceptually presented box and is cubic. For 'that box' in this context refers to the box presented in experience as located in a certain region of space; while the experience

---

[30] In the first section of the next chapter there are examples of types of m.p. which are identificationally basic but not constitutively so.

presents the box located in that region as cubic.[31] In these circumstances, the thought 'that box is cubic' could be false because the experiencer has a retinal defect which distorts his experience of shape, or the object may not be a box, or it may be that it looks cubic only from that angle; but it could *not* be false by the m.p. 'that box' referring, there being something cubic in the given region, while the box is not the thing which is cubic. Since none of the features of the m.p.'s which guarantee this impossibility is contingent, the account equally explains the fact that such demonstratives are not just identificationally basic, but are constitutively so. The reference to the given region of physical space is crucial in the argument. The example of th box can be contrasted with one in which the thinker is watching a sprinting race, in which it is hard to distinguish which legs belong to whom. Then, naturally, the thought 'that fair-headed runner is wearing red shoes' does rest on an identification: that that runner is the owner of the legs with the red shoes.

We often have the ability to recognize objects and particularly people with whom we are very familiar. Someone who can recognize a particular thing will be able to think of it in a distinctive way, in virtue of his possessing this recognitional ability. We will use 'c' as a variable over this kind of m.p. Modes of presentation based on recognitional abilities never belong to any identificationally basic kind. Suppose you are able to recognize Michael Dummett (MD); and suppose you come on the basis of your perceptual experience to believe something about MD under the mode of presentation c. The belief can be knowledge, but it will still rest on an identity concerning c, viz., that this (perceptually presented) person *is c*. This will be so even if, as one would expect to be the case when a recognitional ability is exercised, the m.p. c enters the representational content of the experience. It is not a matter of judgement alone — rather the experience itself represents c as thus-and-so. The fact that in such an example the beliefs that MD is thus-and-so and that this man is MD may well be acquired simultaneously does not prevent the former from resting on the

---

[31] Note that it is the region of physical space in which the object is presented which matters here, rather than the region of sensational space in which it is presented. Two different material objects located at different places at a given time may in a sense have the same location in the visual field: a circular panel of grating and a larger opaque circular disk at a suitable distance behind it may occupy the same region of the visual field when the scene is viewed monocularly.

latter. An experience can cause one to acquire a structure of beliefs simultaneously, a structure in which some beliefs are rationally dependent upon others, beliefs which would be abandoned if those others were abandoned. The structure of beliefs suddenly acquired by a detective when he is struck by the solution to a murder may have this property. There is no contradiction in a belief both resting upon an identity in the sense of being causally and rationally sustained by it, even though it did not initially result from a temporal sequential process of conscious inference.

The difference between m.p.'s based on recognitional abilities and perceptual demonstratives is shown also in the fact that if an experience is totally hallucinatory, an attempt to think of an object under a perceptual m.p. will not result in the subject's thinking a thought about a perceptually presented object at all — for there is no object to which he stands in the relation requisite for thinking of an object in this type of way. But in judging on the basis of his hallucinatory experience 'c is amused', his thought is still about MD — for it is MD who played a special causal role in the generation of his ability.

Perceptual m.p.'s can be said to be *experience-dependent* in the following sense: whether a type on a particular occasion really has a corresponding token depends on whether there is an object standing in a certain relation to a particular token experience, and it is contingent whether any object stands in the relation to such an experience. More particularly, the existence of a token of a given perceptual type will depend upon the relations of the particular sensational features of the experience which are definitive of the type of perceptual m.p. in question. If an object seems to be presented in a particular region of the upper left of one's visual field, then whether there really is a corresponding token m.p. of this type on a particular occasion will depend specifically on what causally explains (and how) the features of the particular region in the upper left of one's visual field. Modes of presentation based on recognitional abilities are not in this way experience-dependent. In an analogous sense we can say that memory demonstratives made available by one's memory images ('that Greek island') are in a corresponding way image-dependent. But perceptual m.p.'s and their memory analogues are not the only m.p.'s which are experience-dependent. The demonstrative types [this ^{T} place] and [this ^{T} time] we introduced earlier are also experience-dependent. Whether in a given context these types have a corresponding object, whether they have an associated token m.p., depends on the contingent relations of the given experience of type T. This is true even though places and times are not literally perceived. Nor should one conclude that all demonstrative m.p.'s are experience-dependent; for [self] is not. Though experience plays a certain part in its constitutive role, it will not be contingent that there is an associated object. Nor is [now] experience-dependent.

It may be wondered whether the evidential account of demonstratives we have outlined is not going to give a false description of which of our judgements rest upon other judgements. Suppose you have a memory image of type M of being on an ocean liner, and suppose this causes you to judge that you were once on an ocean liner. Now it is not *a priori* true that the person with *these* conscious states — here you think demonstratively of your own conscious states — is the person who was at [that ^M_x place]. So does not my view force us to say that in this example your judgement that you were on a liner rests on your two beliefs (i) that the person at [that ^M_x place] was then on a liner and (ii) that you are identical with the person who was at [that ^M_x place]? The view that the judgement does so rest we label 'the identity-based view', or view (A). The advocate of (A) might note that it is certainly the case that you would *ceteris paribus* abandon the belief that you were on an ocean liner if that belief were not overdetermined and you came to judge that you are not identical with the person at [that^M_x place]. This could be either because you come to believe that the image is not veridical, or because this apparent memory is a q-memory in Shoemaker's sense — it is caused in an appropriate way by an experience of past events of the kind it depicts, but the events did not happen to you. View (A) stands opposed to a view at the other extreme; this is the view (B) that the judgement rests on no identity, since the fact in our world there are not q-memories which are not memories is partially constitutive of your concept of yourself; in worlds of the kinds described by Shoemaker and Parfit,[32] our actual concepts of personal identity would have no application — the concepts we would exercise in those circumstances would be new ones. View (B) can be labelled 'the different-

[32] S. Shoemaker, 'Persons and their Pasts', *American Philosophical Quarterly* 7 (1970), 269–85; D. Parfit, 'Personal Identity', *Philosophical Review* 80 (1971), 3–27.

concept view'. *Its* advocate is likely to note that judgements about one's past based on memory-like images are noninferential, and that it is doubtful that anyone whose noninferential judgements lacks such a causal sensitivity has the full first-person m.p. in his conceptual repertoire.

There are difficulties with both of these extreme views (A) and (B). We can take (A), the identity-based view, first. We have indeed already agreed that a belief may be both acquired noninferentially and sustained by an identity belief. But the advocate of (A) needs more than that. For he takes it that anyone with a first-person concept must have the concept either of [that ^M_x place], or of a quasi-memory, and this seems to be false. From the fact that if someone were to come to doubt that he was at [that ^M_x place], he would abandon a given belief, it does not follow that the latter belief rested all along on the belief that he was at [that ^M_x place] — he might not in the actual world, consistently with the truth of that counterfactual, even possess the concepts required to frame that belief. For this reason the case is unlike that of the detective. If we followed the lines suggested by the advocate of (A), we would also have to say that some very primitive judgements rest on some highly sophisticated identities. Consider the judgement 'the door is now shut', based on a visual experience as of the door being shut. Suppose this experience is of type T. Now it is in a very weak sense epistemically possible that [this ^T_t time] $\neq$ [now $_d$] — for instance there could be a very long time lag in perception. In such circumstances, one could truly think: 'These events [perceptually presented] are not happening now'. By the standards of the advocate of (A), we would have to conclude that the ordinary judgement 'the door is now shut' rests on the identity '[now $_d$] = [this ^T_t time]'. Indeed by his standards, even the present-tense judgement 'there is a door in front of me' caused by a visual experience would be counted as resting on an identity, since my optic nerve might be connected by radio links to someone else's retina. The advocate of (A)'s use of 'resting on an identity' is too permissive.

It is difficult to attack view (B) decisively since 'concept' is a term of art, and there must be some sense or other (a sense perhaps more happily picked out by 'conception') on which Shoemakerian worlds where some q-memories are not memories of the subject's own past, people will have a different 'concept' of themselves. But if 'concept' here is used as cognate with Fregean *Sinn*, then there are arguments against (B). If two people differ in what they take as sufficient for judging a content of a given type – e.g. 'I was on a liner' – to be true, this difference cannot show the contents of their judgements to be distinct if they also differ in their background beliefs. But there will be such differences of background beliefs between someone in our world and someone who knows himself to be in a Shoemakerian world – the former will take for granted something the latter will disbelieve. So there is no straightforward argument from these different evidential sensitivities to difference of content. This point also applies to [now]: in a world in which people do occasionally have long time lags in perception, it would not be surprising that they require more than we do before being prepared to judge 'the door is now shut'. It does not follow that they have a different concept of the present. Finally against (B) one should note that in the weakest sense of epistemic possibility, for someone who in the actual world *does* have the concept [that ^{M} place], it *is* epistemically possible that he was not the person at [that ^M_x place]. This gives another reason for saying that in the Fregean sense the content of first-personal thoughts in the actual and the Shoemakerian worlds are not distinct: their places in patterns of cognitive significance in the weakest sense seem to be the same. In fact, if the world were to become Shoemakerian, someone with an actual first-person concept would no doubt initially make mistakes in his past-tense first-person judgements, but eventually his practice would be like those who had permanently inhabited a Shoemakerian world.

If these objections are good, there must be a third view which avoids the difficulties of (A) and (B). One third possibility is this. There are many concepts which have all of the following features. (i) It is constitutive of possession of the concept that its application is sensitive to evidence of a certain kind; (ii) someone who has the concept will not in all possible circumstances take evidence of that kind as conclusive for its application – he would in some circumstances withhold application even though the evidence is present; and (iii) someone can have mastery of the concept without possessing the concepts necessary to formulate fully what would be the case if some possibility of the sort in (ii) were realized. The concept of a cylinder possessed by a blind man who can identify (some) cylinders by feeling them would be an example. Here we distinguish, as before, between a property — that of being cylindrical — and an m.p. of that property; so we can distinguish the blind man's from the sighted man's concept of a cylinder, without denying that they are thinking of the very same physical shape. The blind man's concept has a constitutive sensitivity in its application to certain tactual sensation (feature (i)), but in circumstances in which he has evidence of a tactual hallucination he will withdraw an earlier judgement that an object was clyindrical (feature (ii)); and these properties are consistent, if he is an unsophisticated subject, with his lacking the concept of experience (feature (iii)), at least before he has any tactual hallucinations.

The type [self] seems to have properties (i)–(iii). The constitutive role 'the person with these conscious states' was intended to capture what is essential to the first-person m.p., in the sense that it does not take any background beliefs or presuppositions for granted. There is no inconsistency (thought of course the general phenomenon needs to be better understood) in a thinker's never having contemplated certain possibilities — for instance that of q-memories which are not memories — while his concepts have determinate applications were those possibilities to obtain.

Still, it may be questioned whether what I have said is consistent. Earlier, I expressed scepticism about the intelligibility of nonconclusive canonical evidence which is not entailed (at least in important specified conditions) by the thought for which it is evidence. But in the case of clause (i) above, in relation to past-tense first-person thoughts, do we not have precisely such a case? For the memory image is not conclusive; even if we add as an 'important specified condition' that it is a genuine q-memory of some past experience, the experience may not have belonged to the subject now making the past-tense first-person judgement. This certainly needs clarification. It is true that a particular q-memory the thinker possesses need not represent any of his past encounters. What is not possible is that almost all his q-memories be q-memories of some past person with whom he is not identical (or, better, to whom he does not stand in the relations which matter in personal identity), precisely because of the role of memory in personal survival. So indeed a sensitivity of past-tense first-person judgements to the subject's q-memories does not require sensitivity to any given apparent memory: there has rather to be such a sensitivity to a preponderance of those apparent memories. This point shows that the advocate of (B) in citing the constitutive character of some such sensitivity was not making a point that can be explained only by his own theory.

The type [now] is not perfectly analogous to [self]. We noted that a thought of the form '[this ^T_t time] is not [now $_t$]' can be true, and this without failure of perception; such thoughts could even be generally or universally true. So clause (i) above is not true of [now]. It is plausible, though, that if someone is not conceptually and theoretically sophisticated, in making present-tense judgements about the perceptible world, he must at least start by taking an experience as telling him about the world at the time the experience occurs of its occurrence. He may revise this supposition later, in the light of a theory of perception, but without that initial base, it is hard to see how he could reach the stage of obtaining evidence which suggests that that first base should be abandoned. But if someone is at that initial base, (ii) and (iii) above can still be true of him; so we still have an account of how he can be employing an m.p. with the constitutive role we assigned to [now], and why experience plays a distinctive role in present-tense judgements, without falling into either of the extreme views (A) and (B).

It should be emphasized that these points are not meant to imply that there are no types of example for which the attitudes expressed by the advocate of view (B) are appropriate. There can be cases in which, because of what we take for granted, our actual concepts are genuinely different from any of those we would employ if we knew what we actually take for granted to be false. An example would be a case in which someone judges 'this book is the same as the one I was reading yesterday', and in which, because of some trick set-up and contrary to his beliefs, the book he now feels is distinct from the book he now sees. There is no reason that his judgement must have a determinate truth value, for there is no reason that it should have been settled that one of the tactual and visual m.p.'s is to take precedence over the other. The m.p. exhibiting this indeterminacy is genuinely different from the more refined m.p.'s which would be employed were such divergences common. The point of the earlier paragraphs has just been that the first-person m.p. is not like this case: there is no indeterminacy as to whether 'I was φ', based on a quasi-memory which is not a genuine memory of the subject, a subject who never was φ, is true or not — it is not.

The idea of guaranteed reference is found in some discussions of demonstrative thought. What is its relation to identificational basicness? In fact it appears that neither the range of identificationally basic types, nor the range of constitutively identificationally basic types, coincides exactly with the class of m.p.'s guaranteed to have references. 'Guaranteed reference' needs some elucidation. Suppose a type with guaranteed reference is a type with this property: that whenever someone supposes himself to be thinking a thought containing an m.p. of that type, there is indeed such an m.p. and it refers. In that case some identificationally basic types lack a guarantee of reference. Perceptual m.p.'s when the subject fails to realize he is hallucinating provide an obvious example. Nor is a guarantee of reference in this sense sufficient for identificational basicness. Modes of presentation of the form 'my paternal grandfather' have an empirical guarantee of reference for normal humans, and m.p.'s of the form 'the oldest person now alive if there is a unique such person and me otherwise' have an *a priori* guarantee of reference in that sense. But neither is identificationally basic.[33] Nor is it sufficient for a type to be identificationally basic that if a member *m* of that type refers to a particular object, then a thinker using *m* in a thought believes of that object, (relationally) that it is the thing which falls under *m*. (With more apparatus this could be formulated more precisely.) That is insufficient because m.p.'s based on recognitional abilities also pass this test. If you have been hallucinating in seeming to see MD, you will indeed believe of MD that he is MD. In fact this test will be passed by any m.p. which is relational, in the sense that which object it picks out depends not upon the object's fitting a definite description, but upon which object stands in certain complex relations to the thinker. Not all relational m.p.'s are identificationally basic, and this is something an adequate theory of indexical thought must explain.

Finally, to say that a type of m.p. is identificationally basic is not in any way to imply that some substantive identity involving an m.p. of that type is guaranteed to be true. The definition of the

[33] Let us abbreviate the phrase 'the oldest person . . .' specifying the second of these examples by 'β'. Then it is true that if I am hungry, then I am in a position to know the empirical truth 'If there is no unique oldest person alive now, then β is hungry'. But this does not make β identificationally basic: for this knowledge is inferred from my belief that I am hungry.

identicationally basic adverts only to ways of coming to know thoughts which do not rest on other beliefs; it does not guarantee knowledge of substantive identities. At one point, Anscombe writes that 'I' is an expression X which has guaranteed reference in this sense: 'not just that there is such a thing as X, but also that what I take to be X is X'.[34] It is difficult to take this literally and to make it come out true and distinct from the senses of 'guaranteed reference' already considered. Anscombe would surely allow that a bishop can see a woman dressed as a bishop in a mirror and take that woman, wrongly, to be himself.

[34] 'The First Person', p. 57. This passage must be just a minor slip on Anscombe's part, for taking her words at face value would require attributing to her a position seemingly incompatible with her later positive theory of 'I am this thing here': she says that an utterance of this sentence means 'this thing here is the . . . person . . . of whose action *this* idea of action is an idea, of whose movements *these* ideas of movement are ideas, of whose posture *this* idea of posture is the idea . . . of which *these* intended actions, if carried out, will be the actions' (p. 61). One can mistakenly identify someone else as meeting these conditions.

6

Demonstrative Content II

A Criterion, Evidence and Action

From the preceding chapter emerges this necessary condition for a type of m.p. to be demonstrative:

> A type of m.p. is demonstrative only if at any given time its constitutive role concerns the then current psychological states of the thinker.

Thus the constitutive role of [self] is 'the person who has *these* conscious states', the constitutive role of [now] is 'the time of that thinking', and so forth. The basic idea is that for a genuinely demonstrative component $[\Delta_x]$ of a thought, the pattern of evidential sensitivity someone must display in his willingness to judge thoughts containing that component is distinguished by its relation to some of the thinker's current psychological states, in the way specified by the constitutive role of Δ.[1]

It may be tempting to suppose that the states mentioned in the constitutive role of a genuine demonstrative must be conscious states. But this would be tendentious. It would exclude the possibility of unconscious judgements which have exactly the same demonstrative contents as may be possessed by conscious judgements. We ought not to deny the conceivability of some psychological theory which claims that persons sometimes have unconscious beliefs to the effect that it is now the case that so-and-so, or that that (perceptually presented) person is thus-and-so. An unconscious judgement of the former type would contain an m.p.

---

[1] In the case of experience-dependent types, some of these judgements (such as 'That (perceptually presented) apple is green') will be caused by the token experiences mentioned in the type's constitutive role at a given time. But such judgements are not always caused by the psychological state mentioned in the constitutive role. The constitutive role of [now] is 'the time of that thinking', and it would be absurd to say that thinking one is cold causes one's judgement that one is cold.

whose constitutive role is 'the time of occurrence of that judgement', where the judgement referred to is not conscious.

Is the necessary condition for types being demonstrative also sufficient? It is not. The mixed descriptive–demonstrative 'my paternal grandfather' has a constitutive role which concerns the thinker's current psychological states: it is 'the paternal grandfather of the person with *these* conscious states'. Similarly, the m.p. 'the best friend of the architect who designed this (perceptually presented) city' has a constitutive role concerning the thinker's current experiences of a city, but is no demonstrative m.p. of that best friend. One cannot exclude these cases by noting that the English expressions here formulating constitutive role contain descriptive functors ('the best friend of ξ', 'the paternal grandfather of ξ') applied to demonstrative phrases – for two reasons. First, as we said we are concerned to explain a distinction in thought, not language; and second, the exclusion would be too strong, if one can think of oneself and the present demonstratively. For the constitutive roles we have given to these m.p.'s are of the form 'the person who has these conscious states' and 'the time of that thinking', and these contain descriptive functors applied to demonstrative expressions.

To provide a sufficient condition proves to be complex. So that we can take the problem in stages, let us initially confine our attention to the problem of a sufficient condition in the special case of perceptual demonstratives. We will generalize later.

Is it necessary and sufficient for a type to be a perceptual demonstrative type that, on the basis of the token experience which its constitutive role concerns, one knows where the presented object is located? This would certainly exclude 'that man's paternal grandfather' and 'the best friend of this city's architect'; but it would also exclude too much. Looking at the moon, I may think 'the Americans landed in that crater (perceptually presented)'. I may think this, and also know that atmospheric conditions are bending the light rays, so that I do not know in which direction from me (let alone distance) the crater is located. This can also happen in cases closer to home. One may be walking on the beach and see a life-saving wire stretched out from the beach into the sea. If there are no cues for distance, one may see the wire now as close, now as far; but such oscillation does not prevent one from all the time remaining capable of thinking of that wire in a perceptual demonstrative way. Should the suggestion then be weakened by the proposal that in experience the object be presented as in a certain location, or at least direction, whether or not this is known? This would still prevent one from thinking in a perceptual demonstrative way of a shot fired from a gun or of an oboe on the basis of a monaural auditory experience.

These examples suggest that we should give a simple criterion to the effect that a type is a perceptual demonstrative m.p. 'that F' iff in any experience mentioned in the constitutive role of a token of that type, the object presented by 'that F' is perceived as an F. This condition is to be understood in turn as a constitutive requirement: there must be an experience with this feature whenever the type is employed in thought. Thus, though of course when looking at a city one might happen to see the architect's best friend, one can employ the mixed descriptive–demonstrative m.p. 'the best friend of this city's architect' in thought without seeing him and still pick out an object; but for 'this (perceptually presented) man' to refer, one must perceive the man. Strictly, it may be too strong to require for 'that (perceptually presented) F' to refer that the referent be experienced as an F. It seems to be sufficient that it be presented as a G, for some kind G of members of which F may be predicated. Thus one may judge 'that acid is damaging the table', but one sees the liquid just as a liquid, not as an acid. An alternative stance, one on which we do not need to decide here, is that the stronger principle is true and the thought itself (as opposed to its natural linguistic expression) should be analyzed as 'that liquid is an acid and is damaging the table'. Both requirements are stronger than the requirement that the concept of a man must enter the representational content of the experience. For that condition would be met by an experience in which at night one sees a shadow of a man in front of oneself, and sees it as stretching out from behind one. One sees it as a shadow of a man behind one, and the content of this 'as of' clause is specified using the concept of a man. But in these circumstances one does not think of the man under a perceptual m.p.: one thinks of him descriptively as 'the man casting that shadow'. On the present suggestion this is because one does not see the man as a man or as anything else.

There is no immediate generalization from this test for perceptual demonstratives to a test for demonstratives of other types, since in thinking of a place as 'here' or a time as the present, the object thought about cannot be perceived, and in thinking of oneself in the first-person way one need not be currently perceiving oneself. But there is a less direct generalization to the other cases; for the criterion for perceptual demonstratives exemplifies a more abstract principle which can be applied to the other cases.

When the concept F specifies the aspect under which the referent is perceived in an experience which allows employment of the perceptual demonstrative 'that F', the following seems to be true:

> An ability to make noninferentially, knowledgeably, and non-derivatively on the causal basis of that experience, empirical judgements of the form 'that F is thus-and-so' is constitutive of possession of that concept F.

Someone could no doubt in some sense think of the property of being an apple by means of a descriptive biochemical specification of the genetic structure of apples; but it is by now a familiar point that, by a Fregean test, such a thinker would be employing a different m.p. from that we use. Anyone not disposed to judge on the basis of visual experience in which an apple is obviously presented 'that apple is green', 'that apple is not shiny', and so on for other true thoughts containing observational concepts he possesses is not employing our concept of an apple. (This does not exclude the presence of natural kind elements in the concept.) We can call the principle displayed above and which generalizes this idea 'the strong principle'.

Perceptual demonstratives also exemplify a weaker abstract principle:

> There are some circumstances such that it is partially constitutive of the presence of perceptual m.p.'s in a thinker's repertoire that he be disposed in those circumstances to make empirical, knowledgeable, nonderivative judgements of thoughts containing such m.p.'s.

This principle is weaker because it concerns only what is required for possession of perceptual m.p.'s of the form 'that F', and not for possession of the general concept F.

It is the weaker, and not the stronger, principle which generalizes to give a criterion of demonstrative type. To generalize the stronger principle would have the following consequences: that one could not have the concept of place without that of [this ^{T} place] and [that ^{M} place], nor that of time without that of [this ^{T} time]. This must be wrong, since we had the concepts of place and time before we introduced these invented demonstratives. The stronger principle also has implausible consequences for demonstratives we normally employ. It would entail that no one could have the concept of a dog, say, without having memory-image demonstratives ('that dog') in his repertoire. But in fact there seems no contradiction in a man's having the concept of a dog, of the past, having propositional memories, recognitional abilities and the ability to find his way around, while not having any memory *images*.

Generalizing the weaker principle, we obtain this:

A type is demonstrative iff

(a) its constitutive role at any given time concerns the thinker's then current psychological states, and

(b) there are circumstances such that it is constitutive of the presènce of m.p.'s of that type in a thinker's repertoire that he is, in those circumstances, disposed to make empirical, knowledgeable, nonderivative judgements of thoughts containing components of that type.

Thus take [this ^{T} place]. In the absence of reasons for believing he is hallucinating, a thinker must be prepared to make such judgements as that there is a tree at [this ^{T} place] if an experience of type T represents a tree as being in front of him. Not to be so prepared casts doubt on the hypothesis that the thinker is really employing the type [this ^{T} place] in his thoughts. Analogous remarks apply to [this ^{T} time] and to [that ^{M} place], and also to memory demonstratives.

By contrast, there is nothing in the m.p. itself which requires that one should, on the basis of one's experiences, be able knowledgeably and nonderivatively to judge empirical thoughts of the form 'the place five miles north of [this ^{T} place] is φ'. 'The place five miles north of [this ^{T} place]' has a constitutive role concerning the thinker's current conscious psychological states and so meets part (a) of the general criterion, but it fails on part (b). For the same reason, 'my paternal grandfather' is not a genuine demonstrative: it is not a requirement for employing this m.p. that one be able to make empirical, nonderivative judgements to the effect that one's paternal grandfather is thus-and-so. Nor do recognitionally-based ways of thinking pass the test. A thinker may be able to recognize Mrs Thatcher visually and correspondingly may employ a special recognitionally-based way c of thinking of her. The circumstances which seem the most likely candidate to fulfil part (b) of the criterion are those in which the thinker sees Mrs Thatcher, and she presents an appearance of the type by which he recognizes her. But even in these circumstances, as we argued in the previous chapter, judgements to the effect that c is thus-and-so and which are caused by the visual experience still rest on the identity belief 'That (perceptually presented) person is identical with c'. The judgement is derivative, whereas (b) required nonderivative judgements.

This clearly leaves a theoretical question unanswered. Why is the stronger principle true of perceptual demonstratives but not of the other demonstratives, of [this ^T_x place], or of memory demonstratives? Here is a tentative suggestion. When one has an observational concept F, thoughts to the effect that . . . F . . . are thoughts about a property so conceived that in normal circumstances, one encounters an F (and so is in a position to judge 'that's an F') iff one has an experience as of an F. This entails that in normal circumstances, if one has an experience as of an F, one is disposed to judge 'That's an F'; and so for any observational concept one possesses, one will be in a position in those circumstances and with suitable experiences to judge whether 'that F is φ' for an observational concept φ. But there is no comparable connection between possession of an observational concept and what, if anything, it is like for one to *have* encountered an F; so it is not surprising that memory demonstratives do not meet the stronger criterion.

If this suggestion is correct, is it purely contingent? Could there be a being whose thoughts about a kind G are thoughts which involve some conception of what it is like to *have* experienced a G? The problem is that in a certain sense memory is memory of an experience. A memory is a memory of what it was like to encounter a G then – an encounter that would then have been registered in the present tense. (This is not to say that the propositional content of the memory is about experience.) For this reason it seems barely intelligible to suppose that someone could know what it is like to have encountered a G without being in a position to know what it would be like to encounter one now – for a present experience of a G is simply an experience of the same general type as the one remembered.

As one might expect, there are connections between general epistemology and this criterion for demonstrative type. Just as a belief that τ is φ may rest on an identity concerning τ, so it may also rest on a condition thought to be sufficient for being φ. Someone may for example believe that this (perceptually presented) rod is magnetic, and this belief may rest on his two beliefs that (a) if it attracts iron filings, it is magnetic, and (b) it is attracting iron filings. We can introduce the notion of the belief 'τ is φ' resting on a φ-sufficient belief: the belief so rests iff it is causally sustained appropriately by two beliefs of the forms (a) that if τ is ψ, it is φ, and (b) that τ is ψ. Just as not all singular beliefs that τ is φ can rest on identities concerning τ, on pain of infinite regress, similarly not all such beliefs can rest on φ-sufficient beliefs. Now an inferred belief is knowledge only if the beliefs from which it is inferred are known. So if inferential knowledge about particulars which does not rest only on general beliefs is to be possible, some beliefs 'τ is φ' which do not rest on any identities or φ-sufficient conditions must be knowledge. The second part of the criterion for demonstrative type in effect says that some demonstrative beliefs fulfil that requirement.

In 'Demonstrative Thought and Psychological Explanation', I argued for what I labelled 'the Indispensability Thesis' (IT).[2] This thesis states that no set of attitudes gives a satisfactory propositional attitude explanation of a person's acting on a given object unless the content of those attitudes includes a demonstrative m.p. of that object. There should be a connection between the IT and a proper criterion for demonstrative type; for if the IT is true and the criterion for demonstrative type is correct, one ought to be able to say why the IT is true on the basis, in part, of that criterion. Such an explanation would show that the evidential conception of

[2] Section III.

content as applied to demonstrative types can explain the connection of those types with the rational explanation of intentional action. We will give here just the beginnings of an account.

Consider an example in which we explain your walking up to a particular man by citing your intention to shake hands with that (perceptually presented) man. The direction in which you walk varies systematically with the position your experience represents him as occupying relative to yourself. If in an intention you think of a man descriptively, as when you intend to shake hands with the richest man in London, then there is no saying on the basis of your then current psychological states in which direction you would or should walk. There is equally no saying if you have a similar intention in which you think of a man in a way based on an ability to recognize him. Now both m.p.'s based on recognitional abilities and indexical m.p.'s may be described as relational, in that a subject's ability to think of someone in one of these types of ways is dependent upon the relations in which the thinker stands to that person. So we would not obtain a true principle were we to replace 'demonstrative m.p.' in the Indispensability Thesis with 'relational m.p.' The special feature of demonstrative m.p.'s is this: when you think of an object demonstratively, there is a relation in which you stand to that object and in which you stand in virtue of the relations of your current psychological states, the psychological states mentioned in the constitutive role for the demonstrative. Systematic variation in the subject's actions dependent upon his current psychological states will systematically alter his relations to the objects demonstratively presented to him. It will not in any systematic and regular way alter his relations to objects not demonstratively presented to him.

Consider a man who has to catch a train. At first he does not judge any thought of the form 'I must leave now if I am to catch it'; ten minutes later he does judge a thought of that form. There is an event of his judging such a thought true. The constitutive role of [now] is 'the time of that judgement'. So if the man acts simultaneously with the state of his judging the thought true, he will be acting at the time demonstratively presented in the thought. Here we have a clear case in which it is the fact that some current psychological state enters the constitutive role of [now] which allows [now] to be so closely tied to intentional action on or at the object demonstratively presented. Because the time presented by [now$_t$] is the one bearing a certain relation to the state of judgement, actions suitably related to that state bear systematically corresponding relations to the time t demonstratively presented. One could equally develop a similar illustration for the case of perceptual and other demonstratives. Here then is an outline, which will need more filling in, of how the criterion for demonstrative type can explain the truth of the IT.

One feature of this outline of the connections between the evidential and the action-related properties of demonstratives is that it can also explain the restrictions on the IT. We would not necessarily expect any actions on an object if the only way it is demonstratively presented in a subject's thoughts is by a memory-demonstrative. As originally formulated, the IT was restricted to present-tense demonstratives; that is, to those types Δ such that necessarily for any object x if someone employs [Δ_x] in his thought at some time, then x exists at that same time.[3] This restriction is motivated intuitively by considering examples, but the outline above suggests a general explanation of the need for the restriction. We have said that the action-related features of a demonstrative exist because the subject can make his actions bear certain relations to the psychological state mentioned in the constitutive role of the demonstrative. In doing so, the agent will bring himself into certain relations with the object demonstratively presented. But there is a systematic, uniform connection between the actions and the relations the agent ends up bearing to the object only if an object, demonstratively presented in a particular way, necessarily bears certain *current* relations to the psychological state mentioned in the constitutive role. This will not be true of memory demonstratives: in fact it will be true only of present-tense demonstratives. This explains the restriction on the IT.

What then is the relation of this notion of a demonstrative m.p. to the other concepts that have occurred in this discussion? There are three cases of interest: the relation of the notion of a demonstrative m.p. to (a) demonstrative expressions of English, (b) the identificationally basic types, and (c) the constitutively identificationally basic types.

There are demonstrative m.p.'s which are not expressed by any indexical word or phrase of English — the demonstrative type

---

[3] 'Demonstrative Thought and Psychological Explanation', p. 205.

[this $_1^T$ time], is one such. What of the converse? Is every indexical word of English a word which expresses a demonstrative m.p.? Let us take 'yesterday' and raise the question of whether this expresses just the mixed descriptive–demonstrative m.p. 'the day immediately before today', rather than a demonstrative m.p. of a day. It is hard to see any objection to the view that it expresses a mixed m.p. on the grounds of concept possession: it is hard to see how someone could entertain thoughts containing the m.p. expressed by 'yesterday' without having the concept 'today' and the relation 'before'.

We can imagine someone who often remembers as much about the past as we do, but occasionally forgets altogether what happened on a particular day. It is not merely that he forgets the day upon which certain remembered events occurred, but rather that he forgets the events of that day altogether. Knowing that this sometimes happens to him, he never has noninferential beliefs about what happend to him yesterday based on memory and if he did, they would not in his circumstances be knowledge; such beliefs he has rather to reach by inferences concluding 'so that day must have been yesterday'. This person is still capable of the same thoughts we can have, but does not have all the ways of reaching them which we possess. He stands to us as we ourselves stand to a being who knows on occasion without inference what he did seven days ago. Such a being has a way of coming to believe thoughts that we can also believe, but he can come to believe them in a way we cannot. The argument for saying that such a new way of knowing does not bring with it a new m.p. is that the m.p. employed in thought by someone in connection with the new ability does not have a new place in the pattern of epistemic possibilities. In fact it seems to have exactly the same place as the m.p. 'seven days ago'. Similarly, our actual ability to know noninferentially thoughts of the 'yesterday' type is not constitutive of possession of that type.

This is not to say that temporal abilities never give rise to new m.p.'s: on the contrary, they sometimes do. Someone may have the ability reliably to indicate a temporal interval of a certain length from any initial moment he chooses; for such a person the thought '*that* interval from *now* to . . . *now* (of the length he can repeatably indicate) is five seconds' can be informative, and there are thoughts such as 'the time from *that* event to *that* event (both presented by memory images) took *that* interval of time'. These are thoughts not available to the thinker without the temporal ability. The same applies to a spatial ability which might be exercised using the hands (and 'that length (indicated by the hands) is twenty centimetres' would equally be informative). A spatial example with properties corresponding to those we are attributing to the sense of 'yesterday' is this. Someone taking a long walk may at its conclusion know the direction (shown by pointing) and approximate distance from him of his starting point, and this without any process of working out or calculation. His walking companion may lack this ability, but can still reach by laborious reasoning the very same thought about the direction of their starting point which the first walker knows without calculation. As in the case of 'yesterday', an ability to reach such a conclusion noninferentially and knowledgeably does not seem required of anyone who can employ in thought the m.p. of the day or direction or else day.

We may tentatively conclude, subject to the opponent of the mixed view producing a better account of its constitutive role, that the m.p. expressed by 'yesterday' consists of a descriptive component 'the day just before ξ' applied to the genuine demonstrative 'today'. Most of us in fact have the ability automatically to realign our temporal indexical thoughts as time passes. You have the ability, if you believed yesterday 'today is φ', to believe today 'Yesterday was φ' without any reasoning. Our conclusion about 'yesterday' does not involve denying that to be capable of temporal thought a subject must have *some* ability to realign his temporal thoughts noninferentially. It is denied only that, for every English indexical which picks out a time a certain interval earlier, to understand that expression one must have the ability to realign noninferentially with respect to that interval.

Now we can turn to the second concept, that of the identificationally basic. Is every identificationally basic type demonstrative? We have already argued that the sense of 'yesterday' is not purely demonstrative; so if we can show it to be identificationally basic, some identificationally basic types are not purely demonstrative.

Suppose you learn on Tuesday that interest rates have fallen earlier in the day. You entirely forget who told you this and in what circumstances: by Tuesday afternoon you just retain the information that interest rates fell that day. On Wednesday your thought is realigned and you remember that interest rates fell yesterday. Does this belief of yours rest upon any identity concerning yesterday? That is, is there some m.p. τ such that your belief that interest rates fell yesterday rests upon the two beliefs 'Yesterday = τ' and 'Interest rates fell on τ'? It seems there is no such m.p. Indeed even in a case in which you do remember the occasion on which you were told, there would still be a belief concerning yesterday which rests on no identity concerning yesterday. For if one's belief that interest rates fell yesterday rests just upon the beliefs that interest rates fell the day of *that* conversation (presented by a memory image) and that that conversation took place yesterday, this second belief is still a belief about yesterday resting upon no identity concerning yesterday. Certainly, in the original case in which you have purely propositional memory, not resting upon other beliefs, that interest rates fell yesterday, you would suspend belief if you came to believe that you were not keeping track of time correctly. But this does not show the belief to be *derivative* in the sense we have been using since the last chapter, since the method employed is not one possession of which is required for employment of thoughts containing 'yesterday'. The case is analogous to the case in which one finds, walking in total darkness, that it is wet underfoot, then walks on several paces, and then thinks 'It was wet underfoot over there'; again this judgement rests on no identity concerning the demonstratively presented place over there, but it would be suspended if one came to believe that one was not keeping track of places correctly (say from a very disturbed sense of radial direction produced by malfunction in the inner ear).

There is a sense in which the ability to realign one's thoughts correctly as time passes does not rest upon the possession of any calendar or clocking or dating system; for someone can make judgements of the form 'Yesterday was fine', 'The day before that it rained', and make the appropriate realignments as time passes, without using any such system. (This person can also lose track of time if he sleeps for many days, and does not know how many.) Indeed the ability to use a calendar or dating system rests upon a primitive ability to realign one's thoughts. Provided he does not have information from testimony or indirect evidence, a man's judgement tomorrow that it is Wednesday is caused by his earlier belief today that today is Tuesday; if he did not have this belief, he would not know tomorrow that it is then Wednesday. If there were not this dependence, his knowledge tomorrow that it's then Wednesday would be inexplicable and apparently magical. But it is not inexplicable, and his judgement tomorrow 'Now it's

Wednesday' rests upon his ability to realign yesterday's thought 'Today is Tuesday' into 'Yesterday was Tuesday', together with his grasp of the order in which the days of the week follow one another.

The type m.p. [Yesterday] does then belong within the class of identificationally basic types of m.p. For in the case of propositional memory, it is indeed possible to know that yesterday was thus-and-so without the judgement resting on any identity concerning yesterday, or being inferred from any other belief. It does not conflict with this that there is a sense in which, when someone, unbeknownst to himself, mistracks time, he may be mistaken in thinking that yesterday was thus-and-so but not mistaken in thinking that *some* day was thus-and-so. For this last occurrence of '*some*' has narrower scope than 'thinking that'. Someone who has mistracked time may indeed even know that some day was thus-and-so, but there need be no particular day such that he knows that *that* day was thus-and-so. The sense of 'Yesterday' is then an example of a type which is not genuinely demonstrative but is identificationally basic.

The third notion was that of the constitutively identificationally basic. It follows immediately from the criterion for a demonstrative type and the definition of the constitutively identificationally basic that any demonstrative type is constitutively identificationally basic: this is guaranteed by the second part of clause (b) in the criterion. (Whether the converse is true will be left open here, though it is difficult to see how there could be a counterexample.) The relations between demonstrative type and the other notions can then be diagrammed as in Figure 5 – an arrow from one box to

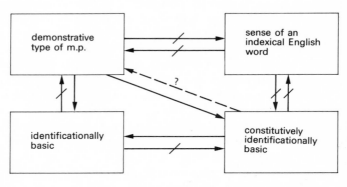

Figure 5

another indicates that anything in the first is also in the second, while a crossed arrow indicates that is not so.

Cognitive Significance

We now turn to the question of the cognitive significance of identities between objects demonstratively presented. Corresponding to each demonstrative m.p. in the identity, there will be a relation in which a thinker must stand to an object in order to be capable of employing that m.p. to think of that object. Abstractly and schematically, the claim of this section is that such an identity is (potentially) cognitively significant iff it is epistemically possible that distinct objects should stand to a thinker in the relations corresponding to the demonstrative m.p.'s in the identity. It will prove convenient to have a notation for such relations in virtue of which an object can be thought of in a particular way. Associated with each demonstrative type Δ there is a relation R_Δ. A person stands in the relation R_Δ to an object at a given time if he is capable of thinking at that time of that object in the type of way Δ. So the main claim can be formulated thus:

(CS) The thought that $[\Delta_u]$ is $[\Delta_v']$ is potentially cognitively significant iff

$$\text{(E)} \quad \exists p \exists t \exists x \exists y (R_\Delta pxt \;\&\; R_\Delta pyt \;\&\; x \neq y).[4]$$

(CS) attempts to explain how cognitive significance depends on type of m.p. It has a natural extension to identities between an object demonstratively presented and one descriptively presented: the thought that $[\Delta_u]$ is the so-and-so is informative iff it is epistemically possible that the thing that bears R to a thinker and the thing which is so-and-so are distinct. In (CS) I follow Evans to the extent that any neo-Fregean theory of demonstratives must: in a Fregean theory cognitive significance must depend upon the identity of the ways in which the objects are presented, and these ways are given by the relations R_Δ.[5]

---

[4] Strictly, of course, one should write 'the thought $[\Delta_u]^\wedge\langle\text{is}\rangle^\wedge[\Delta_v']$', where '$\langle\text{is}\rangle$' denotes the sense of the 'is' of identity, and '$^\wedge$' stands for the operation on thought components which is the natural analogue of concatenation in syntax.

[5] See G. Evans 'Understanding Demonstratives' in *Meaning and Understanding,* ed. H. Paret and J. Bouvresse (de Gruyter: Berlin and New York, 1981). A minor difference is that Evans sharply distinguishes *accounts* of what makes a thought about an object from

Though this account (CS) is abstract and assessment of it must wait upon details of the relations R corresponding to particular m.p.'s, it does have one consequence. This is that cognitive significance depends only upon the *types* of the m.p.'s and not upon the particular objects presented. That this is so is shown in the fact that the variables 'u' and 'v' do not occur in the right hand side of the biconditional in (CS). On this account, if a thought is potentially informative for one thinker at one time, any thought of the same type, differing only in the objects demonstratively presented, will equally be potentially informative, no matter who its thinker or when he thinks it. This does indeed seem to be the case. 'I am Cicero' is equally potentially informative for you and for Cicero (imagine a case of amnesia). 'It is six o'clock' is potentially informative — though of course 'its' truth values will vary with time.

It is constitutive role that we can use to put flesh on the skeletal account given by (CS). Suppose that a subject thinks that $[\Delta_u] = [\Delta_v']$ and that for him then the constitutive role of Δ is C and of Δ' is C'. Then consider the hypothesis that the identity is potentially informative for him iff it is epistemically possible that

the thing that is C $\neq$ the thing that is C'.

Given the meaning of 'constitutive role', this hypothesis in effect says that an identity $[\Delta_u] = [\Delta_v']$ is potentially informative iff it is epistemically possible that the object about which the canonical types of evidence associated with Δ and Δ' give information are distinct. We can test this hypothesis on some examples. Thus take an identity between an aurally and a visually presented object 'this F is identical with this G'. This thought is potentially informative because it is epistemically possible that the F which causes (in the way required for perception) this aural experience is distinct from the G which causes (in the way required for perception) such-and-such features of the token visual experience.[6] Similarly,

[this $_x^T$ place] = the wettest place in Europe

---

types of account: for him $R_\Delta pxt$ and $R_\Delta pyt$ will be different accounts if $x \neq y$. He makes cognitive significance turn on identity of accounts, not on identity of types of account. See the next paragraph of text for reasons in favour of the contrary view.

[6]The thought remains informative even if the experiences represent the object as being in the same place; for in respect of represented location an experience of an object may fail to be veridical and yet a perceptual demonstrative based on that experience can still refer to that object.

is potentially informative because it is epistemically possible that the place determined by the objects perceived and the perspective on them, in an experience of type T, is distinct from the wettest place in Europe. The informativeness is not dependent upon the identity of the particular indexing object x, nor upon the identity of the particular token experience of type T which allows the thinker to employ [this $_x^T$ place].

Here are two more examples: the thought

$$[\text{this } _t^T \text{ time}] = [\text{now}_t]$$

where the first m.p. is the experience-dependent m.p. of a time we mentioned earlier, and the second is a pure present-tense m.p., is potentially informative, as we noted earlier. In accordance with the hypothesis about constitutive roles, this is because it is epistemically possible that the time of occurrence of the events represented in the given experience of type T is distinct from the time of judgement of the displayed identity.

The second example is a transtemporal identity. A person knocks on the door of your office, comes in, and then leaves; a little later again a person knocks and comes in. The thought that that (first) person is that (second) person is informative. We can take it that the second m.p. here is perceptual. Most likely in such a case the thinker has a memory image of the first person to come in, and then his thought is informative because it is epistemically possible that the person who produced and matches that memory image is distinct from the person appropriately responsible for a perceptual experience of such-and-such sort. Less likely, the thinker thinks of the first person in a mixed descriptive–demonstrative way, as the person who came into this office a few minutes ago. The resulting identity in this case is also informative, and can be treated on the model for identities between objects descriptively and demonstratively presented in each half of the identity thought.

I turn now to apply this apparatus to a suggestion made by Thomas Nagel in his first Tanner Lecture.[7] He is concerned with the thought, entertained by him, 'I am TN'. This thought poses the problem that on the one hand it seems to express a genuine fact not captured in an objective description of the world from no particular

[7] *The Tanner Lectures on Human Values 1980*, vol. I, ed. S. McMurrin (Utah and Cambridge UP, 1980), §10, pp. 91 ff.

point of view; while on the other hand it seems that there cannot be any irreducibly first-person facts. Nagel's solution is that

TN, like the rest of you, turns out not merely to be a particular creature with a very specific perspective on the world from his position inside it. Any human being also contains a very different kind of subject [an objective self] . . . with the potential for indefinite further impersonal and objective apprehension of the world. The 'further fact' that I am TN is the fact that this impersonal conception of the world can close over itself by locating the subject that forms it at a particular point in the world that it apprehends. It is attached to . . . the perspective of TN. And since that is not an irreducibly first person fact, it can be part of the real world.[8]

Does Nagel here really succeed in giving a fact that can be part of the real world? In his phrase 'locating the subject that forms it' there is a tacit indexicality which comes out more clearly in an earlier passage, in which he writes:

When I have the philosophical thought that I am TN I am recognizing that the particular objective self that is the subject of *this* centerless conception of a world in which TN is located, is also viewing the world from within through the perspective of TN. [My emphasis][9]

Conceptions may be general public types, in which case one and the same conception may be shared and exercised by many different people; or they may conform to the principle 'one thinker, one conception', even though the conception may be exercised on many occasions. Nagel must be using the latter notion, because in the type sense there is no such thing as the subject of a conception. But in the token sense, it seems that what Nagel gives as the content of his philosophical thought that he is TN is after all something indexical. It is the thought that the person with *this* objective conception is TN. Now this is admittedly not a first-person thought. But the motivation Nagel gives for saying that the world cannot contain irreducibly first-person thoughts, viz., that 'the world really doesn't have a particular point of view'[10] seems to apply to all demonstrative m.p.'s.

   Suppose Nagel is currently reflecting on his objective conception

[8] Ibid., p. 95.
[9] Ibid.
[10] Ibid., p. 92.

of the world, and thinks 'I am TN'. This will be potentially informative for him, according to our earlier claims, if it is epistemically possible that the person with these experiences and thoughts, including those in which his objective conception is exercised, is not TN. This is epistemically possible; and it is what makes Nagel's philosophical thought 'I am TN' informative, and what helps to make it a natural way of expressing in the circumstances the thought that the subject of this objective conception is TN.

Nagel rejects the view that his problem over 'I am TN' is a pseudo-problem caused by misunderstanding of the logic of indexicals. It may well be that he has in mind here a theory of indexicals which does not employ in its treatment of first-person thought a notion of demonstrative m.p. other than character in Kaplan's sense.[11] But if we do employ such a notion, it is not clear that we can state Nagel's problem in just his form: that an m.p. of a state of affairs – as opposed to the state of affairs itself – should be irreducibly indexical is not so puzzling (though of course highly worthy of investigation). The fact, emphasized by Nagel, that we are able to step back from a standpoint and form a more objective conception in which that standpoint is located is obviously of the greatest philosophical interest; but it should be formulated in terms of the distinctive way of thinking of ourselves that we employ when we engage in such detachment.[12]

A Comparison

The above treatment of demonstratives differs from that of Evans in two main areas: the areas are those of perceptual (and memory-image) demonstratives on the one hand and of first-person thought on the other.[13] In both areas there is a different treatment of examples, and this difference reflects underlying theoretical differences. We will take perceptual and memory-image demonstratives

---

[11] 'On the Logic of Demonstratives': the character of an expression is a function from contexts to contents, and these contents do not, on Kaplan's theory, incorporate any indexical m.p.

[12] In formulating the issue as one concerning modes of presentation rather than a new kind of object, we also say farewell to the troublesome question 'Is this objective self *mine*?' It may well be that on Nagel's views this question could be pointless only if 'this objective self' were a *façon de parler* for 'the person who has *this* objective conception'.

[13] *The Varieties of Reference* (Oxford: OUP, 1982).

first. I will assume familiarity with Evans' theory, but will provide reminders about his use of technical terms.

Evans held that perceptual demonstrative m.p.'s of objects are possible because the following conditions are met:

> In the ordinary perceptual situation, not only will there be an information-link between subject and object, but also the subject will know, or will be able to discover, upon the basis of that link where the object is. Given the subject's general knowledge of what makes propositions of the form $\ulcorner \pi = p \urcorner$ true, for arbitrary π [where π is an identification of a place in terms of a public, nonindexical frame of reference] when p is an Idea of a position in his egocentric space, and given that he has located, or is able to locate, the object in his egocentric space, he can then be said to know what it is for $\ulcorner$ This = the object at π now $\urcorner$ to be true (for arbitrary π). Hence he can be said to have an adequate Idea of the object (p. 170).

Evans' 'Idea' is synonymous with our 'mode of presentation'. As a substantive thesis about Ideas, he held that

> we can take the subject's Idea-of-the-object, a, to consist in his knowledge of what it is for an arbitrary proposition of the form $\ulcorner \delta = a \urcorner$ to be true (p. 110).

In the passage just quoted, 'δ' ranges over fundamental Ideas of objects: and

> one has a fundamental Idea of an object if one thinks of it as the possessor of the fundamental ground of difference which it in fact possesses (p. 107).

The fundamental ground of difference of an object is what differentiates it (at a time) from all other objects. So for material objects, their fundamental ground of difference is given by specifying their kind and their location (at the given time).

We have already mentioned examples in which it seems that the thinker cannot locate, in egocentric space, a perceptually presented object. There was the case of thought about the perceptually presented crater on the moon, seen from earth. If the thinker suspects that the atmosphere may be refracting the light rays, he may not even know in which direction that crater is located; nor need he have the belief that there is only one moon in order to be thinking perceptually about a particular crater. Again, we can imagine at some fairground stand an apple, seen in a mirror which is amongst various other moving mirrors: the set-up may be so complicated that it is beyond the subject to locate that apple in egocentric space. But it seems he can still think about it, wonder where it is now, and so forth. It is true that in both these examples the presented object has an (approximate) apparent location, or at least direction, in egocentric space: but this can hardly suffice to fulfil the requirement of knowledge, or the ability to attain it, which Evans gave. (In the case of memory-image m.p.'s, it is even clearer that there need not be so much as apparent location in one's current egocentric space.) Now I would agree that in these examples, there must be some conceivable additional evidence, experiences, and devices (if necessary, spacecraft) which would allow the subject to locate the presented object. If this were not conceivable, and indeed conceivable to the subject himself, it would show that he was not really thinking of an object in the public spatial world. So one can agree with Evans that an information-link between an object and a person is not sufficient to allow him to think demonstratively about that object. But this is less than requiring that the thinker can actually locate the object in egocentric space. The weaker requirement just mentioned also allows memory-image m.p.'s of objects without knowledge or (in the actual circumstances) the ability to obtain it. It is enough that some conceivable additional evidence, experiences, and devices can lead one to identify its location when presented in such circumstances. Evans said that in some cases in which one cannot locate an object, one may indeed think of it in the mixed descriptive–demonstrative way 'the one producing this experience', but held also that this is an incorrect description of the normal case; and it also seems an incorrect description of the crater and apple examples.

There is in fact a curiously unmotivated asymmetry in Evans' important theory. He wrote that an Idea p of a place in egocentric space is an adequate Idea of a place in public space.

provided the subject can be credited with a knowledge of what it would be for $\ulcorner \pi = p \urcorner$ to be true — where π is a stand-in for an arbitrary *fundamental,* and hence holistic, identification of a place (p. 162).

This knowledge consists in a general ability to impose one's cognitive map of the objective spatial world upon one's egocentric space. Now this ability is, in more detail, an ability so to impose one's cognitive map in the presence of suitable evidence and experiences. In some circumstances, one will not be able to impose it: one is lost, one has been kidnapped and transported to unfamiliar territory, and so forth. But when one is lost, one can still use the m.p. 'here' and perceptual m.p.'s of objects; and one's thoughts are still thoughts about places in public space. Evans gives a reason which allows us to say that they are still such thoughts:

provided that the subject does maintain a stable dispositional connection with a place, there is just one proposition of the form $\ulcorner \pi = p \urcorner$ (where p is an egocentric spatial Idea) that is true, and the subject knows what it is for it to be true (p. 164).

So Evans' theory does not require for thought about a place in public space the ability to give some public, non-egocentric individuation of it in one's thought. It suffices that one is suitably related to a position in public space in a way other than one which requires that ability in all circumstances.

The problem is that exactly analogous points can be made about perceptual demonstrative m.p.'s. Suppose a subject perceives material object x of kind F, in way W. (Here W is an experience-type, a type which fully determines the intrinsic properties – sensational and representational – of an experience.) So the subject is in a position to employ in thought a perceptual demonstrative 'that F', or more precisely the token demonstrative m.p. we can indicate in the notation $[W, F_x]$. Then there is just one proposition of the form $\ulcorner p =$ the location of $[W, F_x]$ now $\urcorner$ that is true, and the subject knows what it is for it to be true. Why here, but not in the former case, demand that the subject also know which p (or which π in the former case) is mentioned in the unique such true proposition? Why require an actual as opposed to a general ability in suitable circumstances in the second but not in the first case? The situation is particularly puzzling when we consider a perceptually presented object, presented by $[W, F_x]$ say, whose location in egocentric space *is* known, although the subject himself is lost. Evans' theory allows that $[W, F_x]$ is here an adequate idea of an object, although the subject has no fundamental idea of it. If we insist that he *could* have such a fundamental idea of it with more evidence, why is an analogous possibility not also sufficient for adequacy in relation to egocentric space?

It seems, then, that there are only two uniform, motivated positions here. The liberal position finds the general abilities to locate in the presence of suitable evidence, plus uniqueness of actual location in the relevant space, sufficient for genuine m.p.'s or adequate Ideas. The strict position finds these insufficient in both cases and requires knowledge of actual location in both spaces. The position I have adopted is uniformly liberal, while Evans was liberal about public space and strict about egocentric space. The uniformly strict position seems quite untenable. It entails that whenever you are lost, you cannot think, using perceptual demonstratives, about the objects you see around you. This would amount to an *a priori* demonstration that, after being kidnapped, you cannot coherently think 'I wonder where this city is?'

To adopt the uniformly liberal position is not to deny the importance of fundamental Ideas in thought about objects of a given kind. In examples in which a thinker is perceptually presented with an object but is unable to locate it in either egocentric or public space, he must still suppose that it has some fundamental identification. To come to believe that it has none is to come to believe that there is no such presented object. This would be the situation of someone who came to believe he was in the situation described by Anscombe, in which a man looks through two pinholes, one at each eye, each eye being stimulated by a different matchbox in such a way as to look as if there is only one matchbox in front of him.[14] In these circumstances, the subject really does not know what it is for a supposed thought 'that matchbox is F' to be true.

The uniformly liberal view permits a thinker to employ memory-image dependent demonstratives, even though the thinker has no idea where in public space or at what time he encountered the presented object. Evans raised an objection which can be applied to any theory which admits this possibility. It is not completely clear whether the case to which he himself was objecting involves memory images or existential 'propositional' memory, but this does not matter to the objection:

They will say that the subject's knowledge of what it would be for his supposition [that this presently seen ball is identical with that (remembered) ball] to be true is, at least partly, constituted by the fact

---

[14] 'Comment on Professor R. L. Gregory's Paper' in *Philosophy and Psychology*, ed. S. Brown (London: Macmillan, 1974).

that his Idea is causally derived from an encounter with a particular ball. But the fact that they say this surely makes their case worse rather than better. For this suggestion entirely subverts the very logic or grammar of the concept of knowing what it is for it to be true that *p*. This is the concept of a *capacity*, and the proof of its possession at a given time must surely reside in facts about what the subject can or cannot do at that time (p. 116).

But an ability can be such that experience of it in a given environment involves exploiting in appropriate ways the causal chains which are there: this is clearly a correct description of the ability to locate in egocentric space an object seen in a mirror. This is a partially sensori-motor skill, and may, in the case of an unfamiliar type of mirror, involve manipulating objects to see if one's experience alters appropriately. The ability, exercised in a given context and exploiting the causal chains of that context, homes in on one particular object rather than another. The dichotomy set up by Evans thus seems spurious: it can be simultaneously true that someone bears R to x, that this holds partly in virtue of the causal relations between the subject and x, and true too that being capable of standing in R to objects is a matter of the subject's abilities. In the case of the remembered ball, the ability is not a sensori-motor skill, but rather the ability to reason in certain ways – for instance 'That ball could only have been x, y or z; but my path and z's never crossed; and y did not ever look like that ball looked then; so it must have been x I saw'. Such ways of reasoning presume upon causal connections between the past encounter and the present memory image: they would be unsound were there not such connections. The same applies to the reasoning by which a cognitive map is imposed on egocentric space. In neither case does it follow that the presented object, remembered or perceived, is *thought of* in explicitly causal terms: the mode of presentation remains genuinely demonstrative.

The second main area of difference from Evans is in the treatment of first-person thought. There are several differences here, and developing one of them will lead naturally to the others. In the account we developed earlier, the various examples of immunity to error through misidentification involving the first person fell into two different classes. There were some cases in which the immunity seemed to be absolute ('I'm in pain'), and

some in which it seemed to depend on general presumptions about
the world — presumptions which if false would open the possibility
of misidentification without someone's use of 'I' ceasing to pick out
anything. Within this latter class were 'I was on an ocean liner',
where the judgement is based on a memory image, and 'I'm sitting
at a desk', based on visual, tactual and kinaesthetic experiences.
Now it is a fact about the first-person m.p. in need of explanation
that there is this distinction between the two types of case. What is it
about 'I' which makes 'I'm in pain' based on an experience of pain
totally immune to error through misidentifying who is in pain,
while the memory and perception cases are not thus totally
immune? We have an account of this in terms of the constitutive
role of [self], 'the person with these conscious states'.

It seems that the examples of absolute immunity are those
traditionally regarded as infallibly known judgements, and Evans
does indeed offer an account of how they can be infallibly known:

> the judgement's being a judgement with a certain content can be
> regarded as constituted by its being a response to that state (p. 229).

From this account I would not dissent. The problem is whether this
infallibility can be reconciled with the remainder of Evans' theory.
For Evans holds that 'I' in thought can fail of reference.[15]

But how can 'I'm in pain' be infallibly known and yet 'I' possibly
fail of reference? It is not easy to see how to weaken the content of
the judgement that 'I'm in pain' is infallibly known so as to
circumvent this problem. Conditionalization does not help. If, as is
common ground between the account I have been suggesting and
Evans' theory, indexical thoughts are existence-dependent, so that
where there is no object picked out, there is no thought-content,
then equally 'If I exist, I'm in pain' cannot serve the purpose: the
existence of a thought here still requires 'I' to refer. The same
applies to 'If my uses of "I" refer, I'm in pain', since 'my' is to be
explained in terms of the first person. Can one advance matters by
using a memory-demonstrative, purportedly referring to one's
earlier attempts at using the first-person m.p., as in 'If *those* uses of
"I" refer, I'm in pain'? This does not help either: Descartes' evil
demon could give you apparent memories of someone else's
thoughts.

<hr/>

[15]p. 253.

But Evans would equally object to the constitutive role I suggested for [self], on the ground that it is incapable of illuminating first-person thought. In particular, he would disallow the possibility of the subject whose brain has been in a vat since birth even from thinking his own experiences demonstratively:

Mental events are distinguished from one another, and from all other things, by reference to the distinctness of the person to, or in whom, they occur . . . a subject can gaze inwardly with all the intensity he can muster, and repeat to himself 'this pain', 'this pain', as he concentrates upon his pain, but he will not thereby be able to know which pain is in question unless this provides him with a basis for identifying the pain with a pain conceived as an element in the objective order – which means a pain conceived as the pain of this or that person in the objective order. Consequently, he cannot have an adequate Idea of these mental events unless he knows to which person they are happening (p. 253).

On the uniformly liberal view, however, even the vat subject can be credited with thoughts about his pains, provided that in suitable circumstances and with suitable evidence he would be able to give a fundamental identification of the person who has them. This he could do, provided his nerves were properly connected with perceptual devices and limbs. So if we accept the liberal view, we could simultaneously hold on to our account of constitutive role and also to the thesis that token mental events are individuated by the persons who have them. In any case, we have already considered cases which are counterexamples to the principle that if the identity of an F is dependent upon the identity of the G to which it stands in some relation, one cannot think demonstratively of an F unless one can identify the G to which it stands in that relation. The identity of material objects in the sense in which Evans was concerned with it depends upon their location: but one can apparently think demonstratively of a perceived material object without identifying its location, as in the case of the apple at the fairground set-up, or the case of the moon mentioned above.

This general comparison might end here but for the fact that it is not at all clear to me that 'states, or experiences, . . . *owe* their identity as particulars to the identity of the person whose states or experiences they are, despite the distinguished support the view has received.[16] Consider someone who has, temporarily, a split brain

[16] P. F. Strawson, *Individuals* (London: Methuen, 1959), p. 97.

because his *corpus callosum* has been severed. We can make sense of the possibility – and indeed it sometimes happens – that there are two distinct but qualitatively identical experiences grounded in (different) states of the same brain: the experiences might be distinct, qualitatively identical monaural experiences, for instance. It seems that if we speak of two distinct minds or centres of consciousness in these circumstances, we do so because the token experiences are themselves distinct. One should not of course speak of one of the two centres of consciousness that exist after the division of the brain as *newly* existing, and the other as that of the original person. This would be as ungrounded as insisting of a river which divides and then reunites farther downstream that one and not the other of the two segments in the stretch in which it is divided *is* the original river.

There is a clear motivation for saying that in the split brain there are two token experiences, a motivation which does not appeal to the identity of persons. The two experiences have different causes – for example, one results from the stimulation of one nostril, the other from stimulation of the other nostril – and they may have different effects too. This motivation for distinguishing the experiences does not have the consequence that in normal, undivided brains there are really two distinct minds, co-operating in harness. For in the normal case, one single experience of smell is caused by the stimulation of both nostrils (and so is over-determined).

When we reflect on these cases and similar possibilities, it seems clear that as a rule for individuating token experiences of a given type, 'Same person, same experience; different person, different experience' works only if there is no close tie of 'the identity of persons at a given time to the identity of bodies at that same time. In the actual world, split-brain cases aside, two contingent facts hold which it is not difficult to imagine otherwise: (a) stimulation of different parts of one human body produces experiences which are co-conscious, if it produces experiences at all, and (b) stimulation of different bodies does not produce one and the same token experience. Condition (b) would be false if I felt something in my left arm iff both the left arm of my body and the left arm of another body were being stimulated in the right way. (If we say in such cases that there is only one person with two bodies, or if we treat split brain cases as ones in which there is a divided mind, the individua-

❡ tion of token experiences seems to be determining respectively that of persons or the number of divisions in the mind.)

There is an undeniable truth which may seem to support the above quotation from Strawson. It is the principle that

(1)   One person or mind cannot have two token experiences of the same type at the same time.

This is precisely what one would expect if token experiences were individuated by the time of their occurrence, their type, and the person to whom they occur. It would be structurally analogous to the fact that

(2)   One place cannot be the location of two material objects of the same kind at the same time.

This is guaranteed, as Wiggins has said, by the fact that material objects are individuated by their kind and location at a given time.[17]

Nevertheless, if what we have said, about the individuation of token experiences in causal terms, and the apparent priority (at least in individual cases taken singly) of the individuation of experiences to the individuation of minds or centres of consciousness, is correct, that cannot be the right explanation of the truth of (1): for the *explanans* is false. There must be some other explanation. I suggest the following. Token experiences, which are *total* in the sense that their type fully specifies what it is like (visually, aurally, etc.) for someone who has that experience, individuate minds or centres of consciousness. Distinct total token experiences at a given time must belong to different persons or minds; and there are no further distinctions between minds at a given time than are determined, directly or indirectly, by this principle. (I speak of minds rather than persons only, for it is not clear that it is right to say that there are two *persons* in the case of a temporarily split brain.) This principle also explains the truth of (1), but in a different way: for by this principle, if there are two total token experiences at a given time, they must belong to different persons or minds. Admittedly, (1) speaks of all token experiences, total or not: but any

---

[17] 'On Being in the Same Place at the Same Time', *Philosophical Review* 77 (1968).

token experience is a component of at most one total token experience. This explanation is compatible with the examples we considered. There is on this view still an analogy with the case of material objects, but by a different projection. The analogue of (1) would be not (2), but rather (3):

(3) One material object cannot be located at two places at the same time.

Persons or minds are individuated by reference to token experiences rather than conversely, and material objects are individuated by reference to places. Token experiences, with their place in a complex pattern of actual and potential causal relations, provide the framework for the individuation of persons or minds, as places do for material objects.[18]

[18]It may be true that there are complex and general dependencies in both cases in the reverse direction too. Also none of this should be supposed to lead inexorably to the view that the nature of someone's experiences is necessarily unknowable by anyone else. Everything in the text is consistent with the view that, for instance, pains necessarily have certain, behavioural manifestations in certain circumstances. Indeed, this is a matter of their causal connections, and could be integrated into the account of the text.

7

The Principle of Acquaintance

Russell's Principle of Acquaintance states that '*every proposition which we can understand must be composed wholly of constituents with which we are acquainted*'.[1] The Principle has not had a good press. It has been regarded as a legacy and an endorsement of a Humean empiricism as, in part, it was; and one commentator has even adopted the maxim 'whenever possible, attempt to defend Russell's doctrines independently of the Principle of Acquaintance'.[2] In this chapter I intend to argue that when separated from inessential epistemological accretions, the Principle of Acquaintances states a correct and fundamental constraint on the ascription of content.

Russell held that a thinker is acquainted with his sense-data, with some objects presented by immediate memory, and with universals. He at first held that the thinker is also acquainted with himself, but later abandoned this view. The thinker can also be acquainted with what Russell called 'complexes'; a complex might have the form *aRb*. In assessing whether there is anything in the Principle of Acquaintance (PA), one should not take the relation of acquaintance to be *defined* by the extension Russell took it to possess. For it could be that Russell had a correct underlying conception of acquaintance, but a false view of its extension. The most salient feature of Russell's conception of acquaintance, emphasized by Russell himself, is its relational character: in being acquainted with something, one is presented with the object itself, and not something going proxy for it. He wrote of 'an assumption which I

---

[1] See 'Knowledge by Acquaintance and Knowledge by Description', reprinted in Russell's *Mysticism and Logic* (New York: Barnes and Noble, 1971), p. 159; and *The Problems of Philosophy* (Oxford: OUP, 1973), p. 32.

[2] R. M. Sainsbury, *Russell* (London: Routledge, 1979), p. 36. In fact Sainsbury expresses sympathy for some revised formulation of the Principle of Acquaintance which he describes as 'weakened'. The remainder of this chapter is very much in the spirit of Sainsbury's more sympathetic remarks, but goes beyond the concern solely with names in his reformulation.

believe to be wholly false. The assumption is that, *if anything is immediately present to me, that thing must be part of my mind*'; neutral monists, held Russell, were right at least in holding that 'constituents of the physical world can be immediately present to me'.[3] In general, judgements do not consist of ideas: 'On the contrary, I hold that acquaintance is wholly a relation, not demanding any such constituent of the mind as is supposed by advocates of "ideas".'[4] A thinker can also have noninferential knowledge about the things with which he is acquainted: Russell was explicitly opposed to the view 'that it can only be by inference that we arrive at a knowledge of anything external to ourselves'.[5]

In trying to formulate a claim in the spirit of the PA, we need to concentrate on two key notions: that of acquaintance, and that of something occurring as a constituent of a judgement. My procedure will be to give a brief revised elucidation of each of these notions as a preliminary to assessing a Principle of Acquaintance which connects them.

I argued in the preceding chapters that some modes of presentation m of an object have this feature: that, as an *a priori* and necessary matter, a subject's disposition to judge the thought 'm is φ' is sensitive to the presence of evidence that the so-and-so is φ, where the condition 'so-and-so' relates to the subject's own current psychological states. Thus a thinker's disposition to judge that a perceptually presented object is heavy is constitutively sensitive to evidence that the object that causes certain properties of his visual field is heavy; or again his disposition to judge that it's raining now is constitutively sensitive to evidence that it's raining at the time at which he makes the judgement. Modes of presentation with this feature we can call 'm.p.'s governed by a Sensitivity Principle'. It is not only demonstrative m.p.'s which are governed by a Sensitivity Principle. There will be some complex relation such that the thinker's judgements that c is φ, where c is such an m.p., are sensitive to evidence that the thing that bears the complex relation to the kind of experience which produces recognition is φ. Purely descriptive m.p.'s on the other hand are not governed by a Sensitivity Principle. A thinker's judgements that the F is G need not be sensitive to any particular kind of evidence that the thing that bears

---

[3] 'On the Nature of Acquaintance', reprinted in *Logic and Knowledge,* p. 147.

[4] 'Knowledge by Acquaintance', p. 161.

[5] 'On the Nature of Acquaintance, p. 173.

a certain relation to one of his current psychological states is *G*. In the case of an m.p. that is governed by a Sensitivity Principle, the thing that bears the relation to the appropriate psychological state of the thinker is the object presented by the m.p.; thus the fact that descriptive m.p.'s are not governed by a Sensitivity Principle is one (perhaps the) source of the irreducibility of demonstrative to descriptive m.p.'s.

I propose, then, this reconstruction of Russell's concept of acquaintance for the case of objects: a thinker is acquainted with an object if there is some m.p. (within his conceptual repertoire) which is governed by a Sensitivity Principle and he is in any appropriate current psychological state which is required if he is to think of that object under that m.p. We will also need to use a three-place relation between a person, object, and type of m.p.: that of the person being acquainted with that object relative to that type. This relation holds if m.p.'s of that type are governed by a Sensitivity Principle and for that person (at the given time) the type picks out that object in his thoughts. 'Picks out' is here used neutrally, without prejudice to whether the object is a constituent of the thought – for that is something the relation is to be used to explain. Thus I am acquainted with the pen I am now using relative to a certain perceptual type of m.p., which presents a pen in a certain way in my visual field. These definitions preserve at least two features of the Russellian conception. First, they retain a sense in which in being acquainted with something the subject is able to think of it in a particular way in virtue of his bearing a certain *relation* to it. Second, the reference to psychological states may retain what Russell meant to capture in writing of acquaintance as a relation of presentation: in many cases, it seems that it is by means of the psychological state that an object with which the thinker is acquainted is presented. 'To say that S has acquaintance with O is essentially the same thing as to say that O is presented to S'.[6]

The other key notion was that of an object occurring as a constituent of a thought. This we will interpret as an object indexing a type of m.p., the type thus indexed occurring as a constituent of the thought, as discussed at the start of Chapter 5. So we will not be allowing an object to occur as a constituent of a thought by being the *only* component of the thought which corresponds to a singular term

[6]'Knowledge by Acquaintance', p. 152.

in a sentence which expresses that thought. In this sense we will be incorporating the PA within a neo-Fregean theory, for an object will be permitted to occur as a constituent of a thought only as presented in a certain way. It is not only demonstrative m.p.'s which consist of a type indexed by an object. An m.p. of an object based on an ability to recognize that object can also be regarded as having this structure.

Suppose I can recognize Michael Dummett, and my *Doppelgänger* on Twin Earth can recognize Michael Dummett's *Doppelgänger* in the same way: a certain type of m.p. is indexed with MD when I think of MD in a way based on my recognitional ability, and the same type is indexed with MD's *Doppelgänger* in the m.p. employed by my *Doppelgänger*. There are of course important differences between recognitionally-based m.p.'s and demonstratives, but both sorts of case involve acquaintance with the presented object as we have reconstrued acquaintance.

So for the case of objects the reconstructed PA says this: only objects with which the thinker is acquainted can occur as indices of type m.p.'s in thoughts to which he is in a position to have attitudes. It is the universally quantified claim that:

> For all objects x, persons a and types M, if a is in a position to have attitudes to thoughts containing the m.p. $[M_x]$, in which a type is indexed with the object x itself, then a is acquainted with x relative to M.

Acquaintance is a necessary condition of putting the object itself (albeit clothed with an m.p.) into the thought.[7]

Suppose we construct a theory of thoughts which not only conforms to the reconstructed PA, but also indexes types with objects in any case in which the reconstructed Principle allows it. We can call this *enthusiastic* acceptance of the Principle. Enthusiastic acceptance of the Principle, then, consists not just in holding the Principle but in holding in addition its converse:

[7] Besides any intrinsic merits the reconstructed PA may possess, it could also be argued that the reconstructed version helps us to understand what was going on when Russell said that 'this' (with a reference of the kind he gave it) was the only genuine purely referential device. Here Russell was in effect allowing as objects of acquaintance only those things he took to be involved in possession of the particular psychological state mentioned in the appropriate instantiation of the Sensitivity Principle for a relational m.p., rather than the objects having a distinguished relation to that state. See p. 199 below for Russell's reasons for doing so.

For all objects x, persons a and types M, if a is acquainted with x relative to M, then x is in a position to have attitudes to thoughts containing the m.p. [M_x], in which a type is indexed with the object x itself.

Are we then in our enthusiasm open to the objection that the thoughts thus introduced are psychologically redundant? Does such a theory with objects as constituents of the thoughts under the specified conditions draw distinctions where no psychological differences exist? In the previous chapter, we mentioned the Indispensability Thesis[8]: and that Thesis, if true, can contribute to an argument that the fact that a demonstrative type is indexed with one object rather than another can feature in a propositional attitude explanation of why the thinker acts on one object rather than the other. But the constitutive features of thoughts containing objects as indices are not restricted to the causal consequences of attitudes to them. There are also constitutive conditions concerning the causes of attitudes to such thoughts. In normal circumstances, which thoughts containing a token m.p. [C_x] are judged true will depend causally in part upon the properties of the object x. The properties a perceptually presented object is judged to possess will in part depend causally upon that object's properties (and also of course upon much else); whether 'it's φ at [now_t]' is judged true will depend causally on what is the case at t in a way which it does not depend upon what is the case at other times; and so forth. The nature of the dependence needs to be made explicit, but that some significant kind exists does not seem doubtful.

It is because of these distinctively relational causal antecedents and consequences of thoughts containing objects as indices, that it is not an arbitrary or psychologically irrelevant stipulation to say that if some other object had stood to the thinker in the relation in virtue of which he is acquainted with a given object, then he would be having a different thought. The thought would be of the same type as his actual thought, but the potential causal relations of attitudes to that thought, its antecedents and consequences, would be different.

It will be observed that there are certain loose joints in what we have so far said. For we gave as one of the reasons for saying that attitudes to object-involving thoughts are not psychologically

[8]p. 158.

redundant that they can explain actions on particular objects, the very objects which occur as constituents of those thoughts. But if we were to make such potential effects a requirement for a thought to be object-involving, we would be making it a necessary condition of being an object-involving thought that the thought be demonstrative or indexical. As we noted earlier, thoughts containing recognitionally-based m.p.'s do not have such constitutive connections with the explanation of action. If I intend to shake hands with Peter, whom I know well, and am not sure which of the men in front of me is Peter, since they are dressed for a masked ball, this intention will not cause my action of handshaking until I acquire an additional belief of the form '*this* man is Peter'. The strict line of requiring these action effects if the thought is to be object-involving would also not include all demonstrative ways of thinking of an object as object-involving. Memory-demonstratives available to a thinker because he has a memory image of an object would be excluded, for these have no special connection with action.

We can take the following less strict line. There is a series of analogies with the central demonstrative cases, analogies of gradually diminishing strength. In those central cases, attitudes to object-involving thoughts have both distinctive potential consequences for action on particular objects, and are normally the effects of the properties of particular objects – in both cases, the objects being the very ones which are constituents of the thoughts. Consider this principle, upon which we often rely in attributing propositional attitudes:

> If someone perceives x in the way W, and x has an observational property of which the perceiver has some concept φ, then he is likely to come to judge, if the question arises, that that object (perceptually presented in way W) is φ.

It is less likely, but still likely, that a corresponding principle is true when the m.p. in question is not a perceptual demonstrative one, but a recognitionally-based one of the object perceived, if we are given also that the object is presented in a way which produced recognition. It is less likely, because it is always a possibility that, where c is the recognitionally-based m.p. in question, the thinker should refuse to accept that that perceptually presented object is what falls under c (he might suspect a fake). But both these cases stand together in contrast with that of definite descriptions. There is no reason at all to believe that in general

> If someone perceives x and x is the F and x has some observational property of which the perceiver has some concept φ, then he is likely to judge, should the question arise, that the F is φ.

In brief, there are no principles we want to state which quantify over objects which also occur as constituents of the thoughts, and which tell us when someone is likely to judge the thought that the F is thus-and-so, in the way there are in the demonstrative case, and (to a lesser extent) in the recognitional case. What properties demonstratively presented objects themselves have can in normal circumstances be a good guide to what beliefs someone will have about them, thus presented; but if we want a guide to what beliefs of the form 'the F is thus-and-so' a thinker is likely to have, we would do better not to look at the F itself, but at what evidence the thinker has for the Russellian general thought 'there is one and only one F and it is thus-and-so'.

The position of enthusiastic acceptance of the reconstructed PA is intermediate between two more extreme classes of position. In one direction lie those views which impose more restrictive conditions before an object is allowed to occur as a constituent of a thought; in the other direction lie those views which impose less restrictive conditions.

It is impossible to survey all the views which might be found at these extremes, but we can get an impression of the sorts of difficulties which arise when we veer away from the intermediate position. Take the more restrictive views, all of which in some case or other omit the indexing object from the thought. Since these thoughts leave open which is the object with which the thinker is acquainted, attitudes to them cannot by themselves have the potential relational antecedents and consequences we mentioned. These potential antecedents and consequences certainly seem to play a role in common-sense psychology, and provision must be made for them somewhere. Perhaps this more restrictive theorist envisages these relational consequences as emerging not from the thought and attitude alone, but from these together with a description of some of the relations in which the thinker stands. But such a restrictive theorist will still have to give principles for distinguishing between the types of case in which such a supplementary account is needed to capture the role of attitudes in common-sense psychology, and those in which it is not. It is that distinction with which I am at present concerned. No objection is being offered here to a theory which regards truth value, reference and the explanation of action on particular objects as determined jointly by some notion of content less fine-grained than mine, together with environmental relations. Indeed the account I have been offering must be inter-translatable with some such theory. My concern is rather with the principles which determine the line between those cases in which, to have a satisfactory account of propositional attitude psychology, one needs to take into account (somewhere or other) environmental relations, and those in which one does not.

Another line a more restrictive theorist might take would be to replace an indexed type $[\Delta_y]$, where y is the object presented, by some triple (Δ, x, t), where Δ is still the type, and x and t are respectively the thinker and the time the type is employed. The sense in which you and I when at the same place at the same time may have the same belief in judging 'It's cold here' would have on this view to be captured by taking equivalence classes of triples by means of the relation of picking out the same object, but this could be done. But unless it collapses into a notational variant of the enthusiast's middle view, this more restrictive account is not able to deliver the result that if a different object had been suitably related to the thinker, in having a thought about the object then demonstratively presented to him, he would have been having a different thought. For if the singular component of the thought is given by the triple of type, thinker, and time, this can remain the same even if a different object were to stand to the thinker in the relation R_Δ (the relation in virtue of which someone can think of something in the type of way Δ). Like a descriptive thought, the content would be the same while the 'referent' varies.[9] Note that in giving this argument, we are appealing to the conditions under which a thinker would or would

[9]The preference expressed here for a structure of demonstrative thoughts in which Δ and y are constituents, over one in which Δ, x and t are constituents, is not in conflict with the statement in 'Demonstrative Thought and Psychological Explanation' that '$[\Delta_y]$' and (Δ, x, t)' are equally good notations for demonstrative m.p.'s. The latter statement was concerned with whether both these formal linguistic expressions (relative to an assignment to the variables) determine uniquely a token m.p.; and both of them do. The issue discussed in the present text is the nature of the token m.p. itself— the thing picked out by both the complex terms '$[\Delta_y]$' and '(Δ, x, t)'.

not be having the same thought, and not to the properties of a given thought in respect of *its* truth value in other possible circumstances.[10]

At the other extreme there are the less restrictive theorists amongst whom we can consider one who proposes to add objects which satisfy definite descriptions as constituents of purely descriptive thoughts. (Some of the theorists who would be classified by Chisholm as 'latitudinarians' may fall under this head.[11]) Here we really do have psychological redundancy, and the point can be argued without reference either to vacuity or to modal properties of a given descriptive thought. There are descriptive m.p.'s 'the F' such that something other than the actual F might have been the F. In such circumstances, it will be the case that someone who thinks 'the F is thus-and-so' will have thoughts, attitudes to which have exactly the same relational consequences in action and exactly the same relational causal antecedents, provided none of his other attitudes alter. On the other hand we can consider m.p.'s whose employment requires acquaintance with an object: it is not possible that some other object be picked out by such a demonstrative m.p. of a given kind, and yet these relationally characterized dispositions to act on particular objects or the objects which cause his attitudes remain unchanged. Certainly in some cases, if a different object were to satisfy a definite description, different objects will be the ones on which he is disposed to act if he forms certain intentions. If someone other than the actual Master were Master of the oldest

---

[10] Such a modal appeal might run as follows. Suppose that in the actual world $R_\Delta xyt$, and the thinker x judges that $[\Delta_y]$ is φ. Now consider a world w in which (1) $R_\Delta xzt$ and (2) y is φ and (3) z is not φ. Is x's actual thought '$[\Delta_y]$ is φ' true with respect to this world w? We certainly have a strong intuition that it is not. The problem, though, with the argument is that it makes uncritical use of the notion 'true with respect to w'; an objector could reply that the correct use of this phrase in the language is tied, in our example, to the properties of the object to which x actually bears R_Δ at t, but that this shows nothing psychologically significant. The availability of this reply suggests that one should appeal directly to psychological considerations in arguing for enthusiastic acceptance of the PA.

[11] See R. Chisholm, 'Knowledge and Belief: "De Dicto" and "De Re" ', *Philosophical Studies* 29 (1976), 1–20; at p. 9 the latitudinarian theory is defined as the theory 'S attributes the property of being F to $x = _{Df} S$ accepts a proposition which implies x to have the property of being F'. Chisholm, on p. 8, makes it clear that such implication by a proposition needs only that x *in fact* have certain properties. I say that only some latitudinarians are less restrictive theorists, for it would be open to a latitudinarian to accept the distinction drawn below (p. 196) between belief sentences and a *Bel* relation to thoughts. A theorist who allows such latitude only at the level of belief sentences needs not reject the reconstructed PA.

college in Oxford, it might be that the thinker would meet that different Master; so the thinker would then act in relation to a different object if he formed certain intentions concerning that demonstratively presented man to whom he is introduced, an object different from the one in relation to which he would be disposed to act were a different person Master of the oldest college. He would also have beliefs whose content is explained causally by the properties of this different Master. But this does not undermine the asymmetry. For in this example, the satisfaction by a different object of the definite description 'the Master of the oldest college' causes the thinker to have demonstrative beliefs he would not otherwise have. The alteration of the class of objects in relation to which he is disposed to act, and which causes some of his beliefs, is attributable to this different demonstrative belief. If a different person were to satisfy the definite description but the subject's indexical and demonstrative beliefs remained the same, there would be no relevant alteration of the objects to which the thinker stands in these relations.

In giving this argument against the less restrictive theorist, we just concentrated attention on possible circumstances in which something other than the actual F is the F. But this was merely for vividness. It illustrates the underlying general point that no particular relation of the kinds we have been discussing has to hold between a thinker employing the concept 'the F' and the object which is the F. This underlying point applies even when nothing other than the actual F could be the F.

The reconstructed PA given here is very different from the interpretation proposed by Hintikka. Hintikka suggests that the gist of Russell's PA can be taken 'as a thesis to the effect that only demonstrative methods of crossidentification (individuation by acquaintance), not physical (descriptive) ones, are indispensable'.[12] Russell held judgement to be an ordered relation between the judger and various other entities; so we have to construe Hintikka as holding that under the appropriate possible-worlds formulation of Russell's conception, the PA comes out as stating that only demonstrative methods of crossidentification are indispensable. Now it would be quite consistent for one who holds the reconstructed PA also to hold that a table with which he is

---

[12] 'Knowledge by Acquaintance— Individuation by Acquaintance', in *Bertrand Russell* (New York: Doubleday, 1972), ed. D. Pears, pp. 69–70.

acquainted in perception has a 'descriptive' crossworld identity condition – perhaps a Kripkean one requiring certain origins. Whether one stands in the right relations in the actual world to be acquainted with a given object is one question; the crossworld identity condition of that object is another. One can maintain this distinction even if it is one's aim (though it is not mine) to give a semantics for propositional attitudes in terms of possible worlds. For one could take it as a sufficient condition for quantifying into a belief context that in every world compatible with the subject's beliefs there is something standing in a certain relation to him, without maintaining that the things standing in the relation to him in different worlds are in some sense identical.[13] Any such theory will clearly take it only as a necessary, and not as a sufficient, condition of the subject's believing something that it hold with respect to every possible world compatible with his beliefs. But some such point must be made by any purported possible-world theory of propositional attitudes: conditions which hold in every world compatible with the subject's beliefs but which cannot be formulated in his conceptual repertoire will always need special treatment by such a theory.

What of acquaintance with universals? Russell held that we are acquainted with universals and that they are constituents of our thoughts. Hintikka has described the view that we are acquainted with universals as a desperate remedy to try to save the Principle of Acquaintance.[14] Russell's own arguments for his view that we are acquainted with universals are certainly weak. He wrote:

It is hard to see how we could know such a fact [as the transitivity of 'before'] unless we are now acquainted with 'before', and not merely with actual particular cases of one given object being before another given object. And more directly: A judgment such as 'this is before that', where this judgment is derived from awareness of a complex, constitutes an analysis, and we should not understand the analysis if we were not acquainted with the meaning of the terms employed.[15]

[13] Hintikka also remarks that Russell would not be able to accommodate the cases in which we quantify into belief contexts, where according to Hintikka the quantifier ranges over public 'descriptively identified' individuals (ibid., pp. 70–1). Hintikka compares the principles of descriptive identification with those we would employ to solve a *roman-à-clef;* it is unclear than that many of the cases in which Hintikka would wish to quantify in on the basis of descriptive identification could not be classified by Russell as cases of general thoughts to the effect that the person with such-and-such properties is thus-and-so.

[14] Ibid., p. 79.

[15] 'Knowledge by Acquaintance', p. 155.

This seems to beg the question. It also leaves it unclear what relation has to hold between a thinker and a universal for him to be acquainted with it. The reconstructed PA for objects, however, does suggest a model for making sense of acquaintance with universals: we can enquire whether some concepts are governed by constraints analogous to the Sensitivity Principles to which relational m.p.'s of objects conform.

Earlier in this book, I emphasized the distinction between properties and m.p.'s of properties. A person may think of a certain shape property under a tactual m.p.: it may be essential to this m.p. that some of the things that in fact fall under it can be determined to do so in normal circumstances by certain tactual procedures and experiences. The same person may also think of the same shape property under a visual m.p. – the shape in question might be that of a star of David. The thought that the physical property tactually presented is the same as the physical property visually presented can be informative for someone who employs both m.p.'s in his thought. It may be that such a person must be in a position to work out the identity; but if this is so, it no more throws doubt on the distinctness of the m.p.'s than does the fact that someone who employs the different m.p.'s shown by '25 × 25' and '625' must be in a position to work out that $25 \times 25 = 625$. We use the notation '$[\Sigma_P]$' and '$[\Sigma'_P]$' for modes of presentation of the same property P. It is not excluded that in some cases, an m.p. of a property may collapse into the property itself, as we earlier argued that it does in the object case for token experiences and other conscious events. The sense of 'red' may be such an m.p. of a property.[16]

Whatever properties are, if in some cases they are constituents of thoughts, it would be quite out of the spirit of the present position to take them as either Fregean extensional concepts or as courses-of-values. Fregean concepts and courses-of-values will in one way or

[16]Thus it might be said that identities between pure secondary qualities thought of in a way determined by sensory experience are all either obviously true ot obviously false ('being green is being blue', 'being sour is being noisy'). In parallel still with the case of objects, this mitigates the effects of having the property itself, rather than an m.p. of it, as the constituent of a proposition. It would also provide a limited answer to David Pears' remark that 'It is, in any case, impossible to suggest that acquaintance with a universal is ever entirely free from any mode of presentation' ('The Function of Acquaintance in Russell's Philosophy', *Synthese* 46 (1981), 149–66, at p. 162). But it should be clear from the text that such a defence of Russell cannot carry over to all the objects and properties mentioned in the present chapter: Pears' remark is surely true outside some special cases.

another contain particular objects to which a thinker need not stand in any relation (beyond the trivial one of thinking of a property under which the object falls) in order to think of a property which has that Fregean concept or course-of-values.[17] As a final notational stipulation, we will continue to use 'φ' as a variable over m.p.'s of properties, that is over concepts in a non-Fregean sense.

Some concepts φ have this feature: there is a type of experience such that constitutively a thinker is disposed to judge 'τ is φ' in the presence of evidence that the object falling under τ bears a certain relation to experiences of that type, experiences in which that object itself may be perceived. (The notion of evidence needed here is analogous to that of 'evidence*', used in Chapter 5.) We can say that concepts with this feature are governed by a Sensitivity Principle, and can use this in explaining acquaintance with properties. A thinker is acquainted with a property if there is some concept in his repertoire which presents that property and which is governed by a Sensitivity Principle. The concept expressed by 'is red' and the visual concept of a shape property are both governed by Sensitivity Principles. Judgements involving these concepts must be sensitive to the occurrence of the appropriate type of experience in the thinker or to evidence that such experiences would occur in suitable circumstances. The concepts expressed by 'has John's favourite property', 'has positive electric charge', and 'is a gene' are not governed by a Sensitivity Principle. There is no type of experience, characterized by its intrinsic properties, to the occurrence of which in actual or counterfactual circumstances judgements involving these concepts must be sensitive. In the case of the concept 'is a gene', the position is complicated by the fact that there could be a scientist so immersed in microbiology that in looking down a microscope, he sometimes has experiences as of

---

[17] In 'On Denoting What?' (*Synthese* 46 (1981), 167–83), Hintikka criticizes Russell for thinking that the elimination of objects with which the thinker is not acquainted from 'singular term' position in a proposition suffices to give the reducibility to acquaintance which Russell sought. Hintikka objects that the quantifiers will still range over things with which the thinker is not acquainted. Hintikka holds that such quantifiers cannot be constituents of propositions consistently with the PA, for these quantifiers 'surely would enter into the proposition through their value-ranges, and these value-ranges do not consist of individuals which we are acquainted with' (p. 182). Russell may well have been guilty of various confusions about quantifiers, but he need not have taken quantifiers to enter propositions by their value-ranges: rather something analogous to the Fregean sense of a quantifier expression could enter the proposition. After all, Russell did not make *first*-level properties enter as constituents solely through their value-ranges.

genes arranged thus-and-so: the notion of a gene enters the representational content of his experience. But we considered this sort of case in Chapter 4. Someone can have the concept expressed by 'is a gene' without having such experiences. All that is required for possession of this concept is the conception of genes as conforming to a certain specifiable role in biological theory.

As before we take the notion of a property occurring as a constituent of a judgement as that of its indexing, or possibly in some special cases its being identical with, a mode of presentation of that property. Does enthusiastic endorsement of this reconstructed Principle of Acquaintance for properties have consequences, analogous to those we considered in the case of objects, for explanation by and of psychological facts? Let us first consider the explanation of actions by psychological states.

Suppose you are driving your car when a red light on the dashboard comes on. You believe that a red light indicates that the petrol tank is almost empty, so you pull in to buy more petrol. Your belief that a red light indicates an almost empty tank is part of the rational explanation of your action. Your action can be explained under a description of the form 'doing so-and-so in relation to the red light', i.e. stopping for petrol when the red light comes on. Now suppose you are driving John's car, and believe that the illumination of the light with John's favourite property indicates that the petrol is low. This is not enough to give a rational explanation of your pulling up when the red light comes on, even if you have all the intentions and desires you had in the case in which you were driving your own car, and know John's favourite property to be a colour property. If you also believed a thought of the form '$[\Sigma_P]$ is John's favourite property', where Σ is an m.p. of the colour property in virtue of which you are acquainted with P, then there would be enough for a rational explanation of your pulling up for more petrol when the light with P is on; but this extra belief would be essential in the circumstances for a rational explanation of your action. We cannot explain actions as intentional only under descriptions of the form 'doing so-and-so in relation to the light with John's favourite property'.

This situation may seem puzzling. When one judges of a presented object that it is red, one exercises a recognitional ability, the ability to recognize a colour. We have just said that the concept of being red has special connections with intentional action on red things. Yet in the case of objects, we have on several occasions emphasized that if someone has an intention to act upon some object of which he thinks in a recognitionally-based way, we should not necessarily anticipate action on any particular object. We should expect that only when he can demonstratively identify the object of which he thinks in the recognitionally-based way. What may be initially puzzling is this difference between the case of objects and the case of properties. But in fact this difference follows from two uncontentious points. The first is that an object which a thinker can recognize has to be located before he can act in relation to it, and its location is an *a posteriori* matter: a thinker can have the ability to recognize an object without being able to locate it. By contrast, there is no relevant sense in which the property of being red has an *a posteriori* location: it is sufficient for an action to be intentional under a description containing the concept 'red' that the agent make his action dependent upon the properties of the things in his environment he sees to be red. The only question of 'locating' this property that could possibly arise is that of finding out which objects have it. The second point relevant to the difference is that there cannot be a fool's red in the way that there can be fool's gold: if an object looks red to someone and his perceptual systems are functioning properly, and the environment is normal, then that object is red. Were this not so, a gap could again open up which would make the connection between the concept of being red and action less tight. Indeed the connection will be less tight in the case of natural kind concepts for just that reason, even if the natural kind concept has an experiential element, and is governed by a Sensitivity Principle.

What of the distinctive causal antecedents of belief in thoughts containing properties as constituents? In the object case we noted in effect that for many properties P, it is a constitutive matter that a thinker's belief in a thought of the form '$[R_x]$ is $[\Sigma_P]$' is *ceteris paribus* causally explained by x being P, as one's belief that a perceptually presented man is tall is explained by his being tall. To assess whether a corresponding point holds for properties with which the thinker is acquainted, we can ask whether properties stand to objects as objects stand to properties in the condition we formulated for the object case. So, is it the case that it is a constitutive matter that for many objects x, a thinker's belief in a thought of the form '$[R_x]$ is $[\Sigma_p]$' is *ceteris paribus* causally explained by x being P? This does indeed seem to be the case, with suitable restrictions on tensing (which would apply in the object case too). Which perceptually presented objects the thinker judges to be green will depend *ceteris paribus* on which of them *are* green, just as the properties he judges a perceptually presented object to have will depend on the properties it does have. (Even if in the case of being green, it is insisted that it is not the property of being green which enters the explanation, but only its physical primary quality ground, this physical property is one which bears a distinguished relation to the property of being green itself.) By contrast, which objects someone judges to have John's favourite property will not *ceteris paribus* depend upon which objects do have John's favourite property. That will depend rather on which concepts φ are such that the thinker judges 'John's favourite property is φ' together with which thoughts of the form 'τ is φ' he judges.

Of course, in some special circumstances the fact that an object possesses John's favourite property can explain the thinker's judging that it does: John may be there in front of the thinker, choosing, and he may know John to be choosing on the basis of his favourite property. In this example the thinker's belief that an object has John's favourite property rests upon the thinker's belief that John is choosing on a particular basis. The example is analogous to the objectual case in which you know the richest man in the world is about to walk into the room, and when he does the richest man in the world's being handsome causes you to judge that the richest man in the world is handsome. Your belief here rests upon your belief that that man (demonstratively presented in perception) is the richest man in the world. There is constitutive causal dependence on properties (or their grounds) in the case of properties with which one is acquainted even when the thinker does not have any particular identity beliefs concerning that property. This is parallel to the case of relational m.p.'s of objects.

One part of Russell's theory of acquaintance, a version of which remains defensible on the present reconstruction of acquaintance, is his view that we are acquainted with complexes. We can make sense of this in the following way. A subject may be enjoying a token experience, and this token may have two features. First, it may be a token experience which is mentioned in some instance of the Sensitivity Principle (in the particularized constitutive role) for some token demonstrative m.p. *m* of an object. Second, it may at the same time be a token experience of a type which is mentioned in the Sensitivity Principle for some concept φ in the thinker's repertoire. In some such cases – those in which, in the token experience, the demonstratively presented object is represented as falling under the concept in question – the two Sensitivity Principles combine to require that *ceteris paribus* the subject be disposed to judge the thought '*m* is φ'.

Some readers will have been wanting to object to the reconstructed Principle of Acquaintance since its introduction. Take the belief that Cicero died many years ago, or that arthritis can be extremely painful. It is widely acknowledged that we can attribute such beliefs to those who sincerely utter the sentences 'Cicero died many years ago' and 'Arthritis can be extremely painful', and who understand the terms in them. Yet for someone who judges that Cicero died many years ago, there need be no psychological state such that his readiness to make that judgement is sensitive to his possession of evidence that bears certain relations to that psychological state. For what psychological state might it be? The subject need not remember the occasion(s) on which he first heard the name 'Cicero', and need not be able to recognize sculptures or pictures of that orator. But equally there seems to be no future in saying 'The subject's belief is a purely descriptive one of the form ''the *F* died many years ago'' because ''Cicero'' must abbreviate a definite description'. The semantic function of the name is simply to pick out an object, and someone understands the name as long as he is able to identify the referent of the name in some way or other: there is no particular way in which one has to think of that Roman orator in order to understand the name. This must surely serve, it may seem, to strengthen the objections to the reconstructed PA. If the name serves solely to pick out an object, then when a belief is truly attributed using a name within the scope of 'believes', the believer must be related to a thought which has that object as a constituent.

My reply to the objection involves denying that last conditional. The reply will be in part programmatic, but I hope the structure and motivation of the programme will be clear. The conditional at the end of the preceding paragraph will be denied by someone who distinguishes sharply between the truth of a belief sentence in which the 'that'-clause contains a proper name and the presence of the referent of a name as a constituent in some (neo-Fregean) thought to which the believer has the attitude which I shall label *'Bel'*. A sentence of the form 'Peter believes that *NN* died many years ago', where *NN* is a name, can be true even though the referent of *NN* is not a constituent of any of the thoughts to which Peter bears the relation *Bel.* '*Bel*' is a piece of notation which is intended for use in making explicit the cognitive features of thoughts to which a subject has propositional attitudes. The reconstructed PA is meant to apply to the relation *Bel:* it has no immediate application, without further argument, at the level of belief sentences.

There are many reasons for wanting to discern an underlying relation *Bel* which is not a straightforward reflection of true belief sentences. Here are three, drawn from familiar recent issues.

(a) We want to say that one cannot acquire new (nonlinguistic) beliefs – and certainly not beliefs containing a constituent object which was not previously a constituent of one's beliefs – simply by introducing a name stipulatively as equivalent to a pure definite description. (We can take the example of 'Bright' and 'the inventor of the wheel' again.) But if some member of a community which has made such a stipulation and who believed that the inventor of the wheel lived in Africa expressed that belief by uttering 'Bright lived in Africa', he would truly be described as believing that Bright lived in Africa. If that is sufficient for having the man Bright as a constituent of one's beliefs, the notion of a constituent is trivialized. The point is not met by noting that if we, the theoretical describers of other speakers, had previously had such a name 'Bright' in our language all along, these speakers would not be described by us as *newly* believing that Bright was thus-and-so. For this too is a trivialization: which objects others have as constituents of their beliefs equally ought not to depend upon what proper names *we* have introduced. One cannot, by linguistic stipulation, make Bright a constituent of the thoughts to which one bears the relation *Bel.*

(b) Consider Kripke's Pierre.[18] Pierre grows up in France and sees pictures of London; while understanding French, he sincerely assents to 'Londres est joli'. He travels to England and learns English by the direct method. Living in an ugly part of London, he sincerely assents to 'London is not pretty' while understanding English. Since he does not realize that 'Londres' and 'London'

[18] 'A Puzzle About Belief', in *Meaning and Use,* ed. A. Margalit (Dordrecht: Reidel, 1979).

name the same city, he continues to assent to 'Londres est joli'. We do not necessarily want to convict Pierre of irrationality. This type of problem arises precisely in the case of those sentences s for which the semantics of the language is impoverished relative to the theory of thought, in this sense: if someone understands s and utters it sincerely, it is not thereby determined what thought he is expressing. Since the semantics of the language determines only which object is the referent of the name, and not a way of thinking of it, sentences containing proper names are in this case, as too are some predicates. Pure indexicals are not in the same case, nor are definite descriptions free of proper names and predicates similar to proper names in the problematic respect. The person x who at t utters 'I'm hot now' expresses the thought ⟨ hungry ⟩ ^ [self$_x$] ^ [now$_t$]; but there is no such thing as 'thinking of something under a name', unless this is thought about the name itself. (This is what makes so plausible one of the claims to which Kripke registers commitment, that a complete and straightforward description of Pierre's situation is possible without embedding 'London' within belief contexts.[19]) Again, it is at the level of *Bel* that such views as that there is no such thing as thinking of something under a name should be formulated, for one should not deny that proper names can often be used in true English sentences of the form 'He thinks that *NN* is thus-and-so'.

(c) In the case of perceptual demonstrative m.p.'s it seems that the m.p., given by the type of the experience in which the object is presented, has a richness which need not be capturable in the language of someone who employs demonstratives. This richness will be captured in the perceptual demonstrative component of the thoughts to which a subject bears the underlying *Bel*.

In distinguishing true belief sentences from thoughts to which a subject bears the relation *Bel*, and applying the reconstructed PA at the latter level, there are certain commitments we do not incur. It is not a consequence of these views that in some of the cases in which someone would normally be said to believe that Cicero died many years ago, or that arthritis can be extremely painful, these ascriptions are regarded as not really true, or are given some reinterpretation. We can still interpret these sentences literally, and not as (say) metalinguistic. Rather, they have to be analysed in

[19] Ibid., p. 259. The present remarks give no particular recommendations on what we should say about Pierre, a question which deserves separate treatment.

some way in terms of the underlying relation *Bel*, and a good analysis should make them come out true.[20]

Let us return to Russell. There remain many aspects of his views on acquaintance which it would be difficult to defend. It is arguable that the implausible components of his views can be regarded as flowing from his underlying presupposition, explicit in *The Problems of Philosophy*, that the existence of anything with which one is acquainted must be known to one indubitably.[21] We can call this 'the Indubitability Assumption'. The Indubitability Assumption immediately restricts the range of objects with which a thinker may be acquainted. (It also greatly alleviates the effects of Russell's denotational theory of meaning, for the reasons we discussed on pp. 130–31.) It may be that Russell was aware that provision must be made in any theory for the possibility of noninferential beliefs, of whose content it is constitutive that they can be arrived at noninferentially in particular ways, and that he thought too that dubitability of a proposition entails that anyone who believes it does so as a result of inference. If he did believe this last point, he never gave sound arguments for it.

But to end this chapter on a more positive note, we can turn to one final aspect of Russellian acquaintance as we have tried to defend it. The Sensitivity Principles supply, for m.p.'s of objects and properties with which a thinker is acquainted, something which has to be provided for any component of a thought. For each component of a thought, there must be some way of establishing (possibly less than conclusively) at least some thought containing that component which does not presuppose that one has already judged the other thoughts containing that component. We can call this the *Grounding Principle*. The argument for this very weak Principle is naturally that were it not true, then in some case there would be a regress involved in attempting to establish thoughts containing a particular component. For some component *K* it would be the case that you could not establish any thoughts containing *K*. You could never get started.

[20] This dual-level conception may have a bearing on the interesting examples in Tyler Burge's 'Individualism and the Mental' (*Midwest Studies in Philosophy*. IV (1979). ed. P. French. T. Uehling and H. Wettstein (Morris: University of Minnesota)). One may conjecture that the pairs of examples which show that which belief sentences are true of an individual can depend on the properties of his linguistic community are examples in which the underlying attitudes at the level of *Bel* remain constant.

[21] pp. 25–26.

Many introduction rules for a connective, if taken as specifications of ways of establishing thoughts containing the sense of that connective, conform to the Grounding Principle. So too do those ways of establishing which concern the perceptual experience of the thinker: experience has a propositional content, but experience is different from judgement, which is the concern of the Grounding Principle. Nor is it excluded that the ways of establishing have a holistic character: they may for instance concern the pattern of perceptions of the thinker over time, and require for application of some concept that these patterns satisfy certain global conditions. None of these kinds of ways of establishing is excluded by the Grounding Principle.

There is one form of radical holism which, if unrestricted, does come into conflict with the Grounding Principle. This is the sense discussed by Dummett when he takes radical holism as the doctrine that the meaning of a sentence (or correspondingly the nature of a thought) is to be given by the totality of ways which exist (in the language in the case of meaning) for establshing its truth.[22] The Grounding Principle must at least restrict the legitimate characterizations of content given by the radical holist so that situations of the following kind do not arise: all the ways of establishing thoughts containing K_0 require us to establish thoughts containing one of $K_1, \ldots, K_n$, while we cannot establish these thoughts containing $K_1, \ldots, K_n$ without first establishing thoughts containing K_0. Such putative ways of establishing do not, because of the circularity, give one a way of establishing anything, and are excluded by the Grounding Principle. This, however, is about as much as one can extract from the Grounding Principle by itself on radical holism. In particular, the Grounding Principle itself is neutral on the analytic/synthetic distinction. The Principle requires there to be ways of establishing some thoughts containing a given component which do not involve establishing other thoughts containing the same component, but this is consistent with the nonexistence of a privileged subset of these ways. It is consistent too with there not existing restrictions on which other sets of ways of establishing something can be regarded as establishing the same content.

---

[22] See 'The Justification of Deduction', reprinted in his *Truth and Other Enigmas* (London: Duckworth, 1978).

Implicit in our reconstructed PA is a commitment concerning the distinction between those thought constituents the nature of which has essentially to be specified by reference to inferential principles involving other thoughts – uniqueness operators, other quantifiers, and connectives amongst others – and those whose nature is not essentially so given. The commitment is to the view that that second class is non-empty. This commitment should be acceptable to anyone who accepts the Grounding Principle: it too, like the constraints on the ascription of content given by the reconstructed PA is independent of the curiosities within Russell's logical atomism.[23]

---

[23] It may be that a more extensive defence of a PA, one which applies to the logical constants too, could be constructed. One might appeal to the idea that certain truth functions themselves, and not just m.p.'s of functions, capture the judgemental properties constitutive of truth–functional operators. Such a development would not, however, be Russellian: in *My Philosophical Development* (London: Allen and Unwin, 1959), at p. 169, Russell explicitly qualifies the PA saying that it is inapplicable to the logical constituents of thoughts.

8

Between Instrumentalism and Brain-Writing

My aim here is to chart a middle course between two more extreme views. One extreme view is an instrumentalist attitude to everyday propositional attitude explanation of someone's actions, the sort given when one uses the scheme of folk psychology. The other extreme view is the claim that there must be a language of thought, and sentence-analogues built up from the vocabulary of this language must in some way be present in the brain of a person with propositional attitudes. The proponents of each extreme use amongst their arguments the difficulties in the views at the opposite extreme. Thus on one side, Dennett writes

the evidence is quite strong that our ordinary notion of belief has next to nothing of the concrete in it . . . [If ordinary folk psychologists insist that in imputing the same belief to different people] they are postulating a similarly structured object, as it were, in each head, this is a gratuitous bit of misplaced concreteness, a regrettable lapse in ideology.[1]

At the other extreme, Fodor writes that to explain an organism's behaviour in terms of its beliefs about that behaviour's consequences and desirability

is . . . to presuppose that the agent has access to a representational system of very considerable richness . . . No representations, no computations. No computations, no model.[2]

So if a coherent middle view between the extremes can be stated, the arguments for both the extremes are weakened. On the positive side, I shall be arguing that an intermediate type of position to be outlined is the closest we can at present reasonably move towards

---

[1] 'Three kinds of intentional psychology', in *Reduction, Time and Reality*, ed. R. Healey (Cambridge: CUP, 1981), at pp. 47–8.

[2] *The Language of Thought* (New York: Crowell, 1975), p. 31.

the hypothesis that there is a language of thought, and that we must move at least that far if we continue to employ the scheme of folk psychology. Such a stand, then, involves disagreement with both the instrumentalist and with the believer in a language of thought. The disagreement with the instrumentalist is direct; the disagreement with the believer in a language of thought will be not over whether it exists, but over the adequacy of his current reasons for believing that it does. I will argue that those reasons can support only the middle position to be outlined: we should be agnostic about anything stronger. This is to be argued not only for experiences and imaginings, where there are special reasons for thinking these may resist capture in a language of thought, but also for beliefs and desires.

An argument for the middle position will then fall into two parts. One part will show that we have to take a view at least as strong as the middle position, while the other will show that that position is the strongest we can reasonably take. The first part, then, will be concerned with instrumentalism about folk psychology.

As an example of an explicit formulation of an instrumentalistic construal of folk psychology, I will take the recent writings of Dennett. In fact the phrase 'instrumentalistic construal' is ambiguous, and may be applied to two different types of instrumentalism. What we can label 'internal instrumentalism' is the doctrine that folk psychology is thought of instrumentalistically by those who employ it: the scheme itself purports to be no more than an instrument for predicting behaviour. 'External instrumentalism' is the potentially revisionist doctrine that, in so far as it is acceptable to employ folk psychology, it must be construed instrumentally, regardless of whether its ordinary practitioners so regard it and regardless of whether there are expressions of folk psychology which seem to require a realistic construal. Dennett's instrumentalism, we shall see, cannot be described as either internal or external without some qualification. Dennett writes:

all there is to being a true believer is being a system whose behaviour is reliably predictable via the intentional strategy, and hence *all there is* to really and truly believing that p (for any proposition p) is being an intentional system for which p occurs as a belief in the best (most predictive) interpretation.

What it is to be a true believer is to be an *intentional system,* a system whose behaviour is reliably and voluminously predictable via the intentional strategy.[3]

In another paper, he endorses the formula '(x) (x believes that $p\equiv x$ can be predictively attributed the belief that p)'[4] His view is that there are general rules for attributing beliefs and desires given the environment of the subject, and that the attribution of beliefs and desires is an attribution which if correct will have consequences for what the subject will do in circumstances other than those on the basis of which the attribution was made.[5] Since it is often true that the behaviour of an organism can be reliably and voluminously predicted by attributing beliefs in accordance with the rules of attribution, on Dennett's view it is often literally true that organisms have beliefs. Dennett's instrumentalism is not of a sort which classifies sentences of folk psychology as untrue or as not even significant.

With those views, one might expect Dennett to classify beliefs and desires as 'calculation bound entities or logical constructs'[6] rather than as posited theoretical entities with causal powers. In fact he writes: 'The *ordinary* notion of belief no doubt does place beliefs somewhere midway between *illata* (theoretical entities) and being *abstracta* (calculation devices)'[7] This apparent tension is relieved by his remark concerning the above account of what it is to be a true believer that 'this apparently shallow and instrumentalistic criterion of belief puts a severe constraint on the internal constitution of a genuine believer, and thus yields a robust version of belief after all'.[8]

I shall argue on the contrary that the causal role of belief, memory, desire and other folk psychological states cannot be adequately captured in this derivative way, by regarding these

---

[3] 'True Believers: the Intentional Strategy and why it works', in A. Heath (ed.), *Scientific Explanation* (Oxford: OUP, 1981), pp. 68 and 55 [Dennett's italics].

[4] 'Three Kinds', p. 59.

[5] Dennett describes his view as non-reductive ('Three Kinds', p. 59), but in fact his 'rules of attribution' which legitimize mental predicates generate a reduction: a system is in a given psychological state if it is counted as being so according to those rules of attribution. Either such a reduction can be given or the rules of attribution are themselves inadequate.

[6] 'Three Kinds', p. 46.

[7] 'Three Kinds', p. 48.

[8] 'True Believers', p. 68; and cp. 'Three Kinds', pp. 52–3.

roles as a consequence of an instrumentalistic account. We can argue by example that the instrumentalistic conditions Dennett gives are not sufficient for the attribution of psychological states. This then will be an argument against internal instrumentalism.

Let us consider a particular human body, henceforth to be designated as 'The Body'. The Body is just like a normal human body, except in containing no brain. The afferent and efferent nerves which would in a normal human be connected with the brain are instead linked by radio to a computer on Mars. This computer, built by highly intelligent Martians who fully understand human neurophysiology, can predict the efferent nerve firing patterns of a human for any given stimulation and past history. The computer has a specification of the past environments of The Body and has been given the vast but finite number of conditionals specifying what a typical human would do with a given past history and current stimulation; so it can cause The Body to behave in any circumstances exactly as a human being would. The behaviour of The Body is voluminously and reliably predictable via the intentional strategy, as voluminously and reliably as for any normal human being. Yet we have a strong intuition that The Body (or The Body plus computer and radio links) does not have propositional attitudes at all: it is just a Martian marionette. So Dennett's instrumentalistic conditions seem not to be sufficient.

What do those conditions omit? What is the crucial difference between The Body and a normal human brain *in vitro* connected by radio links to a body (the case described in Dennett's, 'Where am I?'[9])? One might be tempted to add to Dennett's conditions that a true believer must not be designed and built by some other intentional system, a condition the computer controlled system fails. But such a condition would be too strong: it must be possible for the Martians to build creatures, perhaps even molecule-for-molecule replicas of actual human beings, who genuinely do have propositional attitudes.

The condition The Body plus computer fails is that its behaviour is not caused by beliefs, experiences, memories, desires and the rest. When, for example, someone remembers something, there is some state he has been in (normally) since his participation in the

[9] *Brainstorms.*

remembered event, and this state can play a role in explaining his current behaviour. The computer is not in such states. There will indeed be the history of previous stimulation of the Body with which the computer is equipped, and we can suppose too that the continuing stimulation of The Body plays a causal role in updating this stored history; but although the stimulations caused by the remembered event will be described on this list, this description as an entry in that list can hardly be identified with a memory trace. An intention may, for instance, have been formed too at that past remembered encounter and may have persisted. We cannot say this too has the description of that encounter in the history as its categorical ground. There are no states of The Body plus computer related as folk psychology takes belief, experience, memory, intention, and so forth to be related to one another.

The case of the Martian marionette suggests that having propositional attitudes is more than having a complex and interlocking family of dispositions to behave, however complex that family may be. It suggests it is more too than having such a family of dispositions together with some categorical grounds for them: all the dispositions of the Body may have categorical grounds in the realization of the computer program and the history of previous stimulation.[10]

The case of The Body makes the need for a position between instrumentalism and brain-writing more pressing. If there were no middle ground, such examples might seem, if we want to continue to believe in parts of folk psychology as literally true, to force us into the arms of the language of thought theorist.

The hypothesis that there is a language of thought is (at least) the hypothesis that for any given attitude a person may have such as belief, there is a language such that for him to believe that *p* is for him to store some sentence in this language, a sentence which has

---

[10](i) The case of The Body shows that the way Dennett tries to explain the causal interaction of attitudes with other events will not be available in every case in which his instrumentalistic conditions for belief are fulfilled. He explains such interactions in terms of the causal properties of the 'core elements' ('Three Kinds', pp. 49–50) which in some complex way realize our beliefs: in The Body case, there are no such appropriate core elements.

(ii) It is plausible that The Body system does not have experiences. This can also be developed into a case for saying that it has no propositional attitudes.

the content that *p*. Thus Field: '*organisms which are sufficiently comp-licated for the notions of belief and desire to be clearly applicable have systems of internal representation in which the sentence-analogs have significant grammatical structure.*'[11] Storage of a sentence of the language of thought need not be a spatial matter. It could have to do with firing patterns of neural circuits or with components of some wave form instead of storage of some particular molecule pattern. All that is essential for the idea of a language of thought is that tokens of the sentence have some analogue of syntactic structure, structure which is relevant to the content of the sentence. In principle, then, given the correlation between symbols and content it would be possible to know the content of a sentence of the language of thought (LT) which one had not previously encoun-tered. This also leaves open the possibility that the sentences of the LT are in different languages for each of the attitudes of belief, desire, intention, etc. The hypothesis that there is an LT can also be extended not only to cover propositional attitudes of common-sense psychology, but also to apply to states discovered by cognitive psychology, such as iconic storage of the information that *p*.

The LT hypothesis is regarded by most of its proponents as an empirical hypothesis, albeit a high-level one based on very general considerations. Three different reasons have been offered in its favour. The first argument relies on acceptance of common-sense psychology together with a functionalist theory of psychological states and a physicalist attitude to functional states. On this view, very clearly formulated by Field, a propositional attitude to a proposition must be realized by some physical relation, and the only account in the offing seems to be that this physical relation can be analysed into a relation to a sentence, together with the sentence's meaning a proposition, with meaning to be physicalist-ically analysed too. For Field's argument, the notion of realization is pivotal. A second argument, espoused by Fodor, is that the common-sense psychological theory of a rational agent, in which the expected utilities of various courses of action are computed, requires the existence of an LT: for, he says, computation requires a system of representations, a medium in which the computation is carried out. Here the pivotal notion is computation.[12] This argument does not in itself lead to physicalist conclusions, but can

---

[11] 'Mental Representation', reprinted in *Readings in Philosophy of Psychology*, vol. II, p. 85.
[12] *The Language of Thought*.

be combined with a form of physicalism to yield physicalist conclusions about the sentences of the LT. The third argument, also given by Fodor, again turns on the notion of computation. It is claimed that particular theories in cognitive psychology, notably theories of perception and concept formation, are computational and again require symbols in a language in which the computations are carried out.[13]

The middle position to be defended here holds that there is an alternative model which does not postulate an LT and is consistent with the premises of these three arguments. It is of course no business of philosophy to engage in unfounded neurophysiological speculation. My aim will just be to give a clear sketch of an account in which there is no LT and which would be capable of many different physical and neurophysiological realizations. Nothing to be said here will entail that the LT hypothesis is false: rather the point will be that the commonly cited reasons do not support it. I will not discuss all the arguments that have been offered that particular theories in cognitive psychology require the existence of an LT: I hope the reader can generalize from the cases I do treat.

We can begin to move towards the alternative model by considering a specific example. Fodor suggests that 'what must go on in perception is that a description of the environment that is *not* couched in a vocabulary whose terms designate values of physical variables is somehow computed on the basis of a description that *is* couched in such a vocabulary'.[14] The former description might be 'There's a robin on the lawn', the content of which could be a possible content of perceptual experience; the latter description, Fodor says, will be encoded in messages from peripheral cells, and will in the visual case be something like 'there is light of physical magnitude M at (retinal) location *l*'. Let us consider this last content, and ask: when a retinal cell fires and transmits this information, what is the token of the LT which refers to the location *l*?

It seems that the answer must be that there is none. A qualitatively and physically identical type of cell at another place in the retina may be registering information about light at another location *l* by firing in exactly the same way as the first cell. What makes one cell's information concern one location and another

[13] Ibid.
[14] Ibid., p. 47.

cell's another location is not a difference in any terms of the LT they contain, but simply their different *relata*: one is attached and causally responsive to one place on the retina, the other to another.[15] An exactly similar point applies to line detectors slightly deeper in the perceptual system. One such detector is capable of registering that there is a line in one region rather than another because that is the region to which it is causally connected. This suggests a relational paradigm: that the possession of content by a state is a matter of the relations in which the state stands. Possession of a structured content need not require corresponding physical structure in the state, but may rather reside in the pattern of relations in which that state stands.

A clear sketch of a system satisfying the premise of the first argument for an LT which conforms to the relational paradigm but which does not itself have an LT must have several features. It must show how one can still reasonably ascribe a particular propositional content to a state even though it is not syntactically structured; it must allow for the ascription of relatively complex contents to syntactically unstructured states; and, what is implicit in the first of these, it must show how these states can interact in the right ways with perception and behaviour. Each of these features is one which might be thought to require an LT, and if any one of them is not present at least in embryonic form in a simple account, there will be doubts that the model can be extended to something of realistic complexity without bringing in an LT.

In a sketch, we can restrict our attention to those contents built up from atomic components *a, b* and *c,* where these are ways of thinking of three objects based on a visual capacity to recognize

[15] It may be objected that Fodor could construe the retinal cell's firing as partially analogous to an utterance of a sentence 'Foggy!', which we stipulate to be synonymous with our indexical sentence 'It's foggy here now'. 'Foggy!' has no semantically relevant syntactic structural, but in an utterance of it there will be reference to a particular place and time. (Actually, more central units in the nervous system must in *some* way receive nonindexical information from the periphery: a man who receives a hundred telegrams saying, e.g. 'it's bright here', 'it's raining here' . . . is in no position to draw up a weather map unless he knows where they come from.) But such an indexical strategy cannot work for more complex contents. Because of its links with other cells, one cell's firing may have a complex truth-functional content determined from the content of those other cell's firings. The given cell may be neurophysiologically indistinguishable in kind from another cell with a totally different firing content; and may be very different from another whose content (conceptually) overlaps with its content. If these relations which give content are counted as part of the syntactic structure of a state, the claim that there is an LT is trivialized. There would be no genuine sentence-analogues.

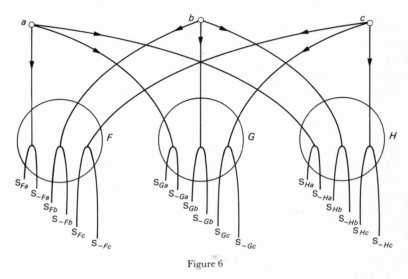

Figure 6

each one of them, and three visual observational properties *F, G* and *H*. In Figure 6, the small circles at the top labelled with these three ways of thinking pick out whatever physical assembly or state of an assembly which is the ground of the subject's ability to recognize the object in the given way when he has a visual experience.[16] The large circles labelled with the concepts represent whatever grounds the ability to tell, of a presented object, whether it falls under the given observational concept by which it is labelled. The states S_{Fa}, $S_{\sim Gb}$, etc. are the physical states which realize the subject's having the belief that *Fa*, that $\sim Gb$, etc., if he has such a belief. The lines in the diagram indicate that if the subject is in any such realization of a belief state, he may be so as a result of the activation in the past of a causal pathway passing through whatever is the ground of those abilities associated with the components of the content of that belief. It is consistent with this description of the case so far that each of the states S_{Fa} through

[16]The small circles might correspond to something highly complex, in which information is stored in 'distributed' form, as in an optical filter or holographic photograph (see for instance, K. Pribram, *Languages of the Brain* (Englewood Cliffs, N.J.: Prentice-Hall, 1971), Ch. 8). Here indeed it would be the case that, as Dennett speculates, 'the core *elements*, the concrete, salient, separately stored representation tokens (and there must be some such elements in any complex information processing system)' store information that is entirely unfamiliar from the standpoint of folk psychology ('Three kinds', p. 49).

$S_{\sim H_c}$ be syntactically unstructured in the sense that there is in S_{F_a}, $S_{\sim F_c}$ and S_{F_b} no type of common component corresponding to the common property F which is a component of each of their contents. No one could even in principle here examine some of these physical states themselves and, if told their content, reasonably predict the content of the remaining states. (This is not to say that the states may not be physically highly complex.)

One could indeed reasonably predict the content of the state $S_{\sim F_c}$ if one knew all of (i) the content of the states S_{F_a}, S_{G_c} and $S_{\sim G_c}$, (say), (ii) their relations to the assemblies labelled by a, F and c, and (iii) the relations of $S_{\sim F_c}$ to the assemblies labelled by c and F. But (iii) here is hardly an analogue of syntactic structure in the state $S_{\sim F_c}$: no more is it a syntactic matter that a token of a given type of sentence a man utters is caused by a particular intention. The psychological irrelevance of the particular physical nature of the state S_{F_a} in this example is shown in the fact that we could replace some parts of the brain of such a subject so that a quite different physical state is produced by activation of the causal line passing through the assemblies associated with a and F without altering his psychological states at all.[17]

---

[17]This is a technical note for those who find quantificational formulations worthwhile. Let f be a function with brain symbol types in its range, and left 'F' and 'a' range over predicates and singular terms of English respectively. Fodor's view is then that there exists a relation R such that

(1) $\exists f \,\forall F \forall a$: ⌜John believes that Fa⌝ is true iff R (John, $f(^\frown)((F), f(a)))$.

There is a uniformity here, as indicated by the $\exists \forall \forall$ form. There is also a certain kind of separability. Given the attitude in question is belief, we can say with which neurophysiological symbol an English a is correlated without reference to the full content of the belief. In the example just given in the text, on the other hand, we could not do this: the states designated by terms of the form 'S_{-a-}' may have nothing intrinsically in common. They share only the relational feature of being linked in a certain way to the node labelled by 'a'. In the example of the text, the following conditions *are* met. First, where g has state types in its range

(2) $\forall F \forall a \exists g$: ⌜John believes that Fa⌝ is true iff R' (John, g (⌜Fa⌝));

this is a weak claim which involves no more than what is sometimes called the realization relation. Second, we can also formulate a principle which expresses the fact that there is a relational feature shared by all beliefs with contents expressed using a. Let h be a function verifying the existential quantification '$\exists g$' in (2). Then

(3) $\forall a \exists C \forall F$: $C(h(⌜Fa⌝))$.

Here 'C' ranges over possibly complex relational neurophysiological properties (to avoid triviality, C must not be specified by alternation or some equivalent for each belief). A

Examples of this type could be further elaborated. One can imagine a creature whose brain contains layers of spatially organized 'maps', each layer corresponding to the layout of things in his environment as it is believed by him to be at some particular time. If a particular place is believed to fall under a given concept at a given time, the corresponding place in the appropriate layer is linked to some assembly corresponding to that concept. Again, there need not be an LT with syntactically structured brain-states. This could clearly capture much of a simple creature's view of the world.

Belief in a complex — say a distjunctive — content could be accommodated as follows. We know from the theory of circuits and switching how one device may be linked with two others so that it is triggered if at least one of the other two is. A syntactically unstructured state may be related in this way to the states S_{Fa} and S_{Gb}, and so be a candidate for realizing the disjunctive belief that *Fa* or *Gb*. Such a model should also provide a third route which when activated can place the subject in the state realizing the belief ⌐Fa or Gb⌐, a state corresponding to logical and other reasons for believing a disjunction which do not give reasons for believing either disjunct alone. The model can also be modified to allow for the fact that a person will not always draw the disjunctive consequences of his beliefs: it may for instance be the case that some component of the line linking S_{Fa} with the state realizing the disjunctive belief is not always in place. 'In place' here is, like many of these abstract characterizations of a system conforming to the relational paradigm, again somehting which may be realized in many different ways: it may, for instance, be a matter of some substance reaching certain concentrations in a particular collection of neurons, or a matter of its distribution within them.

Deductive inference is something easily accommodated on the hypothesis that there is an LT. A deductive mechanism has only to look at the analogue of the syntactic structure of various states and to make any new structural states it produces dependent upon the syntactic structure of these states which correspond to premises of the inference. It seems plausible that in the case of beings who have a language many beliefs will be coded at some level in a form systematically related to the sentences that would

---

question worth consideration, even if we are not in a position to accept (1), is whether (3) is constrained to hold by our conception of propositional attitude psychology, or by that plus physicalism.

be used to express them, and a deductive mechanism could operate on these forms. Nevertheless it is not true that we can make no sense of deduction if the states realizing beliefs are not sentences in an LT. A device could check that the state which is in fact $S_{Fa \lor Gb}$ is a disjunctive one because it is suitably linked to two belief states; if the system is in this state, and also in one of the states which is the realization of the negation of one of the states to which it is related in the way characteristic for disjunction (e.g. $S_{\sim Gb}$), the device can cause the system to go into the state S_{Fa}. Such a device would show the feature emphasized by some defenders of the LT hypothesis, that it would need no information about the content of the two halves of the disjunction. In the case of this device, that is shown in the fact that in the operation corresponding to an inference by *modus tollendo ponens* there was no need to check which of the concept assemblies — *F, G* or *H* — or singular assemblies corresponding to *a, b,* or *c* the states S_{Fa} and $S_{\sim Gb}$ are linked with.

In the operation of such a device, we have an instance of a generally applicable replacement tactic available to a critic of the LT hypothesis. Whenever a proponent of that hypothesis claims that some psychological phenomenon is explicable only if there is an LT, and that operations on psychological analogues of syntactic structure are unavoidable, one should always ask: 'Can those operations on syntactic structure be replaced by operations that look at, or are crucially dependent upon, the relations in which a state stands?' If the answer is 'Yes', there is something wrong in that argument for an LT. In fact in pressing this tactic one would only be pressing a move that proponents of the LT hypothesis use in some cases but not in others. To my knowledge, none of those who argue for the existence of an LT go so far as to say not only that there is a sentence *s* stored when the subject believes that *p,* but further that there must also be stored a sentence *s'*, meaning 'I believe that *p*'. Storage of believed sentences in one location, intended ones in another, desired ones in yet another . . . is thought quite sufficient; and the ground for belief in the sufficiency is presumably that it is enough for the content of a stored sentence to be believed (rather than intended) that it be related in the right ways to experience, other states, and behaviour. This is precisely to apply the relational replacement tactic to the question of whether a given state is a realization of belief, desire, or some other attitude.

The replacement tactic can also be used in showing how in the simple model actions can be explained by states with content. It is partially constitutive of an intention to φ that if the subject is acting on it and nothing interferes, such action will continue in the way thought appropriate until the subject comes to believe that he is φ: this is a crude approximation, but it seems clear that the belief that one is φ plays a special role in bringing to an end one's attempts to φ, which is not played by other beliefs. (Part of the crudity of this formulation lies in the fact that a time may well be presented differently in the intention and in the belief.) Under the LT hypothesis, this constitutive link would be reflected in a matching relation – or a relation of matching *modulo* a certain translation scheme – between the syntactic structure of the state realizing the intention and the syntactic structure of the state which would realize the corresponding belief. It is here that in this example the replacement tactic can be employed: an intention that Gb can have its propositional content partly in virtue of the fact that action on that intention is terminated by the subject's being in the unstructured state S_{Gb}, which has its content in virtue of its relations. Another example in which the tactic could be employed would be in an account of practical reasoning: an intention that q must be able to interact with a belief that if p were to be the case q would be the case, to produce an intention that p. So here some device would have to be able to pick out whatever state realizes the belief that $p \,\square\!\!\rightarrow q$; it would have to do this, if the states were unstructured, by the complex relations that state bears to a belief that p and a belief that q.

This simple model based on the relational paradigm seems then to have the features needed: it admits of answers to the questions of the form 'In virtue of what does this state have the propositional content it does?', it allows inference, and the states can interact to produce action. In fact, in a sense, the LT hypothesis can be seen as a special case of a type under which the simple relational model falls. For where the simple model has states standing in various relations which give it its content, the LT theorist supposes for each such relation it is also the case that some analogue of a syntactic component of that state exists and that *it* stands in corresponding relations.

The simple model can also be extended to undermine the second of the three arguments we distinguished at the outset for the existence of an LT. That was the argument to which Fodor appeals when he challenges any opponent of an LT to provide an account of action explained by maximization of expected utility, without at some point requiring the existence of a language in which computations are carried out. Suppose what is in question is whether the agent should φ. When Fodor describes the agent as computing the expected utility of φ-ing under condition C, what actually goes on in an extension of the simple model might be the following. That the subject has a certain degree of belief in the proposition 'C given that I φ' may be realized in the possession, by the state which realizes the belief, of a physical feature in a particular degree; that the state has the content it does can again be a matter purely of its relations. Similarly a certain physical feature of a state may realize his attaching a certain level of utility to the proposition 'C and I φ'. Now the two physical features may interact to produce that feature which realizes the expected utility of φ-ing under the condition C. It seems that nothing here requires an analogue of syntactic structure in the realizing states – a language in which the computations are carried out. Nor does acceptance of this extended simple model require an instrumentalist attitude to the psychological theory of a rational agent: on the contrary, if someone satisfied this model, realism about the postulated mechanisms of rational belief–desire psychology would be vindicated.

If an organism can be in psychological states with content without in any way storing analogues of sentences, then it can also engage in computations without having an internal language. For computation is a matter of states with content resulting from one another in a systematic way; this requires a certain pattern in the order and causal relations of states with content, but it does not impose a further requirement that there be syntactic structure in their realizations. It is not necessarily true to say 'No representations, no computations'.

This suggests that the many arguments Fodor brings to show that psychological processes are computational do not suffice to establish the existence of an LT. Towards the end of his book Fodor states what he regards as the consequence of the type of psychological theory he believes true as follows:

It won't be possible to construct a psychology of the kind that I have been envisioning unless organisms have pertinent descriptions as instantiations of some or other formal system . . . What pertinency requires is (a) that there be some general and plausible procedure for assigning formulae of the system to states of the organism; (b) that causal sequences which determine propositional attitudes turn out to be derivations under the assignment; (c) that for each propositional attitude of the organism there is some causal state of the organism such that (c1) the state is interpretable as a relation to a formula of the formal system, and (c2) being in the state is nomologically necessary and sufficient for (or contingently identical to) having the propositional attitude[18]

This condition can be met without the existence of an LT. This is because there are at least two different types of case in which an organism is counted as 'instantiating' a formal system in the way Fodor says psychological theory requires. In a case of the first type ('Case One'), there are indeed analogues of sentences in the human brain and the procedure for assigning formulae of the system to states of the organism Fodor says exists can be specified recursively: corresponding to atomic symbols of the formulae are components of the sentence-analogues, corresponding to concatenation is some presumably neurophysiological relation between those components of the sentence-analogues, and so forth. This basic mapping between formulae and neurophysiological ('N-P') states determines a corresponding mapping between sequences of formulae, sequences which may be derivations or computations, and sequences of neurophysiological states. So this first case can be depicted as in Figure 7.

In the second type of case, the condition stated by Fodor is fulfilled in a very different way. The formal system is provided with a semantics which, say, correlates its formulae with Fregean thoughts — or with constituents of Fregean thoughts if the formulae use terms rather than sentences. Such thoughts are also independently attributed as the content of some of the N-P states of the organism by general principles of attribution of content (which are

---

[18] *The Language of Thought*, p. 199. This quotation, in a sense which the text following is meant to make explicit, misrepresents Fodor's real view: his real view is stated more accurately in his *Representations* (Brighton: Harvester, 1981), at p. 26; '(d) Mental representations have their causal roles in virtue of their formal properties'. But the quotation from *The Language of Thought* is significant because it *does* state what is required for a psychological theory to be computational. Note also that if a gap opens up between computational theories and LT theories, and only the former are required to justify talk of mental representations, a gap also opens up between the existence of mental representations and Fodor's view.

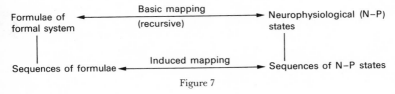

Figure 7

still not fully understood). These two assignments of content together determine an *induced* mapping between formulae of the formal system and the N-P states: a formula is mapped to a N-P state if under the given assignments of content, they are assigned the same content. This induced mapping need not be recursively specified, and as we have seen the N-P states with such content may have no syntactic structure. The induced mapping will as before fix a further mapping between sequences of formulae and sequences of N-P states. So the position in the second case is as given in Figure 8. A psychological theory formulated in computational terms can still be true and important if Case Two obtains, for N-P states may under the induced mapping succeed one another in the way predicted by the computational theory. It is not required that there be an LT for this to be so. Note that in this example Fodor's condition (c) quoted above is met. Condition (c) said 'for each propositional attitude of the organism there is some causal state of the organism such that (c1) the state is interpretable as a relation to a formula of the formal system, and (c2) being in the state is nomologically necessary and sufficient for (or contingently identical to) having the propositional attitude'. The relation of the causal state to the formula which verifies Fodor's (c1) here is that of having the same content.

Cases One and Two are not exhaustive : they are at the two ends

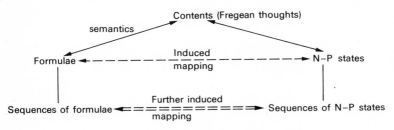

Figure 8

of a spectrum of intermediate cases. There is no reason it cannot be the case that from a specification of a collection of N-P states and their associated contents, when given a further N-P state from outside the collection one can predict some features of its content but not all of them. For example, instead of the fanciful realization given earlier to states with the content of an alternation, it might be that an assembly bearing a certain N-P relation to two others is, if activated, in a state with the alternation of the contents of the two others: and this could be so while those two others were systematically unstructured. Thus from information about the content of other states one could predict that this one had the content of an alternation, but one could not predict which particular content of that form it possessed. One can envisage many other such intermediate cases. The defender of the LT maintains that we have reason to believe that we are at one end of this spectrum. I have been arguing that none of the arguments so far given by such defenders establish any more than that we are at some point or other on this spectrum.

Index